The How-to Guide for

Integrating the Common Core in Mathematics

For Grades 6–8

Author
Karen Gartland
Contributing Author
Linda Dacey
Foreword
Anne M. Collins

LESLEY UNIVERSITY

SHELL EDUCATION

Publishing Credits

Robin Erickson, *Production Director*; Lee Aucoin, *Creative Director*;
Timothy J. Bradley, *Illustration Manager*; Sara Johnson, M.S.Ed., *Editorial Director*;
Lori Nash, M.S.Ed., *Editor*; Sara Sciuto, *Assistant Editor*; Grace Alba Le, *Designer*;
Corinne Burton, M.A.Ed., *Publisher*

Consultant

Dana Strong, Math Consultant

Image Credits

All images Shutterstock

Shell Education

5301 Oceanus Drive
Huntington Beach, CA 92649-1030
http://www.shelleducation.com
ISBN 978-1-4258-1196-9
© 2014 Shell Educational Publishing, Inc.

Integrating the Common Core in Mathematics

For Grades 6-8

Table of Contents

Foreword

Standards by themselves do not impact student learning, rather, how students engage with the standards is the single most important component in a student's mathematics education. It is crucial that the problems students are assigned are interesting, grade appropriate, and accessible to all students. Teachers make all the difference in the world when it comes to effective teaching and learning. The interactions between students and teachers, between students with other students, and between students and the curriculum can either promote and support student learning or thwart it.

The Common Core State Standards identify a set of mathematical content standards that develop in complexity across the grade level but they also identify the mathematical habits of mind successful students employ as they problem solve. The Mathematical Practices articulate those habits of mind that enable students to reason through and make sense of various problem solving situations. Effective implementation of the Common Core State Standards can and will be successful only if students embrace the Mathematical Practices as a way of thinking and reasoning. This book provides samples of lessons aligned with both the content standards and the Mathematical Practices. The author describes strategies, not only for engaging students in problem situations aligned with the content standards as well as the Mathematical Practices but also provides strategies for mathematical discourse and collaborative learning.

The National Mathematics Panel (2008) identified effective formative assessment as having a positive impact on student achievement. In this publication, the author integrates formative assessment examples that go beyond using tests and quizzes to inform student understanding to include Tickets to Leave (Exit Cards), assessing prior knowledge, and appropriate questioning techniques. In addition to the formative assessment examples, the author provides a comparison between the two assessment consortia and how the new tests are similar and different.

Throughout the book the author clearly labels those sample activities and problems that incorporate the mathematical practices and how teachers might incorporate them into their own teaching. Graphic organizers are illustrated, as are suggestions for how to organize the summary component of a lesson. The order in which students report out their findings often adds to the scaffolding that is often necessary and helpful to ensure that all students have entry into the problem. The diversity in activities, classroom practices, and suggested representations will be very helpful to teachers as they implement the Common Core State Standards and help prepare their students for the assessments. More importantly, this book provides tried-and-proven ways in which teachers might enact student-centered classrooms that value perseverance, modeling, multiple representations, and discourse.

—Dr. Anne M. Collins

Acknowledgements and Dedication

This book includes vignettes and teacher voices from a number of classrooms in which I have worked over my career. Numerous colleagues and students have contributed to my understanding of how best to teach mathematics. I am very grateful for their insights and assistance in making this book a useful tool for the teachers and students I have not met. Thank you in particular to my colleagues in the Groton-Dunstable Middle School and to Sophie, Caroline, and Julia for their student work contributions.

To my family: Joe, Joseph, and Amy, for their support and love throughout the writing of this book.

$\frac{1}{2} + \frac{3}{4}$

Chapter

Opportunities and Challenges

 Voice from the Classroom

When the teachers in my school first heard that there were going to be new standards for us to teach, a number of us thought, "What's the big deal? The math is the math." But, as we began to dig into what the individual standards were for each grade level, we slowly began to realize what a difference there was from what we had taught in the past. As important, we realized that the expectations we had for our students needed to change as well.

At first, we just focused on trying to determine whether or not what we had been teaching would still be taught at our grade level. This brought us to trying to figure out what the language of the standards meant and we found that challenging at times. Someone found the "Progression Documents" online, and found out they were written by the same authors who wrote the standards. We hoped that they would help us to understand the standards better, but found that they were challenging to interpret as well. Our school system doesn't have money for math coaches and outside consultant money had been allocated to Language Arts. Our principal said we had to figure the math out together. We decided that the best approach for us was to pick one domain and look at it across the grade levels and then to work in our grade-level teams on the critical areas most connected to this domain. It was so helpful to be talking about this with other teachers.

—7th-Grade Teacher

This teacher's voice expresses what I have heard many teachers say. It's challenging to figure out how these standards effect to our teaching when they are presented to us as a list. We need time to work with others about what they mean and how we can implement them. We need to understand their purpose and to be able to make sound choices among the myriad of resources that seem to pop up online daily. Most importantly, we need to invest in our own learning; to take the time to read, to listen and to talk with others about mathematics, these standards, our students, and our teaching practices.

Each of us is on our own learning trajectory regarding these standards. Some of us have attended numerous workshops and conferences and have coaches to help us explore ideas. Others may only have limited familiarity with the math standards. Regardless of where you are starting from, it is not a journey that ends quickly. I have been able to teach others about these standards from the time they were published and I continue to deepen my understanding of them and what they mean to teachers and classrooms. So, let's begin with a general overview of these standards.

Overview of the Standards

Demand for mathematical knowledge has increased as student performance on worldwide standardized tests continues to disappoint. In response, the National Governors Association Center for Best Practices (NGA) and the Council of Chief State School Officers (CCSSO) cooperated on the development of the Common Core State Standards, standards that were designed with the goal of creating common K–12 learning goals that would prepare students to meet expectations for career and/or college. In mathematics, the standards identify *Standards for Mathematical Practice* as well as content standards. As of this writing, these standards have been adopted by 45 states, something that has never happened before in the history of the United States.

These standards are intended as a set of learning outcomes, not a national curriculum. The implementation stage is where teachers' knowledge of both their craft and their students is most important. Support for these standards clearly varies at local, state, and national levels, but one thing is clear to me and hopefully to you; it is time for educators to take the lead, as we will ultimately be the key to the success of this reform effort.

We all need to do the following:

- ✏ Understand the standards clearly.
- ✏ Gain insight into how these standards could be met within classrooms.
- ✏ Develop assessment strategies to support student success.
- ✏ Recognize ways in which working with others and using available resources can help us to meet our goals.

This book is designed with these needs in mind. It also is written with the beliefs that all teachers want their students to succeed, that given the right circumstances, all students can succeed, and that any change comes with opportunities and challenges. To support the success of our students, we need to embrace the opportunities and find ways to address the challenges in manageable ways.

Teachers know change. No other profession has a complete change of clients every year. Every Fall teachers meet their new students with excitement. Yet those early days can be more tiring too, as we establish routines and classroom expectations with a new group. The routines do get established, and the excitement begins to come not from the newness, but from the progress our new students are making. Just as our task is to get to know our new students and learn how to best support them, our first task here is to get to know these new standards and how to best implement them for student success.

Discussion of these standards often centers on the extent to which they provide focus, coherence, clarity, and rigor. Each attribute is considered here and returned to throughout the book.

Focus

The phrase "a mile wide and an inch deep" has often been used to describe the mathematics curriculum in the United States. Many teachers complain about the range of topics they have to *cover*, and clearly strong instruction involves much more than coverage. The Common Core provides focus on key ideas and understandings, as you cannot gain deep understanding of a great number of topics. Also, critical areas have been identified for each pre-secondary grade level, which provide further focus to the documents.

Coherence

Mathematical ideas need to be learned as a series of related ideas that progress across the grades rather than through exposure in ways that do not connect one topic to the next. Too often, students don't realize, for example, that the concept of division is the same, whether it is applied to whole numbers, rational number, or integers. Similarly, many students do not recognize that properties such as the commutative property of addition also apply to all types of numbers. Such generalizations are necessary to avoid students learning isolated concepts or skills that are then likely to be forgotten. The Common Core provides coherence by providing standards that progress across the grade levels and that connect to one another in clear, recognizable ways.

Rigor

Teachers often feel as if education reform is just a pendulum swinging back and forth between conceptual development and skill acquisition. Similarly, curricular resources may emphasize one end of the continuum considerably more than the other. Conceptual understanding and skill development are both expected outcomes of the Common Core. For example, students are expected to understand the four operations with all rational numbers and use strategies to find sums, differences, products, and quotients, reach arithmetic fluency, and apply their understandings and skills to solve problems. The Common Core also defines mathematical habits of mind (Mathematical Practices) that include rigorous terms such as *persevere*, *precision*, *abstractly*, and *viable argument*, among others.

Clarity

When grade expectations are given for grade-level spans such as 6–8, or if the language used to describe standards is imprecise, teachers remain unsure of expected outcomes. The Common Core provides specific single-grade level standards that indicate what is to be learned when. As teachers we need to develop a common understanding of what students need to know and how they can demonstrate that they know it. Figuring this out is often referred to as *unpacking* the standards.

So though the standards may, at first glance, appear dense and challenging to comprehend, as they are viewed both within and across grade levels, the progressive nature of the standards will become clear.

The Expectations are for All Students

Before looking at specific standards it is important to emphasize the *common* expectation of the standards. Too often we have discovered that schools in lower socioeconomic areas have less rigorous standards than others with greater financial resources. This educational disparity leads to increased differences and does not match our democratic values. All students must have access to learning goals that allow for success. This is also true of students with learning challenges who are often restricted to skill development through rote procedures. "Emerging literature suggests that students with moderate and severe disabilities can learn content aligned with grade-level standards while continuing to work on basic numeracy" (Saunders, Bethune, Spooner, Browder 2013, 24). As we think about implementing the standards, we need to address how we will meet the needs of our diverse students.

Standards for Mathematical Practice

The Standards for Mathematical Practice describe a set of proficiencies, or habits of mind, that students should develop over time. Built on the five process standards, developed by the National Council of Teachers of Mathematics (NCTM 2000) and the five strands of mathematical proficiency identified in *Adding It Up* (National Research Council 2001), these eight standards in Figure 1.1 have the potential to transform mathematics education in ways that would be even more significant than the content standards. They indicate ways in which students should learn and demonstrate their knowledge of mathematics (Hull, Harbin Mills, and Balka 2012).

Figure 1.1 Standards for Mathematical Practice

MP1—Make sense of problems and persevere in solving them

MP2—Reason abstractly and quantitatively

MP3—Construct viable arguments and critique the reasoning of others

MP4—Model with mathematics

MP5—Use appropriate tools strategically

MP6—Attend to precision

MP7—Look for and make use of structure

MP8—Look for and express regularity in repeated reasoning

(NGA and CCSSO 2010)

The goal is to have these standards integrated into all mathematical content areas in K–12 classrooms. Understanding these practice standards takes time and will be the focus of the next chapter. For now, let's consider how one mathematical task might relate to them. In seventh grade, students are expected to understand how to find a percent of a number and to be able to solve two-step problems. Figure 1.2 shows how the following task might connect to the Mathematical Practices.

Natasha is buying a new videogame for $49.99.

She has a 15% off coupon and a $12 off coupon, but the store will only allow her to use one of them.

Natasha decides to use the coupon that will save her the most money.

With a 5% sales tax, how much did she spend, in total, to buy the videogame?

Figure 1.2 Connections Between a Specific Task and the Standards for Mathematical Practices

Practice	How Practices Connect to the Task
MP1 Make sense and persevere in solving problems	Students can interpret the problem information. They have strategies they can use to represent the problem so that it makes sense. They try more than one approach if they get stuck.
MP2 Reason abstractly and quantitatively	Students can identify the important information in the problem statement. They can represent the information in equations, models, diagrams, or drawings.
MP3 Construct viable arguments and critique the reasoning of others	Students can explain and defend their thinking clearly and understand the explanations of others. They can identify strengths and weaknesses among various solution strategies.
MP4 Model with mathematics	Students use models and equations to represent the problem. They can develop a model strategy for determining a logical way to choose between the two options.
MP5 Use appropriate tools strategically	Students successfully use representations, mental arithmetic, and paper and pencil strategies to find a solution.
MP6 Attend to precision	Students use appropriate vocabulary, symbols, and labels to communicate their solution process.
MP7 Look for and make use of structure	Students find a flexible method for finding the percent of a number: for example, they may choose to find 10% and then another 5% and add the two numbers together.
MP8 Look for and express regularity in repeated reasoning	From solving other problems, students recognize this as a problem in which they must solve for the percent of a number and then subtract the discount or they could solve it by finding 85% of $49.99.

According to Silver "...typical classroom mathematics teaching in the United States tends not to use challenging tasks, nor to promote students' thinking about and engagement with mathematical ideas, and thus fails to help students develop understanding of the mathematics they are learning" (2010, 1). For students to develop the habits of mind suggested by these practices, the tasks we present must be complex, especially if we want to incorporate more than one mathematical practice in a lesson or activity. Consider the following tasks. What differences in complexity do you notice among them? What mathematical practices do you think they would each tap?

- Find the volume of this shape. (Shown only Figure A)

- Find the volume of each shape. Explain how finding the volume of Figure A could help you to find the volume of Figure B. (Shown Figures A and B)

- Design a purpose for this figure. Use your knowledge of the volume of this figure to help you. (Shown Figure B)

Figure 1.3 Volume

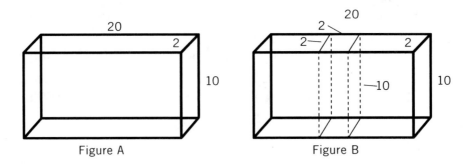

Figure A   Figure B

Content Standards

Domains, Clusters, and Standards

For K–8, content standards are provided for each grade level. It is helpful to understand the ways in which the standards are organized. Domains, which are large groupings of related mathematical ideas, have been specified for each grade level. The domains for the 6–8 levels are summarized in Figure 1.4.

Figure 1.4 Domains Across the Grade Levels

Domains	Grade Levels		
	6	7	8
The Number System	X	X	X
Ratios and Proportional Relationships	X	X	
Expressions and Equations	X	X	X
Functions			X
Geometry	X	X	X
Statistics and Probability	X	X	X

Within these domains, related standards are organized in clusters as shown in Figure 1.5. Standards are identified by their grade level, domain, and cluster (e.g., 7.NS.1 identifies the first standard in The Number System domain at the seventh grade level). Sometimes they list specific standards under a broader one, for instance, 7.NS.1a is standard *a* and is listed under standard 1 in the Number System domain in grade 7.

Figure 1.5 Elements of the CCSSM Grade Level Standards

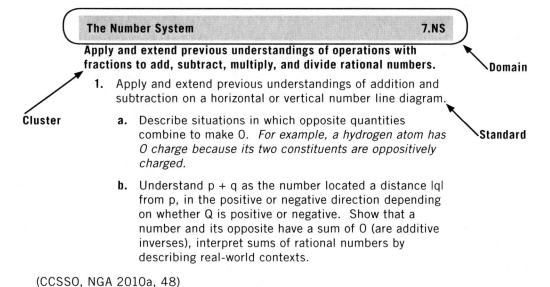

(CCSSO, NGA 2010a, 48)

Critical Areas

Many of us may be so drawn to the standards themselves that we overlook the introduction section to each grade level. It is there that the critical areas for that level are identified. At the 6–8 levels there are two to four areas per grade. These key ideas provide the focus of mathematical instruction for that year and help us to plan the curriculum that will allow the standards to be met. Each area often highlights a particular domain, but sometimes more than one is involved. The critical areas for each level are summarized in Figure 1.6.

Figure 1.6 Critical Areas of Instruction at Each Grade Level

Grade 6:

1. Connecting ratio and rate to whole number multiplication and division and using concepts of ratio and rate to solve problems (RP)

2. Completing understanding of division of fractions and extending the notion of number to the system of rational numbers, which includes negative numbers (NS)

3. Writing, interpreting and using expressions, and equations (EE)

4. Developing understanding of statistical thinking (SP)

Grade 7:

1. Developing understanding of and applying proportional relationships (RP)

2. Developing understanding of operations with rational numbers and working with expressions and linear equations (NS, RP, EE)

3. Solving problems involving scale drawings and informal geometric constructions, and working with two- and three-dimensional shapes to solve problems involving area, surface area, and volume (EE, G)

4. Drawing inferences about populations based on samples (SP)

Grade 8:

1. Formulating and reasoning about expressions and equations, including modeling an association in bivariate data with a linear equation, and solving linear equations and systems of linear equations (EE)

2. Grasping the concept of a function and using functions to describe quantitative relationships (F)

3. Analyzing two- and three-dimensional space and figures using distance, angle, similarity, and congruence, and understanding and applying the Pythagorean Theorem (EE, G)

RP: Ratio & proportions	G: Geometry
NS: Number system	SP: Statistics & Probability
EE: Expressions & Equations	F: Functions

(adapted from CCSS, 2010)

Looking closely at the critical areas gives us important perspectives on the standards. The small number of critical areas per level supports the notion that these standards are focused. At the middle school level you can see that significant attention is given to writing expressions and solving equations. The critical areas highlight the key ideas where several domains coalesce. In this way, these areas support focus and cohesiveness. The cohesive nature of the standards is also demonstrated with the ways in which ideas progress through the grade levels.

There are other standards in each grade level that are not part of these critical areas, and yet they too are important.

In grade seven, 7.SP.8c is not connected to one of the three critical areas at that level. However, it is an extension of a critical area in grade seven. The standard is significant though, as it supports the progression of the students' abilities; students must use their understanding of number and percent to interpret the simulations.

Sometimes we consider standards as a checklist. *Do I understand this one? Move onto the next on the list.* We cannot meet the goals embedded in the critical areas with this way of thinking. Once we understand standards and their progressions over time, we need to think about how the domains work together to support the critical areas at that grade level.

Unpacking a Standard

A standard tells what students need to *know* and be able to *do*. To unpack a standard we grapple with each of the following questions:

- ☞ What must the student *know*?
- ☞ What will the student be able to *do*?
- ☞ How does this standard *relate* to other standards and to the grade level critical areas?
- ☞ What vocabulary and symbols are important to develop?
- ☞ How does the knowledge develop over time (*learning progression*)?
- ☞ What *learning targets* connect to the standard?
- ☞ What *curriculum* and *instruction* support the learning targets being met?
- ☞ How could this standard or its associated learning targets be expressed in student-friendly language?

Let's consider a specific standard in the sixth grade The Number System domain (6.NS.C.6). *Understand a rational number as a point on the number line. Extend number line diagrams and coordinate axes familiar from previous grades to represent points on the line and in the plane with negative number coordinates.* Thinking about the nouns (know) and the verbs (do) can be a way to begin the process. Figure 1.7, also available in Appendix A as a template, is one way to organize the unpacking process. Here is how one teacher completed it.

Figure 1.7 Unpacking an Individual Standard

Standard 6.NS.C.6 Understand a rational number as a point on the number line. Extend number line diagrams and coordinate axes familiar from previous grades to represent points on the line and in the plane with negative number coordinates.	**Organize by Nouns and Verbs** **Understand** • Rational numbers as points on the number line **Extend** • Number line diagrams • Coordinate axes **Represent** • Points on the line and in the plane with negative number coordinates
Relate to Other Standards This standard is in the cluster *Apply and extend previous understandings of numbers to the system of rational numbers.* I will look at each of the other standards in the cluster. It also supports the critical area *Completing understanding of division of fractions and extending the notion of number to the system of rational numbers, which includes negative numbers.*	**Vocabulary/Symbols** Students must know what a number line diagram is and what coordinate axes are. They must also know the (—) sign in front of a number does not mean subtraction but rather represents a negative number.
How Does This Idea Develop? Students need to rely upon previous experiences with number lines as representative of placement of rational numbers, including that the further to the right on the number line the number is (the further to the right from zero), the greater the number is. This concept will be reversed when students consider opposites of the number (the negative of the number), as when on the left side of zero, the lesser the number is. This concept is then extended as students consider the number line as both horizontal (the *x*-axis) and vertical (the *y*-axis).	**Learning Target Examples** • Name a given point on a number line, either to the left or the right of zero. • Place a number in the correct place on a number line, perhaps based on benchmarks. • Identify coordinate points on a coordinate graph, including those with negative numbers.
Curriculum/Instruction • Complete activities on the number line to narrow down where a point is using an applet on the computer. • Play Battleship® with negative numbers as coordinate points. • Use formative assessments such as warm-ups to check for understanding.	**Student-Friendly Language** *I know* what a coordinate graph is. *I can* find where a point is on a coordinate graph.

Glossary

The glossary is another section of the Common Core State Standards that can be forgotten if there is single focus on the specific standards. This aspect of the standards document is meant to augment the standards in that it provides tables that summarize definitions for the terminology used throughout the standards. The tables give problem examples connected to related equations identified within the elementary grade-level standards, but middle school teachers should also keep these different problem situations in mind when they choose or create problems involving fractions or integers. The glossary can help teachers develop common definitions of the terminology used within the standards. When you read a phrase such as *tape diagram* in a standard, it is helpful to refer to the glossary. You may find that you are familiar with this representation provided in the definition, but that you call it by one of the other names, such as bar model.

Assessment

"Asking a student to understand something means asking a teacher to assess whether the student has understood it" (CCSSO 2010, 4). The new standards call upon students (and thus teachers) to deeply understand mathematics. The content progression can only be fully realized if students are able to apply what they are learning in new contexts and connect it to the next related standard(s) as a natural learning path. A variety of assessments help students know how well they understand the material and inform teachers, parents, and administrators about student progress. To be worthwhile, we must make sure that such assessments address both concepts and skills, include tasks that require higher-order thinking, and are accessible.

Formative assessments such as listening to students' conversations in the classroom or reading a child's math journal inform teachers about how to structure the next day's lesson or to determine who might need remediation or enrichment. Purposeful homework provides students with an opportunity to practice the content and to learn to persevere if they find that doing the work individually is difficult. Frequent formative assessment allows us to intervene quickly when a student lacks complete understanding. Time for assessment and intervention should become part of our planning and we must create safe classroom environments where errors are viewed as learning in progress, not embarrassing mistakes.

Questioning techniques are also important. The manner in which we ask students questions should reflect the rigor of the standards, calling upon our students to not only respond to questions such as *What's the answer?* but also, *How do you know...?, What if the problem asked for...?* or *How could you use this information if you were ...?* (See Chapter 2 for further discussion of questioning techniques.) Coupled with the new standards, new standardized tests will be administered. As of this writing, there are two major standardized testing programs being developed. States may choose between The Smarter Balanced Assessment Consortium (SBAC) tests and the Partnership for Assessment of Readiness for College and Careers (PARCC) tests to use for its statewide standardized testing. Both testing programs will require more time throughout the school year as well as a much wider use of technology for full implementation. We need to prepare our students for the particular formats and technology used to better ensure that these tests will capture what our students know.

A chapter of this book is dedicated to assessment of the new standards, including a more detailed look at these high-stakes tests, and a section on assessment is included in every chapter, but let's consider an example here. Most previous standardized tests emphasized multiple-choice questions that were simple to score. These tests will give more attention to open-ended tasks, many of which may be in a puzzle-like format such as the example in Figure 1.8. To respond successfully to this task, students must compute with precision, understand the relationship between multiplication and division with fractions, and be able to explain their reasoning. In this way, expectations for both the mathematical practice and content standards are addressed. We should embed similar tasks in our classroom activities.

Figure 1.8 Sample Assessment Task

Put a number in the start box.

Follow the directions.

Do this two more times.

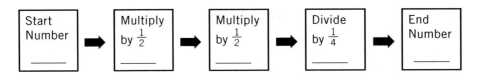

What do you notice?

Explain why you think this happens.

Related Documents

Though the National Governors Association Center for Best Practices and the Council of Chief State School Officers are considered the authors of the Common Core State Standards, many writers and reviewers were involved. Though this document is the only one that is officially approved, drafts of *Progression Documents* provided by those identified as *The Common Core State Standards Writing Team* are available online. These can be a valuable resource for you, though many teachers find them to be challenging to read without guidance or support as they discuss complex ideas related to cognitive development and the structure of mathematics. Ideas from these documents are incorporated into this book so that more teachers will have access to the ways in which writers thought about these standards. Many states have created websites to support educators. We will consider ways to take advantage of such resources and opportunities to work with others in Chapter 10.

Next Steps

As mentioned earlier, understanding these standards and how they might connect to your classrooms is a top priority for your teaching. As the mathematical practices and assessment relate to all of the content domains, those topics are considered in the next two chapters before we turn to each domain separately.

As you read this book, you will notice that instuctional scenarios are presented to model thinking and help facilitate the development of the habits of mind—not necessarily to provide the specific answer. You may want to take notes on what is new to you or about an idea that you want to explore further. Are there special projects that come to mind when you read about a particular standard that you'd like to try with your students? Is there a new model for teaching a concept that seems as though it will work well with one group of students or an individual student that you'd like to learn more about? As you are likely already being asked to teach the standards, think about what new ideas come to mind when you read about a concept or a skill described in this book that you did not understand before. Ideally you would share the reading with a colleague or within a Professional Learning Community (PLC) so that you can discuss it together and perhaps make plans for new ideas you want to try in your classrooms. Also note that you will see icons as you read this book. The Mathematical Practices icon shows where particular MPs are embedded in the mathematical tasks being explained. The classroom connections icon points out activities, lesson ideas, problems, or other classroom ideas that can be used in instruction. The following key will help you navigate through the book.

MP7
Structure

Mathematical Practices

Classroom Connections

Let's Think and Discuss

1. What was your first reaction to learning about the Common Core State Standards?

2. If you were given time to work with colleagues about teaching math, how would you want to spend it?

3. What is an opportunity that adoption of these standards will give you and your students? What is something that will be a challenge for you or your school?

Chapter 2

Standards for Mathematical Practice

 Voice from the Classroom

When we first started meeting about the new standards, our math coordinator decided to have us learn about the practice standards first. A number of us questioned her, as what we wanted to do at that point was to figure out what content we were going to need to teach in our particular grade level. We talked about how important these practice standards were, as they were to drive how we teach the content and that they were far more interwoven into the content standards than we may have realized. It actually turned out to be a very interesting way to start our journey into the new standards.

Learning to decipher what each of the practice standards meant, in our own words, gave us a lot to talk about. As we attempted to unpack these standards, our conversations led us to discuss topics such as when should students be using calculators, how much should students be working in groups, and how to have better discussions in our classrooms. We actually started to form a list of the kinds of learning behaviors that we wanted to see in our students across the board, and how those behaviors might look different and the same, from grade to grade. One grade level even made a booklet to hand out to their students on the expectations that they had for their students about learning in their classrooms. They plan to start the year by modeling and teaching students about some of these expectations.

Now that I look back on it, learning some about these practice standards first has given me a different lens from which to look at the content standards. As I started to think about the math the students are expected to learn, I found myself referring back to these practice standards. There is a great deal more focus on "Understand the concept..." than there used to be in these new content standards, so the practice standards creep back into my planning. I have a lot to learn about how to make these practice standards an active part of daily classroom routines, but I am excited to implement them and hopeful that students will become better mathematicians as a result.

—6th-Grade Teacher

This teacher declares that she and her colleagues gained a new vision for how mathematics could be taught. Does this mean that all of our present teaching strategies need to change? No! It does mean that we need to make sure our students have the opportunity to develop these rigorous expectations for mathematical habits of mind, and that our classrooms are places where students expect to struggle, to reason, and to share their thinking.

The Big Picture

The importance of the Standards for Mathematical Practice can be assumed from their position in the document; they are listed first. Though you may recognize aspects of these standards, their composition and definitions are new and as of this printing, the Common Core writers have not provided a progression document similar to those drafted for the domains. Fortunately, educational consortia, state departments of education, individual writers, and mathematics educators have provided some worthwhile resources. (See Chapter 10.) This is one of the distinct advantages of the national involvement in the Common Core; there are numerous resources available online. You need to have a sense of what these standards are about, however, to evaluate and make good choices about these resources.

While the content standards are grade specific, the practice standards are for all students, K–12. They provide a coherent structure to the study of mathematics and establish the mathematical ways of thinking all students should develop. Like the content standards, the Standards for Mathematical Practice set criteria for learning, criteria that will be assessed. As such, it is important that we understand these standards, envision what teaching and learning looks like in classrooms that embrace them, and develop the teacher moves necessary for their development. As such, the practice standards are referred to throughout the domain chapters. Perhaps most important, we must believe that all students are capable of meeting these goals. While listed in Chapter 1, they are repeated here in Figure 2.1 for your convenience. A listing with their definitions is provided in the Appendix.

While these eight standards each have individual importance, authors of the Common Core have suggested a related structure within them. *MP1 Make sense of problems and persevere in solving them* as well as *MP6 Attend to precision* are identified as overarching standards. The remaining six standards are coupled within three areas of focus: reasoning and explaining thinking, modeling and using tools, and seeing structure and generalizing.

Figure 2.1 Mathematical Practices

MP1 Make sense of problems and persevere in solving them
MP6 Attend to precision

Explaining and Thinking	Modeling and Using Tools	Seeing Structure and Generalizing
• MP2 Reason abstractly and quantitatively. • MP3 Construct viable arguments and critique the reasoning of others.	• MP4 Model with mathematics. • MP5 Use appropriate tools strategically.	• MP7 Look for and make use of structure. • MP8 Look for and express regularity in repeated reasoning.

The content standards are closely related to standards for mathematical practice. Words such as *understand, apply, explain,* and *create* within the content standards suggest reliance on the practice standards. Interweaving the Content Standards with the Standards for Mathematical Practice will help our students view mathematics as engaging and meaningful (Parker and Novack 2012). But first, we need to understand what each of the practice standards requires us and our students to do.

Looking Closer at Each Standard

Make Sense of Problems and Persevere in Solving Them (MP1)

This is one of the two overarching practices that should permeate our instruction. What does it mean to make sense of problems? Ideally, students will dive right into a problem, regardless of the difficulty level, and stick with it until they figure it out. If you have been teaching for any period of time, you will likely agree that this is easier said than done. Many students have a good deal of difficulty with problems that involve any type of challenge and often, as soon as they have read the problem, willingly state, "I don't know how to do this problem." Rather than pondering it even for a moment, they move right away onto to the next one. Research has shown that when students are not able to draw upon a strategy that they have used before, or when the lesson moves from being computation-based to problem-solving oriented, many make no attempt to solve the problem and other students give up easily (Colton 2010). A recent NPR news story suggested that academic struggle is seen in the United States as a sign of weakness, whereas in Asian countries, it is viewed as an opportunity to learn. These are the same Asian countries that, according to international test data, produce strong mathematics students (Siegel 2012). In the U.S. we often applaud students who are naturally good at something or are easily able to solve a problem right away, rather than encouraging students to work through the difficulty, gaining a sense of accomplishment once it is solved. For students to persist, they need to view themselves as capable, with abilities that will increase through their own efforts. According to Carol Dweck, author of the groundbreaking book *Mindset: The New Psychology of Success*, a "...*growth mindset* is based on the belief that your basic qualities are things you can cultivate" (2012, 7).

So, how do we help students learn how to make sense of a problem and to realize that, with effort, they can solve it?

- Choose a clear, appropriately leveled task for students, just beyond their easy reach.
- Group students carefully, varying the groupings from individual to small group, as changing the independence level helps them to learn to persevere on their own or work cooperatively with others when called upon to do so.
- Make sure students have access to the appropriate tools and mathematics vocabulary to solve the task and have a toolbox of strategies from which to choose.
- Provide adequate time for students to work on problems, with extensions given if necessary in order to fully complete the task.
- Set high expectations and give students ample opportunities to reach their own level of success, which helps students gain self-confidence and often leads to a greater willingness to take on more challenging problems.

Reason Abstractly and Quantitatively (MP2)

When students are presented with a problem involving numbers, they must learn to make sense of the quantities provided and consider how several quantities may relate to one another. Students must learn to *decontextualize* given information, meaning to represent what is given symbolically, writing equations, or if appropriate, variable expressions. For example, consider the following problem.

The school chorus group is planning a pizza party for its 60 members. You are in charge of ordering the pizzas. You want each chorus member to be able to eat 2–3 slices of pizza. How many 8-slice pizzas should you order?

Students need to represent the situation in such a way that they can calculate the answer. They do not need to think about the pizza as they work with these numbers. Students must then *contextualize* the answer they found, that is, think about what their answer means within the given context. In this case, students must realize that they can only purchase a whole number of pizzas and will need to adjust their answer accordingly, while keeping the 2–3 slices per chorus member in mind.

Thinking quantitatively, also known as numeracy, entails being comfortable with numbers and being able to use math skills in everyday life. A student who is quantitatively literate is able to support an answer through clear communication and chooses an appropriate format such as words, a table, a graph or an equation (AAC&U 2010). Learning when it is acceptable to provide an estimate, that is deciding *When is the answer close enough?*, through in-class problems as well as real-life questions such as *How many books are on my shelves?* and *How many cars did we pass on our trip?* provide a variety of opportunities for reasoning about numbers.

Teachers can support their students' ability to think quantitatively by providing contexts that are easily related to their everyday lives, with attention paid to their cultural differences and varied learning styles (Darling-Hammond 2012). Research has also shown that including quantitative reasoning opportunities into writing programs strengthens both mathematics and writing skills (Lutsky 2008). Activities involving number sense may include asking questions such as *How long would it take you to drive across the country?* Connections can also be made to topics students are exploring in other subjects, such as figuring out how many garter snakes it would take to make a length as long as a python or comparing data from an historical era being studied to that of today.

Construct Viable Arguments and Critique the Reasoning of Others (MP3)

Understanding is key to the content standards and in the introduction to those standards, the writers of the Common Core state, "One hallmark of mathematical understanding is the ability to justify…a student who can explain the rule understands the mathematics and may have a better chance to succeed at a less familiar task…" (4). To explain how they solved a problem or to understand strategies their peers used, students must learn how to use words, diagrams, mathematical symbols, graphs, or equations to represent and describe their thinking. This process may range from simply turning and talking to their neighbors or participating in class discussions to more formal presentations or written explanations.

In groups, students are often more actively engaged in their own learning and more able to challenge each other's thinking about the strategies they are using. As students become more adept at their mathematical conversations, they learn to communicate with appropriate vocabulary and use clearer strategies to explain their thinking. While students work independently in pairs or small groups, the teacher can interact with students, collect assessment data, or meet with small groups within a scheduled rotation. Wedekind (2011) refers to these meetings as math exchanges. She defines the teacher's focus during these conversations as, "…guiding student talk and mediating thinking as students share problem-solving strategies, discuss how math works, and move toward more effective and efficient strategies and greater mathematical understanding."

As is true with the other practice standards, the more interesting and in-depth the task, the more fully this standard can be realized. Students' willingness to converse about an open-ended task such as *Bryan has 35 cents. What coins could Bryan have?* is far greater than when the tasks are simply right or wrong answers. Of course, having students sit together in a group with an interesting task does not always produce meaningful conversation on its own. Ways teachers can support mathematical discourse are suggested later in the chapter.

Students must also learn to systematically explain their thinking in writing to convince others, teachers and students, that their solution is correct. It is not uncommon for some students to resist justifying their thinking, stating, "I just know that's the answer." We need to consider such responses to determine if the task was too simple for the particular learners and they did "just get it" or if such responses are coming from reluctant learners. The latter must be encouraged to justify their thinking in writing so that when problems get more complex, they will have gained experience justifying their thinking. It's important to remember that a student's solution process does not always have to be documented in words; creating a diagram or drawing a graph may more appropriately describe their thinking. A goal of this standard should be to teach students how to best explain their thinking based on the task.

Throughout the process of discussing and writing about their thinking, students learn to listen to and read their classmates' justifications, to build on what they hear and read and recognize if they need to ask clarifying questions. If a solution does not seem valid, students should engage in meaningful dialogue about how to improve the work, just as they would in language arts.

Model with Mathematics (MP4)

Real-world tasks do not come with instructions for finding a solution. Rather, we must solve problems with no clear solution paths outlined for us. We must, individually or collaboratively, determine what tools to use, identify appropriate mathematics skills and strategies to help us, and design our own solution path. Our problems do not come with a label stating, "Use an array to solve this problem" or "If you need help, look on page 52." We must give students opportunities to address similarly open-ended tasks.

Different than the typical textbook word problem, tasks promoting modeling involve contexts that students are interested in, such as:

- We are going to organize the blocks by shape in the block area. Which ones should go together? How should we label them?

- As the pipes are fixed in our school, we are temporarily not allowed to drink the water in our school's water fountains. If we are going to have bottled water delivered to our school for you to drink, how many bottles of water do you think we should have delivered each week?

- If your family won $1,000 for a family vacation during spring break, how do you think it should be spent?

- The principal has agreed to let you set up an aquarium in the front hallway of the school. How many fish do you think should be purchased for a 20-gallon tank?

These questions, and others like them, allow for multiple entry points as students engage in the processes of gathering appropriate data and considering a variety of solution strategies. Often, such problems result in multiple strategies and solutions. Learning to model a real-world task encourages students to consider how useful mathematics can be to help them solve problems in their daily lives.

You may also wish to engage students in projects that promote the use of mathematics, such as those that embody the principles of Project-Based Learning (Thomas 2000):

- Are central to the curriculum

- Encourage students to struggle with the content

- ✏ Promote purposeful investigations

- ✏ Are student-driven

- ✏ Are realistic

The ultimate intent of this standard is for students to realize that the mathematics they are learning in school may be useful to them in their daily lives, as they engage in activities in which they must consider a complicated situation and simplify it by using mathematics.

Use Appropriate Tools Strategically (MP5)

As is true for an electrician's apprentice, students must first learn to appropriately use the tools of their trade and then put them to good use. This standard requires students to build a toolbox from which they carefully make choices about which tool to use based on the task they are solving. The students themselves must learn to choose the tool without the need to ask, recognizing the power that each tool holds and that the mathematics will make more sense by using that tool (http://thinkmath.edc.org/index.php/CCSS_Mathematical_Practices). But, what does a mathematical toolbox hold? The standards require a number of appropriate tools, heavily relying upon visual models such as using the number line to compare numbers (Figure 2.2), arrays to model multiplication, or tape diagrams to model relationships among numbers. These models are versatile, as they are useful for modeling mathematics at all levels. Students should learn to use the same model in varying contexts; for example, arrays can be used to model multiplication with whole numbers, rational numbers, or polynomials.

Figure 2.2 Number Line

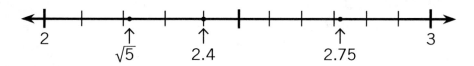

Other models include, but are not limited to:

- ➭ Construction tools such as compasses and straightedges
- ➭ Manipulatives such as color tiles, pattern blocks, and algebra tiles
- ➭ Measuring tools such as rulers, balances, and protractors
- ➭ Technological tools such as scientific and graphing calculators, applets for making graphs, and application programs such as spreadsheets
- ➭ Other tools such as tracing paper, graph paper, and dice

As students become more adept at conceptually understanding the mathematics of the content standards, they learn to transition from using a particular tool, such as the number line to add positive and negative numbers, to instead, drawing upon a rule. Knowing that the tool may be relied upon for reassurance, students keep it in their toolbox, in case the rule is forgotten or misinterpreted. Students should also know when it is more efficient to use mental math as a tool rather than paper and pencil or another tool. Using a calculator to find the answer to 52 x 50 may actually take longer than mentally using the distributive property and thinking: $50(50 + 2) = 2500 + 100 = 2600$.

The intention of this standard is to encourage students to build their mathematics toolbox as they learn more mathematics content. Students should be able to ask themselves:

- ➭ Have I used the right tool for what I want to find out?
- ➭ Has the tool that I chose helped me to learn more math?
- ➭ If asked to, could I explain to someone else how to use this tool? (http://www.weber.edu/COE/CollegePages/appropriate.html)

Attend to Precision (MP6)

Precision is something we want students to consider frequently. Prior to these standards, teachers probably thought about precision in terms of working carefully or checking work. Here we are asked to cultivate precise understanding of mathematical terms and symbols and to use them clearly when discussing a solution strategy. With a focus on mathematics vocabulary, students must engage in activities that introduce them to a term through a variety of experiences, through which students create their own understanding.

Students may develop their vocabulary through using:

- Word walls
- Graphic organizers such as the Frayer model diagram (Frayer, Frederick, Klausmeier 1969; Wormeli 2005)

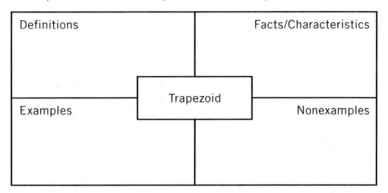

Definitions	Facts/Characteristics
Examples	Nonexamples

Trapezoid

- Math journals, including problem solving strategies or reflections
- Concept maps
- Math dictionaries with visual models and student-created definitions

Using mathematics vocabulary appropriately gives students greater ability to communicate more clearly both in writing and when discussing their solutions (Murray 2004). Murray cautions teachers to take particular care when introducing mathematics vocabulary that may be contrary to how we use the same terms in everyday language. For example, Murray refers to *supplementary* as added on or extra, whereas in mathematics it is used to describe two angles that sum to 180 degrees. Students will, at times, need to distinguish between various uses of the same term, just as they learn to do in their language arts classes.

As teachers encourage their students to learn appropriate use of vocabulary, they, too, must take care to precisely use mathematical terms and to provide a wide range of examples. Geometric figures must be shown in a variety of orientations and, for example, students should be asked to use their definition of prime numbers to decide if the numbers 1 or 2 are prime. Students should also experience various ways of using mathematical symbols, giving particular attention to the equal sign, such as recognizing that $8 + x = 5$ is the same as $5 = 8 + x$ or when to use $=$, $\approx$, or $\cong$.

Accurate calculations, completed efficiently with an appropriate label for the quantity, must be expressed using a level of preciseness appropriate for the situation. For example, students should learn to recognize that providing an answer to a problem about the speed of a car with a label of feet/second might not be as useful as miles/hour. Or, when deciding how many baseballs must be bought based on how many students there are on the team, students must realize that they cannot purchase 6.5 baseballs and determine, based on the situation, whether to purchase 6 or 7 baseballs.

Students who attend to precision have developed, in general, a habit of mind whereby they calculate efficiently and communicate their solution strategies using appropriate vocabulary and symbols. It is expected that, as students gain expertise in the mathematics content, their ability to bring higher levels of complexity to their precision will increase as well.

Look For and Make Use of Structure (MP7)

Consider the following problem:

Describe an interesting way to find the answer to 20 x 16.

Students who look for and make use of structure understand how to reason about the mathematics in the content standards. In actuality, learning to reason about mathematics often means to look for similarities, relationships, or patterns as they are learning. In the problem above, students who look for structure may notice that 20 may be written as 5 x 4 and 16 may be written as 4 x 4, therefore, the problem may be reconstructed as 5 x 4 x 4 x 4 or they may think of multiplying 16 x 10 + 16 x 10 and adding 160 + 160. As students determine a structure for the problem, students are making sense of the mathematics they are learning. Students recognize how ideas are related in a mathematical context, such as the relationship between the number of sides of a polygon and the sum of the angles. Understanding this relationship allows students to draw conclusions that may be used again when seen in other contexts.

Students learn to look for rules as they play mathematics games such as *Guess My Rule?*. While interpreting the attributes of shapes in one part of a Venn diagram versus another part, they determine a category label such as *polygons with right angles* or *quadrilaterals*. Pattern finding is also a considerable component of this standard, as recognizing a pattern can often lead to a rule or a generalization. Finding a pattern; analyzing it; making a generalization; or written rule, expression, or equation prepares students for the algebraic thinking necessary for the related content standards.

Teachers may encourage students to attempt various strategies for noticing structure, including the problem solving strategy of solving a simpler problem (Ray 2011). When students create a simpler problem, they often notice the structure involved in the more complex one. According to Ray, over time students will recognize that if changing the numbers does not change the solution process, then it is the structure of the problem that is most important to their understanding of the mathematics.

Look For and Express Regularity in Repeated Reasoning (MP8)

A student is asked to solve the following problem:

> Austa has decided to build a rectangular garden in her backyard. Based on what she has decided to plant, she thinks that 60 ft² will be enough room. What different lengths and widths can Austa choose from for her garden?

As the student begins working on the task, she decides to build a table of integer lengths and widths that, when multiplied together, make an area of 60. The student isn't sure if she has all of the possibilities so she turns to her friend to discuss what they each have so far. Her friend recognizes that they are making a table of the factors of 60 and uses the strategy they learned previously to assure they have all of the factors.

These students are practicing the habits of this standard by connecting a solution strategy from a prior task to the one at present. In such situations, students are generalizing methods through repeated, similar experiences. Often students who are looking for a general method to solve a problem are looking for shortcuts, a way to make the problem easier to solve. Students who conceptually understand the structure of the standard algorithm for whole number division will recognize the similarity in the structure when solving a decimal division problem. While students are paying attention to the details of how to solve the decimal problem, they are also able to see the bigger picture that the standard algorithm for division still applies. Recognizing that the calculations are the same, despite the introduction of the decimal point, allows students to use reasoning previously applied to this new context.

Students can be encouraged to practice this standard by asking them:

- Does this situation look like one that you have encountered before?

- Can you explain how the solution strategy you used for this problem can be used in another problem?

- Are there situations, given a similar problem, in which this solution strategy will not work? (USD 2011)

Recognizing patterns and generalizations in their study of mathematics, students learn to see mathematics as a cohesive whole, rather than separate unconnected parts. Knowing that they can apply a previously learned strategy in a new situation implies conceptualizing mathematics in such a way that it is ingrained in their thinking and is useful beyond the current task.

 **Snapshot**

It's the first week of school and this seventh-grade teacher knows that she wants to establish expectations as early as possible, for what her students will do in math this year. She wants them to explore a problem that will solicit a variety of ideas so that they will have something to talk about together. She also wants her students to know that she is accepting of different ways to solve a problem and students should work toward understanding a variety of solution methods. She has created a task for the students to explore and presents it to the students with the following introduction:

Today, you are going to work in groups on a task that I will present. I'd like you to think about the task itself, but also be prepared at the end of our class today to discuss how you worked together as a group in sharing your solution strategies. If we have time, I'd also like to discuss how well you persevered through the task when you weren't sure what to do. So, here's the task:

I love ice cream. I don't have it very often, but when I do, I like getting a double scoop. At my local ice cream shop there are 12 choices of flavors. If I choose a different combination of flavors every time I go, how many times will I have to go before I have had all of the combinations?

The teacher asked her students to begin thinking about this task individually. She believes that all students should have the opportunity to think about the problem without influence from another student. She circulates to hear some initial questions, although she chooses not to answer them individually. After about 10 minutes, she brings the class back together and asks them if they have any initial thoughts. Calvin says, "It's really too many to count. This is going to be a lot of work." Kyle raises his hand to ask a question, "I'm wondering if you ever get the same flavor for both scoops." The teacher responds to Kyle by saying that he has asked a good question. She had thought about this aspect of the task when she was writing it for the class, but she decided not to include this information, hoping that someone would ask if it was possible. When she responded, "Yes, sometimes I like double scoops of the same flavor" a good deal of the students said, "Oh, so that changes my ideas." As students continue to ask other questions, the teacher often responds with a comment back to the class, "Do you understand what Brett is asking?", "Did anyone else have the same question?" or "What do you think, Malik?" The teacher wants to assure that all of her students are as engaged as possible in this short, whole class discussion. She finds that asking students to repeat what others have said is a good way to keep them on task and allow students to articulate each other's thinking.

After a short discussion, she then tells the students that they may work together if they wish to work on the task. Several students ask the teacher if she has any post-it notes they can use and others go over to the bookcase to get some multi-link cubes. She is pleased to see that the students are coming up with their own ways to model their thinking. In the past, she has found that, if she gets into solution strategies with the whole class too quickly, the students just follow someone else's thinking rather than devising their own strategies. The conversation among the students becomes animated as they discuss various ideas. The teacher notices that one group wants to go to their lockers to get their calculators and the teacher allows them to do so, but challenges them to try to do their calculating without it at first. The group of students who were using multi-link cubes found they didn't have 12 different cube colors to use to represent the flavors so they abandoned the use of that model and decided to label each flavor with a letter, A-L, and make lists on their paper instead. Yet another group was laboriously writing down flavors of ice cream with long titles, so the teacher sat with that group for a moment, asking them if the exact flavors were important in the task, or the total number of combinations. Sierra and Claudia agreed that perhaps they could abbreviate their flavor names, which would cut down on the time spent on the task. Several groups were writing long lists of combinations, while the teacher noticed others recognizing there was a pattern in the lists and were abandoning writing out all possibilities. Instead, some were working on finding the total using the pattern and two groups were working on finding a rule.

As the students came back together to share their solutions, the teacher first asked students to provide what they found for answers. As the groups reported out several different answers, the teacher didn't say whether or not they were correct, rather she made a list of the possible answers on the board and made a checkmark next to an answer for each group who thought that was correct. She wants to create the kind of environment whereby students can feel free to offer suggested answers without feeling embarrassed if it is incorrect, so she starts by first accepting volunteers to provide answers rather than requiring each group to report. As students began talking about their solution strategies, the teacher asked the students, if they wanted to, to bring their work to the front of the room and display it using the document camera. They could then stay at the front of the room if they wanted to or go back to their seats to share their answers. Once the correct answer was established, the students compared notes on how they found the solution. The teacher was pleased to see how students found the connections between the strategies, and made comments such as, "That's almost how I did it, but I also…"

The teacher is pleased with what the students accomplished. They explained their thinking, listened to each other, built on the ideas of others, made sense of the problem, modeled with mathematics, and reasoned quantitatively. Tomorrow she will ask them about a similar problem with a greater number of flavors. This time she would have the students brainstorm different ways to represent the flavors and different equations they can write to represent their combinations. She wants them to begin to focus on the equations, how they could be different when they must be the same. She wants the students to focus on the structure and repeated reasoning involved by asking questions such as *Is there a shortcut we could use? Will this always be true? What happens as we change the number of possible flavors?*

Teacher Strategies to Support these Standards

As we understand the practice standards more deeply, it becomes clear we must reflect on whether or not our current instructional strategies will support students becoming proficient mathematicians. We need to think about the class environment through the lens of the practice standards. We must make it clear to students that being persistent, taking risks, listening to one another carefully, analyzing errors, and debating ideas respectfully are the expected classroom norms. It is not possible for students to engage actively with for example, sense making or critiquing the reasoning of others without these expectations. Students must also feel safe, that is, that their ideas will be listened to and respected and that sharing mistakes helps everyone to learn. Students must also expect to look to themselves for mathematical insights, rather than relying on the teacher to resolve all mathematical questions. As such, the role of teacher changes from that of *information provider* to one who *chooses tasks* carefully and *facilitates learning* based on knowledge of what students know, what they need to learn, and how they learn best.

Choosing Tasks

One of the most important choices we make as teachers is identifying the instructional tasks we will offer our students. The practice standards should have a significant influence on the tasks we choose. For example, how can we expect students to learn to persevere in solving problems if we don't provide tasks at the right level of challenge? Similarly, how can we engage students in reasoning abstractly if we do not offer tasks that require students to analyze relationships? Figure 2.3 suggests some questions to consider about the tasks we choose in relation to the Standards for Mathematical Practice. The idea is not to consider each question for each task, but rather, to focus on the questions related to the particular practice standards you plan to highlight in a lesson or activity.

Figure 2.3 Questions to Consider When Choosing Tasks

Practice Standard	Task Considerations
MP1 Make sense of problems and persevere in solving them	• Is the level of complexity appropriate? • Will the context of the task engage students? • Will diverse students have a way to begin? • Is the description of the tasks clear? Are there ways I can adapt the description of the task to make it more accessible to ELL students?
MP2 Reason quantitatively and abstractly	• Does this task require students to contextualize or decontextualize mathematical ideas? • Does the task require students to make use of relationships among numbers and properties of operations?
MP3 Construct viable arguments and understand the reasoning of others	• Will the task solicit multiple approaches or opinions? • Will the task uncover incomplete understanding or misconceptions?
MP4 Model with mathematics	• Will this task solicit multiple representations? • Is the context of the task realistic?
MP5 Use appropriate tools strategically	• Does this task support use of a variety of tools or representations? • Does this task require students to choose an appropriate tool to use?
MP6 Attend to precision	• How will this task further students' understanding of mathematical terms? • Does the context suggest a level of precision required? • Will this task require students to think about appropriate labels?
MP7 Look for and make use of structure	• Will this task encourage students to note and make use of patterns? • Will this task help students uncover a mathematical structure or property?
MP8 Look for and express regularity in repeated reasoning	• Will this task help students discover a shortcut? • How might this task support the development of general methods?

Some types of tasks have been identified as particularly worthwhile. For example, Barlow and McCrory (2011) suggest tasks that stimulate disagreements are particularly appropriate as they can stimulate sense making, discussion, and reasoning. They identify three types of tasks that are likely to create opportunities for mathematical disagreements, tasks that: force students to pick a side; reveal students' misconceptions; and ones that have triggered disagreements in previous years. The following are examples of tasks that require students to take sides and that address common misconceptions:

✏ Write about why this shape is or is not a trapezoid.

✏ Do you think Jamie's work is correct? Why or why not?

$$\begin{array}{r} {}^{2}\ {}^{15} \\ \cancel{\cancel{3}0.\cancel{5}} \\ -16.8 \\ \hline \end{array}$$

✏ Jeri said that 1 is a prime number because it doesn't have any factors others than itself. What do you think?

As you consider your students' work, identify those errors that occur a few times. Create a similar example and ask students to "take a stand." Allow them time to debate and clarify their thinking. Sometimes you may be surprised by how deeply some misconceptions or particular misunderstandings are held. Other times you may be delighted by how quickly a common misunderstanding falls away once it is uncovered. Either way you are engaging your students in important sense making and reasoning; you are putting them in charge of their mathematical understanding.

Letting Students Do the Work

Most of us can probably remember a time when we were taking a high-stakes test and were told to *stop working and put our pencils down*. As teachers, we need to put *our* pencils down to make sure students are doing *their* work. Too often, teachers respond to student queries by *showing* them how to complete a task or solve a problem. Even teachers committed to fostering student thinking can fall into this trap. It can be quite challenging to refrain from indicating exactly where a student made an error within a series of steps or from resolving a mathematical disagreement during a discussion, but to do so would eliminate learning opportunities for the students. We will invariably make such an error, especially when feeling the pressure of time, but our intentions to avoid doing so should be firm. We do not want to be so helpful that we lower the cognitive demand of a task (Zucker 2012). Note that the blog of well-known TED speaker Dan Meyer has the motto *less helpful*.

There are other ways we can do too much of the work, for example, when we:

- ✏ **provide too many sub-questions**, which keep students from having to make sense of a problem.

- ✏ **provide a template** such as a coordinate graph, when students should be deciding on the tool to use.

- ✏ **do not give wait time**, but rather, just give the answer when no one responds immediately. The term "wait time" was coined by Mary Budd Rowe (1986) when her research established that merely waiting 3 seconds after posing a question increased student responses. Today, many educators recommend 4–7 seconds for students to formulate their thinking. Such time may help to alleviate some of the differences between genders and support English Language Learners. Too often teachers call on a quick responder or provide the answers themselves, rather than wait for a greater number of students to process their ideas.

Orchestrating Discourse

Class discussions provide opportunities for students to share their thinking and take ownership of their mathematical ideas. Such opportunities can address all of the practice standards depending on the specifics of the discourse. Interest in mathematical conversations has been growing for several years. Chapin, O'Connor, and Anderson (2009) have identified what they called five productive talk moves:

- ✏ Revoicing is a move that allows teachers to check to make sure that what a student has said has been heard and understood correctly. It might begin with a teacher saying, "So I think you are saying that…"

- ✏ Students also can be asked to restate someone else's reasoning, a move that encourages listening carefully by asking questions such as, "How would you use your own words to tell us what Erica just said?"

- ✏ The move to apply their own reasoning to someone else's is another way to focus students' attention on what others are saying and also promotes the critical analyses of the thinking of others. You can encourage such responses by asking questions such as, "Do you agree with what Jasmine just said?"

- ✏ You can prompt for further participation through such questions as, "Who can give us another example?"

- ✏ The authors also include wait time (mentioned earlier) in their identified moves.

It is also important to think about which students you call on and the order in which you ask students to present their thinking. If you want a student to critique another student's thinking, you may want to first ask a student sitting on the other side of the room as a student sitting next to them may be hesitant to take a different position.

Smith, Hughes, Engle, and Stein (2009) encourage us to think carefully about the students we select to present their thinking to the class and the order in which we ask them to do so. As we observe and interact with our students as they explore a task, we should note students whose work would help others to learn and understand. Some questions to consider are:

- ☞ Which students' work samples show different approaches?

- ☞ Whose work illustrates a common error or misconception that will be helpful for others to discuss?

- ☞ Whose work best illustrates a common solution strategy that most students will easily understand that I might want presented first/early?

- ☞ Whose work is concrete and might help other students better understand work presented later?

- ☞ Whose work is the most unique or efficient that I might want presented last?

- ☞ Whose work best demonstrates attention (or inattention) to precision?

Hufferd-Ackles, Fuson, and Sherin have identified four components of a math-talk learning community: questioning, explaining mathematical thinking, sources of mathematical ideas, and responsibility for learning. They describe different levels of each of these components based on the degree to which the teacher (indicating a lower, less preferred level) or students (indicating a higher, more preferred level) are taking the lead. They state, "When student thinking began to be elicited, students became more engaged and involved in classroom discourse as speakers and listeners. Their responsibility for their own learning was indicated by their desire to ask questions in class, their eagerness to go to the board to demonstrate their understanding of problems, and their volunteering to … assist struggling students" (2004, 106).

Asking Questions

Asking our students the right question at the right time can be immensely valuable in supporting these practice standards. Examples of questions to support discourse were identified among the talk moves, but we also need to ask questions directly related to each of the practice standards. Examples are provided in Figure 2.4.

Figure 2.4 Sample Questions to Stimulate Development of the Practice Standards

Practice Standard	Questions to Support Development
MP1 Make sense of problems and persevere in solving them	• What do you think the problem is asking you to do? • What else could you try?
MP2 Reason quantitatively and abstractly	• What would your solution mean in this context? • Are there relationships among the numbers that are useful?
MP3 Construct viable arguments and understand the reasoning of others	• Why did you choose this representation? • Can you tell me what you are doing and why?
MP4 Model with mathematics	• Is there a table or graph you could make to show this information? • Is there an equation you can write?
MP5 Use appropriate tools strategically	• Is there a representation you can make? • Is there a tool you might use?
MP6 Attend to precision	• How are you defining this term? • In this context, how important is it that the answer be exact?
MP7 Look for and make use of structure	• Have you completed other tasks similar to this one? • Do you see a pattern?
MP8 Look for and express regularity in repeated reasoning	• Can you make a generalization? • Will this method always work?

Assessment

As stated earlier in the chapter, assessment must include a focus on these standards. When you wish to focus on a particular practice standard you can translate the description of the practice into a rubric. For example, after rereading the description for MP2 Reason quantitatively and abstractly you could pinpoint the key behaviors students are expected to exhibit and use them to create a checklist.

Figure 2.5 Sample Checklist for Mathematical Practice Standards

Student Name: _____ Date:_____

The student:

❏ noted or made use of numerical relationships among quantities

❏ created an equation to represent the situation

❏ checked to see if the answer made sense given the situation or the numbers involved

❏ used properties of operations flexibly

As standardized tests will include items that require students to explain their thinking in writing, students need ample practice in doing so. Denman (2013) recommends that we familiarize students with the procedural language of such explanations, including:

➯ **What words**: *multiply to find…*

➯ **Why words**: *since, because…*

➯ **Transitional words**: *to start with, first, then, after that, second…*

➯ **Concluding words**: *Therefore I know…*

Encourage students to connect phrases such as *Because I … I started with…* Once students have gained initial expertise for such explanations, perhaps in conjunction with their language arts instruction, students can adapt to an explanation style that fits them best as long as completeness and clarity are maintained.

Encourage students to read and edit their explanations in pairs or small groups, as they would for any writing assignment. You can also have students reflect on their explanations by having others try to match or actually create similar work based on what was explained.

 ## Let's Think and Discuss

1. How will you include the Standards for Mathematical Practice into your daily planning?

2. Which practice standards do you think will have the greatest impact on your teaching? Why?

3. What evidence do you expect to see that your students are mastering the habits of mind required in the practice standards?

Chapter 3

Assessment and the Common Core

 Voice from the Classroom

Now that there is a lot more in the press about the new standardized tests that will be used for assessing the standards, we have begun talking in school meetings about what these tests will look like. Our greatest concern, at this point, is that the tests will all be taken online. While we have begun having greater access to technology in our classrooms, our students are not regularly seeing the technology as a way to learn the content. They often want a "re-explanation" after engaging in an activity online. We know that the online standardized tests will require our students to engage in online material as purposefully as if it were being done with paper and pencil. We recognize that this will take time for teachers to find appropriate, online materials to use and also for our students to fully embrace how the use of the computer can change how they learn new material. Our math coach is great about helping us to look for materials that can engage students to learn a concept in a more open-ended, engaging manner, just as the new tests' questions promise to do.

We are also having a lot of conversations about how the questions are likely to change from being more procedure-based to being more concept-based. We have been reviewing some of the questions that are online as sample questions for the new standardized tests. We have recognized that there are more concept-based questions than what our students may be used to. Some of us feel as though we focus on conceptual understanding in our classroom lessons but we don't necessarily ask enough conceptual questions on quizzes and tests. We tend to stick with questions that rely on their ability to carry out procedures even in application problems, because we don't want our students to struggle too much on tests. We'd like to focus more on engaging our students in questions that challenge their understanding of a concept and ask them to apply it in a new situation. We hope that this will allow our students to, not only be more successful with these new tests, but also to retain the concept.

—8th-Grade Teacher

 ## Big Picture

What role should assessment play in our classrooms? The National Council of Teachers of Mathematics published *Assessment Standards for School Mathematics* that asserted four purposes of assessment: to make instructional decisions, to monitor our students' progress, to evaluate students' achievement on an individual basis, and to evaluate programs (NCTM 1995). All four of these purposes remain important today. Sometimes, though, it can seem as if attention is given only to the evaluation of teachers, school systems, and students based on student performance on standardized tests. Imagine what it would be like if editorials, news reports, tweets, and blogs were filled with as much attention to teachers who knew how to ask a question that gave them access to students' thinking and led to instruction that helped those learners move from a misconception to full understanding.

Assessment is not new to our classrooms. We know that we must collect evidence of learning, use such evidence to plan our instruction, and share data with parents and other stakeholders who have a right to know the success of our teaching and of student learning. We know that no one type of assessment will provide us with all that we wish to know and that important decisions must be made based on several sources of data. Yet, there is new knowledge that we need. The adoption of the Common Core State Standards for Mathematics raises five new issues for educators:

- How can classroom assessment strategies help ensure that students meet grade-level content standards expected in the Common Core?

- How do we support equity through the assessment process?

- What are the implications of so called "next generation" standardized tests?

- How should we assess whether students have met the Standards for Mathematical Practice?

- How can we involve parents and students in the high-stakes testing likely to be associated with these standards?

Classroom Assessment Strategies

With all the attention given to performance on standardized tests, we can sometimes underestimate the importance of the assessment strategies within our classrooms that are conducted on a regular basis. As new standards require students to acquire both conceptual understanding and procedural fluency, we need to make sure that our assessments are attending to both types of learning. As there are expectations for students to perform at grade-level, we need to find ways to uncover learning needs more quickly and to address them. As always, we must make instructional decisions based on the information we collect (Collins 2012).

Assessment decisions must be based on an understanding of how students' thinking becomes more sophisticated over time (Heritage 2008). Such learning progressions are built on research about how students learn. This is why it is important for teachers to understand the standards at their grade level as well as to recognize how they relate to standards across grade levels. Teachers must also have a deep understanding of the mathematics involved in these standards to recognize how to best assess them and how to recognize when student thinking may relate to a misconception at a later grade level.

Assessment strategies may be classified as *summative*, that is, used as assessment *of* learning or *formative*, the assessment *for* learning. In actuality, all forms of assessment data can be used for either purpose, if that is how teachers use it. So, you play a pivotal role in the assessment process and can always use data to inform your teaching.

Summative Assessment

Summative assessments are scheduled to occur after learning is assumed to have taken place and might be in the form of a completed journal or project, a performance, or a test. They are likely to result in a grade or score that is significant in rating students' performance levels. The most familiar type of non-standardized summative assessment is the use of chapter tests or quizzes. Mathematics curricula include such tests in their materials. Some school systems require teachers to have students take these tests and to report student scores to a school administrator. Zorin, Hunsader, and Thompson (2013) identify four concerns with such tests and encourage teachers to become alert to the potential difficulty of items that include:

- ✏ **Poor number choices that may hide important data**. For example, asking a student who may have trouble understanding how to find square roots is given the problem: Find the $\sqrt{4}$. This not a good number choice as the answer is 2 even if the student thought that finding square roots means to divide in half, making it difficult to conclude that the student understands that finding a square root means looking for the same number times itself, not 2 as dividing 4 in half.

- ☞ **Inappropriate contexts for a particular mathematical task**. For example, a story problem about the number of liters of water in an in-ground swimming pool that then asks students to convert the measure to milliliters, a measure that would never be used in this real-world context.

- ☞ **Superfluous graphics that do not help make student learning visible**. For example, including an image of graph paper next to a word problem that requires students to find .8 x .7 for its solution might be helpful to students not quite ready for the challenge or for English language learners. However, more insight into student understanding would be gained if the task required learners to explain how the given representation could be used to justify their response.

- ☞ **Assumptions that must be made to respond to the task correctly**. A problem asks seventh graders to find the speed of an airplane, given the rate and the time. They will assume that the trade winds will be the same. However, later on in their study of such problems, often when studying systems of linear equations, they are told that the winds affect the rate.

These tests should also be examined for their match to the new standards. Are there some items that should be dropped because they are no longer aligned to the grade level? Is there an appropriate balance between the emphasis on procedural and conceptual learning, or do some items need to be adapted? Even recently published materials need to be considered from these perspectives as we are all still learning about these expectations. And, of course, we also should be screening assessment tasks we design according to these same criteria.

Formative Assessment

The National Mathematics Advisory Panel (2008) has reported data that indicate the direct correlation between use of formative assessment and student achievement and recommends regular use of formative assessment. Formative assessment of our students is intended to give teachers and students feedback while they are learning content with hopes of improving teacher instruction and student performance (McManus 2008). Note the emphasis on both teachers and students. We need to make sure students, not just teachers, learn from formative assessment data and that such data are collected throughout the instructional process. When students are given the opportunity to analyze the results of their assessments they are often able to clear up misconceptions and further clarify their own thinking.

A position paper of the National Council of Teachers of Mathematics on Formative Assessment states that, "…by applying formative strategies such as asking strategic questions, providing students with immediate feedback, and engaging students in self-reflection, teachers receive evidence of students' reasoning and misconceptions to use in adjusting instruction" (NCTM 2013, 1). Such reflection and feedback should also help students gain a better sense of where their learning stands in relationship to a standard and what, if any, actions they should take.

So what might this look like in the classroom? Here are some brief examples:

☞ A seventh-grade classroom is investigating finding the missing number in a proportion when it becomes apparent that a small group of students do not understand the strategy of using scale factor. The next day the teacher implements a mini lesson with the students who were having difficulty. Using simulation software, she will have students scale up and scale down several triangles so that students can visually connect how scaling the sides creates equivalent ratios. She carefully chooses numbers that create whole numbers for the scale factor, so that students can focus on the concept rather than the computation. Following several similar visual experiences, the teacher will ask the students to describe the strategy and then try other, more challenging examples.

✏ An eighth-grade classroom is working on explaining their thinking in writing. The teacher has students working in groups and asks them to record their thinking on chart paper. Their responses are posted about the room and students take a gallery walk. Viewing groups are asked to post a compliment and a question to each response. This teacher believes that this group approach is a good way to begin having students assess the work of others as it can be less threatening to some students.

✏ Sixth-grade students have just received their quizzes back with descriptive feedback. On Shanna's quiz the teacher wrote: *You gave a clear explanation of how you solved the first problem. What details could you add to your explanation of the second problem?* On Torry's paper she wrote: *You showed two different ways to multiply. Can you find a mistake that you made when multiplying by 6?* The teacher gives students time to respond to her comments.

✏ A seventh-grade teacher begins a lesson by saying *Tell me what you know about a sphere.* She will use student responses to help her decide the language and examples of triangles she needs to highlight in the lesson.

✏ As eighth-grade students are finding lines of best fit, the teacher asks questions such as *How do you know where to place the line? How do you decide if one of the points should be included or not? How do you know if you think you have shown enough points above and below the line?* She makes brief notes on an observation form as she listens to responses, which she will return to the next time the students are drawing lines of best fit.

✏ A sixth-grade teacher asks students to look at the entries in their math journals. She asks them to choose two samples that show how their understanding of measures of variability has increased. The students are expected to write about their choices, giving specific details about the evidence of growth in understanding.

Use of Journals

Journal writing in a mathematics class is an activity that allows students to write about a particular mathematics topic, knowing they will not be graded on what they write. Keeping the writing private, except to the teacher, gives students the opportunity to write individually and usually, freely. There is a strong relationship between the mental journey needed to write about mathematics and the mathematics itself, as the act of writing may be used to organize and clarify thinking (Aspinwall and Aspinwall 2003). Journal entries are an excellent formative assessment tool, allowing the teacher to view what the students are thinking, sometimes, before and after a class discussion. The teacher can then formulate next steps based on what all of the students are writing, not just on what a few students may say in a class discussion. The following Snapshot shows how the use of journals allows for formative assessment to be integrated into instruction.

 **Snapshot**

The students in Ms. Ramirez's math class have become quite used to writing responses to mathematics tasks as a way of expressing their initial thinking. Today, Ms. Ramirez asks her students to focus on the statement she has written on the board: *We are required to attend school for 180 days of the year.* The students know that they must take out their mathematics journals and write the statement that is on the board. They are then asked to write freely for five minutes about the mathematics that comes to mind about the statement. Ms. Ramirez purposely chooses not to circulate around the room while they are writing. Instead, she sits at her round table in the back of the room, observing her students. She thinks that if she circulates this might distract her students from their writing and she wants them to feel free to write in their journals without having their teacher looking over their shoulder. She watches their enthusiasm for the writing process, observes students who may be struggling, and jots down some notes about particular students' focus on the task.

After a few minutes, the teacher announces that she would like some students to respond to the statement on the board. She records their statements on the whiteboard. Some students make new comments after listening to what other students have said. Several responses are recorded including:

- We go to school lots of days.

- There are about 30 days in a month. Since $30 \times 6 = 180$, we go to school for about 6 months.

- 180 days is less than the number of days in a year.

- Since $180 + 180 = 360$ we go to school about half of the days.

- We go to school about six hours each day. $6 \times 180 = 1080$, so we are in school more than one thousand hours.

The students enjoy this conversation and everyone is able to contribute. They could talk even longer, but Ms. Ramirez wants them to note relationships among the statements. She asks students to tell how these statements are similar. One student comments that most of them include the number 180. Another student comments that many of the statements have something to do with finding another name for 180 days, like about six months. This student suggests they find the number of minutes they are in school. At the conclusion of the whole class conversation, Ms. Ramirez asks each of the students to return to their journals to write some summary statements. Her students know that they can write any number of things in their summaries. They can write:

- something they learned mathematically that they didn't know before

- a question they have about what they have learned

- a comment about the discussion that they didn't get to say to the group that they wish they had

- anything else that comes to mind related to the discussion

Ms. Ramirez looks forward to reading students' math journals. She may just read one entry, she might make a comment or ask a question in the journal in response to something the student has written, or she might record something about what the student has written in her assessment notebook, where she keeps track of information about her students. More than once, Ms. Ramirez and a student have started a running dialogue about a particular topic in the journal. One of her students shared that he was frustrated with division and didn't see why he had to learn it. Ms. Ramirez wrote back that he should tell her his three top interests and she would help him to learn the importance of division in those areas.

Questioning for Assessment

Crowe and Stanford (2010) suggest that the power of questioning is often overshadowed by the attention given to high-stakes assessment. Good questions challenge students and help teachers to uncover misconceptions (Weiss and Pasley 2004). We can probe students' understanding more deeply by asking questions such as:

- What more can you tell me?

- Can you say that another way?

- Is there something you could draw to show me what you mean?

- How do you know that you are correct?

- What does this 1 represent in your computation?

- What do you do to put numbers in order?

- How would you describe a right rectangular prism if you had never seen one?

- What do you know about how to use a protractor to measure angles?

- When would you use this outside of school?

Note that these questions are open-ended, that is, they could be answered in a variety of ways and still be correct or partially correct. This doesn't mean you should never ask basic knowledge questions such as *What is the formula for the area of a triangle?*, but these types of questions don't give as much insight into conceptual thinking or stimulate such thinking.

Quick questions to which a whole class responds will allow you to get a general feel for student understanding and can be as simple as *Show a thumbs up, neutral, or thumbs down to share how well you understand the meaning of the slope in this situation.* A quick look will allow you to assess the most common responses and identify which students are likely to need additional support or challenge. These check-in questions are often most helpful when asked at the beginning of a lesson or right after some information has been shared and you are about to assign students to individual or small-group work. Responses will allow you to adapt your lesson, help you to assign groups, or gather a small group to work with you further.

Some general "rules" about asking questions are:

- ☞ Be sure to give adequate time for students to think before accepting responses.

- ☞ Avoid yes or no questions as they do not give insight into student thinking.

- ☞ Include higher-level questions rather than questions that have only one correct factual answer.

- ☞ Move away from an individual student when you ask a question so that the whole class feels involved.

Sometimes you may wish to pose a question and have students record their responses before their answers are discussed. This allows some students to respond more thoughtfully. After the discussion you can ask students to correct or extend their original answers. Students could also write two-sentence answers on index cards. The cards could be collected and redistributed for other students to read aloud, allowing a variety of ideas to be heard at an early stage of learning, when many might not choose to share their thinking.

Students can also be invited to pose questions themselves by suggesting, for instance, that they write questions to show what they would like to learn about three-dimensional objects or suggest questions that they think should be on the quiz. You can ask students to pose questions that they think will be helpful to their peers. Have students practice asking such questions as *Why do you think this?* to enable good peer teaching and deeper pair shares.

Equity and Assessment

There are many equity issues associated with assessment that we need to re-examine through the goal of career and college readiness. We want to be sure that our assessment practices help our students to meet this goal and that our assessment strategies support equity. Afflerbach and Clark (2011) suggest that assessment can create barriers to learning and thus increase inequities. These authors indicate that conversely, assessment could open avenues of support and improve positive self-identity, two factors that increase the likely success of students who are too often marginalized. The Common Core has set these standards for *all* students; our assessments must increase access to learning, not further limit it.

There are a variety of ways our classroom assessment practices can be beneficial, rather than detrimental. For example, we can:

- **use a variety of assessment formats**, so that all learners have the opportunity to demonstrate what they know. For instance, some learners perform less well on multiple-choice assessment formats as they tend to be less contextualized (Goodwin, Ostrom, and Scott 2009). Instead of asking whether questions should be open-ended or multiple choice, we should think about which formats are best when and for which students:

- **support student self-efficacy** by providing them opportunities to assess their own work and set their own goals.

- **create learning environments** in which students view constructive feedback as helping them to achieve their own goals.

- **give feedback privately** and compare student work to previous work, not to the work of other students.

- ✏ **connect assessment tasks** to students' culture and identity by providing tasks that relate to students' interests, backgrounds, and daily lives.

- ✏ **differentiate assessment items** to ensure access. For example, you can decrease the complexity of the non-mathematics vocabulary for English language learners.

Most importantly, we must use assessment data to provide students with additional opportunities to learn. Struggling students must be given access to additional instruction so that they can perform better. This approach is quite different than grouping students together to focus on less challenging tasks at a slower pace. Similarly, students who are ready should have access to more challenging tasks, so that they too, can reach their full potential.

Standardized Testing of the Common Core State Standards

As a result of the allocation of funds from the federal Race to the Top assessment grant program, two consortia have received federal funding to create these assessments: The Partnership for Assessment of Readiness for College and Career (PARCC) and the Smarter Balanced Assessment Consortium (SBAC). A national testing model allows data to be compared across students, districts, and states. Both consortia are committed to tests that better assess student's critical thinking and problem solving skills as well as their understanding of mathematical concepts. Replacing fill-in-the-blank, "bubble" tests, the PARCC and SBAC both intend to better understand students' ability to solve problems by asking questions that will require students to describe how they solved the problem as well as to provide an answer. As the mode for test taking is technology-based, the test questions can be made interactive and intentionally engaging. This is why these assessments are sometimes referred to as next-generation tests. According to the Smarter Balanced website the overall claim or statement of learning outcomes of the SBAC summative assessments for grades 3–8, is "Students can demonstrate progress toward college and career readiness in mathematics" (http://www.smarterbalanced.org).

Sub-claims of SBAC Learning Outcomes:

Sub-Claim A: Students solve problems involving the major content for their grade level with connections to practices.

Sub-Claim B: Students solve problems involving the additional and supporting content for their grade level with connections to practices.

Sub-Claim C: Students express mathematical reasoning by constructing mathematical arguments and critiques.

Sub-Claim D: Students solve real-world problems engaging particularly in the modeling practice.

The PARCC consortia have articulated similar goals on its website with a strong focus on creating an assessment system that will "build a pathway to college and career-readiness for all students" (http://www.parcconline.org).

Testing Formats

Both assessments are designed to include more than one test session throughout the school year. Tests given at the beginning of the school year, while optional, are intentionally formative, providing early feedback regarding student knowledge and skills. The time commitment on the mathematics component of these assessments is approximately two hours over two sessions. As a result of these formative tests, teachers can learn more about their students in order to inform instruction and to gain supplemental support for their students, if necessary. Teachers are able to score the tests themselves, allowing for timely feedback. The two required end-of-year assessments are designed to first test students' ability to complete performance-based tasks, where skills and concepts are applied through extended tasks. The estimated time commitment for the two sessions is a total of approximately two hours in length. Second, the final assessment is computer-based and will be comprised of questions that may be machine-scored. The two final assessment scores will be combined to make up the students' accountability score. Grade level specific performance level descriptors (PLDs) and achievement level descriptors (ALDs), have been created to determine what knowledge and skills must be demonstrated at a particular grade level. These can be found in detail on the consortia websites.

The SBAC consortium has agreed to create a paper-and-pencil version of all assessments while districts are in the process of upgrading their technology, after which time all assessments will be completed online. The PARCC consortium will create paper-and-pencil tests for those students who require them as written in their Individualized Education Plans. SBAC will utilize computer adaptive testing (CAT), which bases the questions asked of students on their answers to previous questions. Students who answer a question correctly will then receive a more challenging question, while a wrong answer on a question will lead students to an easier question. While not intending to use CAT, the PARCC assessments will also be taken online for both the formative and summative assessments. Both consortia have outlined the technology requirements to allow for use of a wide variety of devices, including tablets, laptops, and desktop computers. The consortia have provided specifications regarding bandwidth for administering the tests, number of required devices, and recommendations for test administration sessions. The intention is to make the administration of the online tests to be as widely available to all districts as possible, within a reasonable timeframe, though some districts suggest that it is impossible for them to afford the necessary technology. Students in grades 3–5 will not be using calculators to assist with answering any questions on the PARCC and SBAC tests, however, middle and high school grade students will use online calculators for some portion of the tests.

Test Questions

Prototype questions have been made available for the purpose of informing educators as to how the CCSS will be assessed using the new technology-based tests. PARCC has designated the questions to be one of three types:

Type I: Tasks assessing concepts, skills, and procedures

Type II: Tasks assessing expressing mathematical reasoning

Type III: Tasks assessing modeling/applications (http://www.parcconline.org)

The SBAC questions also focus on a variety of problem types within each assessment format, described as:

➭ Selected-response items are essentially multiple choice items, however, more than one choice may be made.

➭ Technology-enhanced items take advantage of the use of technology by allowing students to construct answers to questions regarding their understanding of concepts and skills through innovative responses such as drawing a picture.

➭ Constructed-response items act as short-answer questions intended to collect information about a student's understanding of a concept.

➭ Performance tasks require students to integrate meanings across standards and demonstrate depth of understanding.

So How Will Test Items Change?

First, remember that many of the items are likely to look familiar as they will be the same as traditional test items. Also keep in mind that, over time, students' ability to succeed on tasks posed in new test formats will improve as learners and teachers become more familiar with examples and the first few rounds of testing. As our students grow accustomed to engaging in activities that require their conceptual understanding, differences in the test questions will seem less drastic. Whatever your state decides about the use of these tests, these new formats will quickly be included in published curriculum materials so, eventually, many students will be exposed to new expectations on a regular basis.

Types of Responses

Both the SBAC and the PARCC tests will likely ask our students to:

➭ Manipulate representations using technological tools.

➭ Explain how they solved a problem, using written language.

➭ Use or interpret representations.

➭ Interpret the results of given data.

➭ Identify computation results as true or false.

It is likely that the technological format and the expectation of written explanations will be the greatest changes. Figure 3.1 gives an example of how an item might be transformed to take advantage of the technology platform. And, of course, content changes between these and previous standards will affect the design of test questions.

Figure 3.1 Question Transformed to Take Advantage of Technological Test Format

Traditional task:

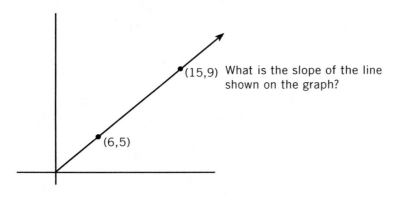

(15,9) What is the slope of the line shown on the graph?

(6,5)

Task that reflects new response possibilities:

Directions: Place 2 points on the graph such that the slope is $-\frac{3}{4}$.

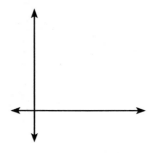

1. Move the slider to the left or right to create an (x,y) point.

2. Do #1 again for a second point.

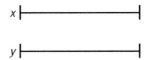

Written Explanations

If your students are not currently familiar with writing mathematical explanations, this change will require considerable attention. You will want to attend to this skill from the beginning of the school year. Provide students with exemplars so they understand expectations; have students use key words such as *first, then, because,* and *so* to organize their explanations; and assign students to begin by writing their explanations in small groups or as a whole class. Use ideas from your process writing curriculum so that students expect to edit their writing for clarity and have them work in pairs to give each other feedback. Examples that require explanations are likely to be multistep and/or have different solution paths.

Tasks requiring such explanations are likely to include a phrase such as, *show or explain how you arrived at your answer.* Your students will need to practice what it means to show and explain their thinking, rather than just arriving at an answer. Providing an explanation of what they are thinking or labeling mathematical steps for solving a multi-step problem may be a daunting task for some students. They will need practice and feedback about their responses as they learn to clearly and succinctly show their mathematical thinking. Figure 3.2 shows such as an example of this change.

Figure 3.2 Comparison of Task Requiring Students to Show or Explain How They Arrived at Their Answer

Traditional task:

Matt has 10 nickels.

Jeri has 3 fewer nickels than Matt.

Kyle has 5 fewer nickels than Jeri.

How many nickels does Kyle have?

Show your work.

Task that reflects newer expectations:

Together, Jeri and Matt have 15 nickels.

Kyle has 8 more nickels than Jeri.

How many nickels do Kyle, Jeri, and Matt have in all?

Show or explain how you arrived at your answer.

Embedded Representations

Particular representations such as number lines and tape diagrams are given new attention in these standards. Middle grade students are also expected to have a deep understanding of our number system. Consider the task change in Figure 3.3. Note that this example includes two representations and a follow up question.

Figure 3.3 Comparison of Task Expectations Involving Representations

Traditional task:

Write these numbers in order: $\sqrt{5}$, 7, 3^2, −2

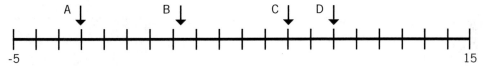

Task that reflects newer expectations:

For each arrow, write the correct number: $\sqrt{5}$, 7, 3^2, −2

A = _____   B = _____   C = _____   D = _____

You have $\sqrt{8}$. Between which two arrows is this number?

Interpret results

Connections to real-world applications require students to do more than compute results; learners must also understand how to apply such results in a particular situation. This figure provides an example of an interpretation students need to make about a remainder.

Traditional task:

Given the equation: $y = 3x + 12$, find the y-intercept

Task that reflects newer expectations:

Maric decided to join a school photography club. The club treasurer asked him to pay an initial fee of $12 to pay for the rental of the darkroom and then pay dues of $3 per week for supplies. Write an equation that will allow him to determine the amount he has paid over the last 20 weeks.

Work with True/False Statements

The emphasis on properties, structure, relationships among numbers, and the use of equations support the use of true and false statements. Such examples are likely to have more than one number on each side of the equation. This figure provides such an example. Students with conceptual understanding and familiarity with this format are likely to be able to respond more quickly than those who are not.

Figure 3.5 Comparison of Task Expectations Involving True/False Statements

Traditional task:

Write $<$, $>$ or $=$ in the blank.

$5 - 12$ _____ 7

Task that reflects newer expectations:

Tell whether each statement is true or false.

$5 - 12 < 5 + |12|$

$18 \div -3 = 18 \div 3$

Equations to Represent Mathematical Situations

Many of the test items will change because the standards have changed. The topic might appear at a different grade level or might no longer be given significant attention. Conversely, new ideas might be considered critical. For example, the use of equations is highlighted throughout the middle level standards. Students are expected to solve equations, but also to use equations to represent mathematical situations.

Figure 3.6 Using Equations to Represent Mathematical Situations

Traditional task:

Solve for t.

$20t = 8.5$.

Task that reflects new expectations:

Represent the following situation with an equation:

Mark is traveling on his scooter at 20 mph. He is driving to his friend's house, which is 8.5 miles away.

Use your equation to determine how long it will take Mark to get to his friend's house.

You can create additional examples by asking yourself:

- ✏ If I posed this question online, what different responses or ways of responding would be possible?

- ✏ What question stems or other scaffolding can I provide as my students learn how to explain their thinking?

- ✏ How might I include information shown in a representation rather than stating it or what representation might I require students to include?

- ✏ How might students need to interpret this computational result?

- ✏ How can I assess knowledge of relationships among numbers and the properties of arithmetic by embedding them in true or false questions?

- ✏ What is a new content emphasis at my grade level?

- ✏ How are ideas among domains related?

Testing Accommodations

Both SBAC and PARCC have published documents describing the accommodations that will be made available to students with learning disabilities, low cognitive ability, and English Language Learners, such as large print versions, Braille options, and tests written in several different languages. Also, two consortia have been granted awards to create alternative assessments for students with significant cognitive disabilities. Dynamic Learning Maps (DLMs) will offer two options; offering questions to students as alternative assessments through day-to-day instruction or a summative assessment that branches based on the students' responses. The National Center and State Collaborative (NCSC) is producing a summative assessment to assess whether these students are achieving higher academic outcomes.

A summary of a number of the key similarities and differences of the SBAC and PARCC assessments is outlined in Figure 3.7.

Figure 3.7 Key Similarities and Differences of SBAC and PARCC Assessments

Similarities	Differences
Tests are taken online except for special conditions by which a paper-and-pencil test may be requested	SBAC: Adapted based on CAT (Computer-adaptive testing: questions are asked based on students' responses to prior questions)
Grades 3–8 will be assessed	PARCC: Fixed form (question sets are static)
Variety of types of items	
Two formative components and two summative components	Re-take option only available through Smarter Balanced
Combination of human and computerized scoring with results expected within several weeks	Optional formative assessments offered by PARCC for grades K–12 students
	SBAC: Grade 11 summative assessment
	PARCC: HS Course-based assessments

Assessment of the Standards for Mathematical Practice

As the proficiencies described in the mathematical practices are standards, they, too, must be assessed. It seems as though high-stakes testing programs will include tasks that rely on the Mathematical Practices, but do not intend to directly measure and report the results of how well our students can apply these standards (Bill and Goldman 2012). This is not surprising, as the Standards for Mathematical Practice are what is most new about the Common Core State Standards for Mathematics. In general, educators are still discerning how to determine mastery of the standards by their students. So what are some ways you can begin to access your students' achievement in relation to these practices?

- Learn as much as you can about these practice standards. Continue to read about them, watch videos intended to highlight them, and attend related professional development.

- Help your students to understand the expectations you have for them. Post them in your classroom in words that students can understand. One teacher shows her students video clips of students learning mathematics and asks the students to find evidence of a particular practice or two. For instance, students might be asked to find evidence that students use correct mathematical vocabulary (MP6) or how they connect mathematics to real-world situations (MP4). Students can also be asked to dramatize responses to a particular task demonstrating a "good" and "not so good" example of persevering in solving problems (MP1).

- Create rubrics for each of the practices based on the example provided in Figure 2.5 and use them to note evidence over time.

- Be sure to ask questions that highlight students' attention to these practices and note their responses. Possible questions include: *How could you be more precise about your description of your results when you solved the proportion? Why do you think a tape diagram is the best representation to use in this situation? Do you know any patterns in your responses that would help you to create a shortcut?*

- Share students' work with colleagues. Give the same task to students in a couple of classrooms at your grade level and sort the responses together based on particular practice standards. You might also want to agree to give the same task across a grade level span to collect data as to how, for example, students' justifications (MP3) become more sophisticated.

The Roles of Parents/Guardians and Students in Assessment

Parents/Guardians' Roles

Ideally, you frequently share student assessments with parents and guardians. Sharing tasks their children completed earlier and later in the year is a wonderful way to document student learning. While this practice should continue, it is important that you also help parents/guardians understand important ways they can support assessment. They can:

- help their children take responsibility for work completed at home by encouraging them to note when assignments are due and to create a plan for meeting that goal.

- support children in the completion of their work, but do not do it for them.

- learn about standards and assessment.

- create a calm environment for their children at home when standardized tests are being taken at school and anticipate children being more tired and irritable during such times.

You and your school are particularly important in helping parents understand the new tests. The 45th annual Gallup Poll, conducted in 2013, revealed that less than half of the parents of school-aged children knew that the Common Core Standards even existed (Bushaw and Lopez 2013). Without a clear understanding of the increased rigor and higher expectations for moving beyond the basic skills required of the Standards, parents of students who have participated in field-testing of the new standardized tests have been left mystified as to why their children have scored so poorly. It is incumbent upon the individual school districts and those on the front lines of communicating with parents and teachers, to provide explanations about how these standardized tests are different from previous state tests and why the scores have decreased. Swanson (2013) provides suggestions to teachers on how to best share information with the parent community:

- Share comparative data from across the nation to give parents a perspective as to the relative nature of the decreases.

- Provide information about their child's progress from the formative assessment results to the end-of-year summative assessment results.

- Show parents how the questions from the state assessments have changed as we have moved to SBAC or PARCC assessments. Allowing parents to see how much the questions have changed to reflect the higher expectations of the new test questions may alleviate parents' concerns about why their child has received a lower score than on past assessment tests.

- Explain to parents that the move from state standards to the Common Core State Standards will take time to adjust to and that their child's scores on the new tests will take time to adjust to as well.

Students' Roles

So often when we talk about classroom assessment, we think about our evaluation of the assessment data we collect. Questions understandably arise about how we will find the time to read student work, interpret it to better ensure learning, and record what we learn. Concern for our assessment responsibilities as teachers can sometimes cause us to neglect the responsibilities of students. Yet, it is essential that students participate fully in this process. Here are some ways we can involve students:

- Have students reflect on their learning through exit cards, journal entries, in responses to feedback on tasks, or by completing rubrics. Ramdass and Zimmerman argue that self-reflection is important to student success. They state that, "Teachers can help students to hone this invaluable self-regulatory skill by giving them frequent opportunities to evaluate what they have learned or where they erred after completing a task" (2008, 41).

- Give students opportunities to set their own goals. For example, students needing to gain better access to geometry formulas could identify an intermediate goal such as, "I will learn the three most commonly used geometry formulas." As it is their goal, they are more likely to attend to it.

- Provide models for students that allow them to see student work samples that meet standards, which allow students to better understand expectations. Students can then give peers feedback and better self-evaluate their own work.

✏️ Help students understand the learning process. Atkin, Black, and Coffey (2001) suggest that students need to understand: Where am I going? Where am I now? How can I close the gap? Teachers can do this by making goals clear, involving students in the assessment process, and having students contribute to a learning plan. Some teachers post learning expectations for a given unit and give students a copy of them as well. Midway through the unit, students might be asked to self-assess their progress on the goals by, for instance, choosing a rating. They can record or talk about what they will do next to continue to improve.

✏️ Provide students with information about standardized tests, similar to that which you give to parents/guardians, communicated in a way that students can understand.

✏️ Provide students with evidence of their growth. Perhaps nothing can sabotage students' performance more than a lack of confidence. Think of students who look at a task and immediately conclude that they cannot do it. Often, with just a bit of support they can be successful. Consider making comments such as *Hmm, just a minute ago you thought you could not succeed and now you are doing just fine. What does that tell you?*

 ## Let's Think and Discuss

1. Think of assessment tasks you give that you find helpful. Can you identify common elements among them that might make them so?

2. Reflect on a time when you discovered particularly helpful information about student learning within a lesson. What instructional decisions did you make or what questions did you ask based on this discovery?

3. What techniques do you use to collect assessment data at the beginning or end of a lesson?

Chapter 4

Ratios and Proportional Relationships

 **Snapshot**

The middle school library is filled to capacity with students from the Gold Team's seventh grade mathematics and geography classes. Each library table houses a computer, a number of travel brochures, books about various countries, as well as handouts describing the assignment. Student teams are working together to create plans for their ideal vacation. Various teams have chosen different modes of transportation, venues and attractions for their trips so they must compute their expenses differently:

✏ Max and Latisha have decided to drive to their destination. They are researching the cost of gas per gallon in several midwest states as part of their plan to calculate their total gasoline budget.

✏ Kaylee and Adela are taking a bicycle trip. They are using an online application to determine how many miles it is from their starting point to their first destination. The students must compute these miles using the scale shown on the online map.

☞ Diego, Angela, and Elena are working with their geography teacher to find an interesting art museum in Italy for kids they can visit on their trip. Their budget constraints require them to spend less than $75 for admission to the museum, so they are computing the total cost for their family to visit the museum, based on knowing the cost for each ticket. They have also realized that the tickets are different prices based on the age of the people in their family.

☞ Olivia and Bryan are calculating what their food costs are as a percentage of their total budget. As they have agreed to not allow their food expenses to exceed 30% of their budget, they must determine whether or not they can afford a night out at a fancy restaurant.

Each group of 3–4 students is working on a different aspect of their vacation plans, using their geography as well as mathematics knowledge in a real-life context. The mathematics teacher has just finished teaching her students about proportionality. Her students must learn to, among other mathematics skills, recognize when they will need to find a unit rate, solve multi-step problems using proportion, and calculate percentages. The proportional reasoning skills learned in the mathematics class seem quite relevant and purposeful to these seventh graders, as the data is a critical component of their vacation planning. The teachers have provided a context for their students where these skills are useful, an aspect of the curriculum that middle school-aged students are continually seeking. Teaching ratio and proportional reasoning skills and concepts within a context allows students to see greater relevance to, and desire for, what they are learning, which in turn gives students the opportunity to learn the mathematics more fully (Posamentier, Smith, and Stepelman 2006).

MP6
Precision

Big Picture

The ratios and proportional relationships domain, while limited to grades 6 and 7, has a direct connection to what students have learned in elementary school with respect to multiplication and division as well as their work with operations with fractions. As students in the elementary grades solve problems such as *Marvin bought an energy bar for $1.25. How much will he pay if he buys a dozen energy bars?* they are essentially solving a special form of a proportion problem. While students in grade 3 begin to understand fraction concepts and continue this work through grade 5, they are building the foundation for understanding ratio in the later grades. Problems involving fraction comparisons or equivalent fractions are also considered to be ratio and proportion problems as well. Students may be asked, for example, to determine which class will get more pie on Pi Day, the class with 15 students and 9 pies or the class with 25 students and 12 pies. Students in the younger grades may solve this problem with fraction comparisons while middle grade students will learn to use ratio and proportion reasoning to determine a solution.

With special attention given to relevance and context in this domain, students will be given the opportunity to see the usefulness of a unit rate and a percent in daily life. As well, middle level students' understanding of these concepts will have far-reaching implications for their high school coursework, with direct connection to the sciences. As described in the progression documents, the concepts of acceleration, density, and the study of equilibrium in a chemistry class require a competence with ratio and proportional reasoning. "Students who have the ability to critically think and utilize RAP [ratio and proportion] to solve stoichiometric problems demonstrate that this ability leads to a greater understanding of general chemistry" (Page, Guevera, and Walton 2012).

MP4
Model

This domain is organized around two clusters:

Grade 6: Understand ratio concepts and use ratio reasoning to solve problems.

Students in grade 6 engage in problems such as *If it took 3 hours to weed 5 beds in the school garden, then, at the same rate, how long will it take to weed all 40 beds?*

Grade 7: Analyze proportional relationships and use them to solve real-world and mathematical problems.

Students in grade 7 engage in problems such as *Last year 155 students attended the end of school year dance. This year the attendance was much higher with 180 students attending. What was the percent of increase in attendance this year?*

These two sequential clusters and their associated standards, considered critical areas for each of these two grade levels, form the basis for understanding ratio and proportional reasoning at the middle level. Definitions, appropriate vocabulary, and conceptual meaning are explored in detail as each standard is described and illustrated in the next sections of this chapter.

Ratio Concepts and Ratio Meaning

A *ratio* is described as relating two or more quantities in a context. Relating 6 cups of oats to 2 cups of almonds uses cups as the units while relating 6 plants to 2 flowerpots uses two different units; yet both relationships are described as ratios. When the parts are related as a part-whole relationship, such as comparing 12 red socks in the drawer out of 22 socks, the ratio may be described as a fraction. Students should understand, when a part-whole ratio is created, their work with finding equivalent fractions will still hold true with ratios. However, ratios may also be described as part-part relationships. The

12 red socks may also be compared to the 10 green socks as a 12:10 ratio. This can be confusing for students if the two types of ratios are not clarified. Students should be given practice distinguishing between the two, especially as they are also solidifying their understandings of fractions in these middle grades.

The language and the notation associated with ratios may at times seem overwhelming as there are many ways to describe the same ratio. The relationship between 6 cups of oats and 2 cups of almonds may be written as "6 to 2", "6 for every 2", and "6 parts for every 2 parts" with the notation written as "6:2" and $\frac{6}{2}$. Each description implies the concept of *for every* regardless of what language is used. Students should experience seeing and writing ratios in many different formats and contexts in order to connect all ways of describing a ratio. In the early part of grade 6, it is easier for students to use the 4:6 notation rather than writing the ratio as a fraction, in order to distinguish their fraction understanding from ratio (Beckmann and Fuson 2012) (6.RP.1).

Consider this example:

There are 9 frisbees and 6 softballs on the school playground.

What is the ratio of frisbees to softballs?

In early work with ratios, students may write their answer as: 9 frisbees to 6 softballs or 9 frisbees: 6 softballs or $\frac{9\,\text{frisbees}}{6\,\text{softballs}}$ before they write without the unit labels.

Early misconception: Sometimes students think that it's okay to write the ratio either way: Frisbees to softballs or vice-versa. Students need to learn that the ratio must follow the way the question is worded. Writing the ratio as 6 softballs: 9 frisbees would not be an acceptable answer as the question asks for the ratios of frisbees to softballs.

It is important to distinguish between additive and multiplicative comparisons when students first encounter ratios. There is often a confusion that arises when students look at two numbers and find the difference between them to create what they believe to be a ratio. Describing the relationship between 5 inches and 30 inches as 25 inches should be emphasized as an additive comparison, whereas ratios are multiplicative comparisons. Students more often see this relationship as multiplication when they learn to describe the ratio as *6 times as great as*. Students who begin to recognize the structure involved in ratios will more easily be able to distinguish between the two comparisons.

MP7
Structure

Figure 4.1 Ratio Structure

Melba has to practice the piano for 1 1/2 hours. It takes her 1/3 of an hour to practice each piece of music. How many pieces of music can she practice in that time?

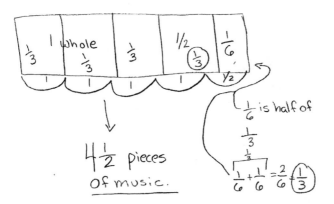

When students first learn to complete ratio tables they often move from one equivalent ratio in the table to the next by adding, using an iterative model (essentially counting up by the same number). The ratio table can certainly be completed in this manner. However, attention should be given to creating a ratio table where students must find ratios with larger numbers, so they will need to use multiples rather than repetitive addition, which, in these instances, would be too cumbersome a solution process. As an example, students may be asked to complete a ratio table (Figure 4.2) where they must use multiplication to find missing values (6.RP.3a).

Figure 4.2 Ratio Table

Frisbees	9	18		81	
Softballs	6		18		90

In an effort to emphasize the change that occurs between ratios, pairs of values may then be plotted on an *x-y* coordinate graph. Students whose learning style necessitates a visual model of ratio will benefit from seeing this change as a straight line on the graph. As the line goes through the origin of the graph, a pattern of increase will emerge as both the *x*-values and the *y*-values increase in coordination. It is the simultaneous change as a multiplication pattern in two variables that differentiates multiplicative thinking from additive. The graphical representation of ratio also allows students to see the possible ratios that exist between those represented in the table.

For example, students may engage in Siera's story, as she is learning to keep track of the money she earns as a mother's helper. She earns $4.00 per hour and she wants to know how much money she will make depending on how many hours she works. She and her classmates make a ratio table comparing the hours worked to the money earned. These data are then graphed as points on an *x-y* coordinate graph. Looking at the graph, Siera is able to find out how much money she will earn for any amount of hours worked.

MP4
Model

Figure 4.3 Graph Showing How Much Money Siera Will Earn

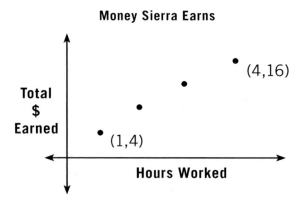

The relationship between the *x*-values and the *y*-values is further explored when sixth-grade students learn to relate the independent and dependent variables in the expressions and Equations domain.

Much of the literature regarding ratio and proportion distinguish between that of a ratio and a rate, however, it is important to note that rate is not distinguished in the standards. Rather, once the concept of ratio is established, students learn to associate a unit rate as related to ratio (6.RP.2).

Consider this example: A ratio describing the cost of 5 highlighters for $3.75 would become a unit rate as the cost of one highlighter is calculated by dividing 3.75 by 5. Students begin to recognize the benefits of a unit rate as they compute equivalent ratios in a table. It is easier to find equivalent ratios in a ratio table if the unit rate is known, as it will allow students to find the ratios of larger numbers without using the iterative approach. Starting a ratio table with the unit rate and then using the rate as the multiplier to find equivalent ratios emphasizes the usefulness of a unit rate.

In another example: It costs $3.50 for 6 mechanical pencils at the school store. Find the unit rate and determine the cost for purchasing other amounts of pencils at the store, using the ratio table.

Total Cost	3.50			
Pencils	6	1		

Many real-life contexts provide examples for unit rates, for instance the hourly rate for a job, the monthly fee for a gym membership, and the cost of a gallon of gas. Measurement conversions relating 1,000 meters to 1 kilometer or 4 cups to 1 quart are important unit rates as they are used in many other contexts. It may take some practice for students to understand that when writing unit rates, the 1 is often eliminated from the denominator. An hourly rate described as $15 for 1 hour is usually written as $15/hour. It is important for students to know that the /hour means per one hour. Students who have difficulty with this idea should write the unit rate as $15/1 hour until this concept is solidified.

Students often do not recognize that, given a ratio, there are two different ways to write a unit rate, however, that one way often holds more meaning than another in a real-life situation. Have students find both unit rates, discuss what each rate would mean and determine which unit rate is most useful.

Other models such as tape diagrams, drawings that look like a segment of tape, and double number line diagrams are useful for visualizing ratios and unit rates and for solving problems. Tape diagrams should be used when the quantities being compared are the same unit while double number line diagrams are best used when the units are different, as each line in the diagram can represent a different unit. Tape diagrams allow students to translate from the words of a problem to a visual model of the number relationships. This model, also known as a strip diagram, a bar model, or a length model, is specifically named in the standards as a tool for comparing ratios. See Figure 4.4 for an example of a tape diagram.

MP5
Tools

Figure 4.4 Tape Diagram

Alex found a recipe for a healthy trail mix by combining peanuts and sesame sticks. The recipe called for 2 cups of peanuts and 3 cups of sesame sticks.

This tape diagram can represent any amount of peanuts and sesame sticks.

Peanuts

Sesame Sticks

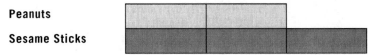

The total amount of trail mix is 5 parts of equal size. If the diagram represents 5 cups of trail mix, each rectangle represents 1 cup. This relationship may be equated to any amount of cups by keeping the ratio of $\frac{2}{5}$ peanuts and $\frac{3}{5}$ sesame sticks.

Double number line diagrams, as shown in Figure 4.6, are named as such because the marks on the number lines relate with two different numbers. Each row describes the whole in a different way, yet each line is equal in length. Students usually start each row of the diagram at 0 and then create another point that is common where the two values that make up the ratio are related. This relationship on the number lines is what allows students to make other equivalent ratios.

Figure 4.5 Double Number Line Example 1

It took Jada 2 hours to make 48 healthy muffins. If she cooks for 5 hours, how many healthy muffins can she make?

In this situation, students can either determine the amount of muffins that can be made in 1 hour and then multiply by 5 to determine the amount of muffins that can be made in 5 hours or can recognize that 2.5 times the pair 2 and 48 will result in the pair 5 and 120.

This cluster brings the introduction of percent to grade 6 students in the context of rate. While rates other than unit rates are not emphasized in the standards, knowing that the concept of percent is a rate with 100 in the denominator is very important to students' foundational understanding. According to the standards, students' work with percent in grade 6 is limited to finding the percent given the whole and the part or finding the whole given the part and the percent. As work with percent does not involve solving with proportions until grade 7, students in grade 6 should learn other strategies for finding percent or the whole, such as a double line drawing (Van de Walle, Karp, Bay-Williams 2013) (6.RP.3c).

Figure 4.6 Double Line Example 2

Martin borrowed money from his parents to buy a new computer program that cost $80.00. As of last week, he has paid back his parents $20.00. What percent of the cost of the program has Martin paid back?

Analyzing Proportional Relationships

Students in grade 7 begin their work within this cluster by, once again, working with unit rates (7.RP.1). Building upon their understanding of unit rates as learned in grade 6, students expand upon these ideas to now include unit rates that are computed with fractions. Partitioning the unit rate into smaller and smaller parts, recognizing that the numbers become more complex each time the ratio is partitioned, may emphasize the use of fractions within a unit rate.

Consider this example: In a grade 7 classroom, students work at stations to practice finding unit rates in different situations.

Station 1: Students use an applet to create unit rates based on the questions provided (e.g., Thinking Blocks [http://www.thinkingblocks.com]).

Station 2: Students are watching a video online, taking notes on how to provide unit rates and then answering questions online.

Station 3: The teacher works with a group of students, pre-determined based on a formative assessment, to practice making double line diagrams to find unit rates involving fractions. These students need more practice multiplying and dividing fractions as well as computing the unit rates.

Station 4: Several students have shown mastery of the unit rate concept and are extending their thinking by reading the book *Gulliver's Travels* as a requirement for both their English and mathematics classes. They are currently working to create a Brobdingnag-sized (larger than life) mathematics textbook, made to scale as related to their own mathematics textbook. As students are asked to make their measurements in inches, they encounter a number of challenging fractional relationships.

MP4
Model

When difficulties arise with students being able to compute these unit rates, it usually stems from being challenged by the division of the fractions rather than understanding how the unit rate should be computed. Finding unit rates with complex fractions gives students in grade 7 the opportunity to practice the work of other domains in a different context and to practice division of fraction skills (6.NS.1).

Working with unit rates in grade 7 also allows for a deeper understanding of the labels given to such rates. What may have previously been thought of as $3.75 for one gallon of gas is now connected to $3.75/gallon, with the one for one gallon of gas being dropped and yet implicitly understood. Knowing that the one is implied within the label of a unit rate is important for students as they extend their thinking of unit rates to that of proportions in this grade.

Students in grade 7 apply their understanding of ratios to the meaning of a proportional relationship. Defined as two equal ratios, students must understand that a proportion is created when the ratios stay constant even as the numbers in the equivalent ratios change (7.RP.2). Understanding that a frozen yogurt machine can make an 8–ounce soft serve cone in 10 seconds is the same as making a 16–ounce cone in 20 seconds, draws upon students understanding of the multiplicative nature of proportions. There are numerous ways for students to recognize a proportional relationship and to create them. As well, students will learn how to solve proportions by being given situations where they know a ratio and one of the two numbers of an equivalent ratio. Discussed in detail later in this chapter, students should learn to solve for the fourth number in the proportion by using a number of strategies, all of which lead students to a deeper understanding of the relationship between the two ratios.

MP2
Reason

Students will have a clearer understanding of how to create proportions as they learn to recognize a proportional relationship among those that are not. Oftentimes, students think that, just because they are given a situation where they have three out of four numbers, they should form a proportion to solve for the fourth number. Knowing that some of these situations form additive rather than multiplicative relationships will highlight which situations are proportional and which are not.

MP7
Structure

In another example, students in a grade 7 small-group class are provided with situations in which they must determine whether or not the situation describes a proportional relationship. Each situation is written on a card and placed at a different table in the classroom. Next to each card, students will find a variety of materials, including a set of color cubes, paper/pencil to draw a pictorial model of the situation and a computer opened to an applet which can be used to represent the situation. Students know their goal is to work with their classmates at each table to represent each situation using the materials provided. A handout, as shown in Figure 4.7, is provided for them to record their thinking. The situations are written as follows at each table:

1. Is this a proportional situation? If Martin can run 4 laps around a track in 6 minutes, how long will it take him to run 6 laps around the track?

2. Is this a proportional situation? Susan will have her 12th birthday this year as her brother turns 9. When Susan is 15 years old, how old will her brother be?

3. Is this a proportional situation? Maya, who is 9 years old, is allowed to have 6 friends over for her birthday sleepover party. Her younger sister, Ava, who is 6, is allowed to have 4 friends at her party. Ava doesn't think that this is fair. Help Ava to determine whether or not the number of friends she is allowed to have come to her birthday is fair.

Figure 4.7 Is It Proportional Activity Sheet

Is It Proportional?

The situation: _____
_____
_____
_____

My representation using
color cubes:

My representation using my
picture model:

My representation using
the applet:

Here's what I think about
whether or not it is a proportion:

Determination of whether or not a situation is proportional may also be found by creating a graph of the related ratios, as shown in Figure 4.8. If the graph of the points goes through the origin then a proportion has been formed. Students learn to recognize the unit rate within this graph as well, stating, "For every 4 problems solved, you will receive 2 points extra credit" and "For each problem solved you will receive $\frac{1}{2}$ point extra credit", is an important step in recognizing proportional relationships.

Figure 4.8 Relating a Table, Graph, and Equation of Proportional Relationship

For every 4 problems solved, you will receive 2 points extra credit.

Problems Solved (x)	Extra Credit Points (y)
0	0
4	2
6	3
8	4
10	5

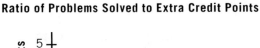

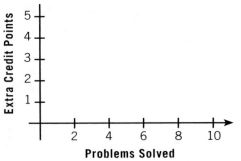

Equation: $y = \frac{1}{2}x$

For one unit you move to the right, you move up $\frac{1}{2}$ unit.

The use of technology is often a helpful tool for students in learning to visualize proportions. Such tools provide students with an opportunity to make a visual representation in order to solve a proportion. Multiplicative reasoning is emphasized as students visually set up the two equivalent ratios in order to find the missing number. Online tools also give students the opportunity to solve the proportion in a number of different ways within the same visual model.

Other examples of technological tools students may use to engage in proportional reasoning include those in which they can:

- compare scale models of airplanes to real-life planes and change the scale using geometric drawing software,

- use graphing software to compare the rate, time, and distance of different runners, and

- collect data on a spreadsheet and write formulas using proportional reasoning to compare the data.

As students become more adept at recognizing proportional relationships, they will need practice with knowing that proportions may be set up in different ways. Understanding that two equivalent ratios may be written *within* the ratios or *between* the ratios is an important distinction. For example, knowing that a major league baseball player can run 90 feet from home plate to first base in 5 seconds, students may be asked how many feet can he run in 8 seconds. The proportion created using the *within* ratios format would look like $\frac{90 \text{ feet}}{5 \text{ seconds}} = \frac{x \text{ feet}}{8 \text{ seconds}}$ with the original ratio written as a fraction and compared to the ratio of the unknown with the new information. The *between* ratios format would look like $\frac{90 \text{ feet}}{x \text{ feet}} = \frac{5 \text{ seconds}}{8 \text{ seconds}}$ with the same unit compared in each ratio. It is important for students to know that the proportion may be set up using either format and both representations are acceptable for solving the problem. As well, students should recognize that the ratios may be inverted and it will still produce the same result.

As students progress in their understanding of proportions, they begin to use the unit rate from a proportional situation as the *constant of proportionality* (7.RP.2b).

Students in an above-grade level class are watching a real-time video of an elite marathon runner. The video shows a close-up of the runner's pedometer, recording the number of steps that she is taking. Students are working in groups to determine, from the video, the number of steps the runner takes each second. As each group reaches its conclusion, they present their findings. As a class, they determine which group best figured the unit rate, or constant of proportionality for this situation and they write an equation so that they can figure the runner's predicted time for the entire marathon. They must describe each component of their equation, $y = 5x$, to demonstrate their understanding of the variables as well as the constant of proportionality. Although the standards do not formally introduce the concept of the slope of a line on a graph until grade 8, recognizing the constant of proportionality on a graph will be an important foundation for this concept.

MP3
Construct

**Marathon Runner's
Steps Over Time**

of
Steps

Time
(seconds)

An important connection to the Expressions and Equations domain may be made by writing an equation to express the proportionality between two quantities (7.RP.2c).

Provided with a wide variety of situations to interpret as well as from which to write an equation, students are given an opportunity to represent proportionality from any given context. Students are specifically asked to interpret a graph of a proportion by providing a contextual description of any (x, y) point on the graph. As they learn to interpret that all graphs of proportional situations must go through the origin, students must be able to describe what the point $(0, 0)$ means on the graph and to see the unit rate as a point on the graph $(1, r)$

MP8
Regularity

where r is the unit rate. This important connection between a unit rate and its representation on an x-y graph emphasizes the x-value as the 1 in the unit rate and that as x increases by 1 the y-value increases by r, the constant of proportionality (7.RP.2c).

Solving for a missing number in a proportion provides students with the opportunity to learn a wide variety of strategies for relating the two ratios (7.RP.3). It has been commonplace to see students learn to solve proportions by cross-multiplying almost immediately after setting up the proportion, often using x to represent the missing number. In contrast, the CCSSM does not require that students learn to solve a proportion using a particular strategy, and accompanying literature (reference to progression documents) encourage students to use the method of cross-multiplication to solve the proportion only under certain circumstances. Recognizing when the unit rate and the scale factor strategies each are practical and, in fact, easier to use than cross-multiplication requires student flexibility. Relying upon understanding the proportion as equivalent fractions and drawing upon previously learned strategies will also help to avoid the immediate use of the cross-multiplication strategy. Even within these two strategies, one is usually easier to use than the other, depending upon the situation.

MP7
Structure

Consider this example: You take a long bike ride with your friend and determine you have gone about 25 miles in 2.5 hours. If you'd like to ride another 15 miles, what do you think your total time riding your bike will be?

Using the unit rate strategy:

$$\frac{25 \text{ miles}}{2.5 \text{ hours}} = \frac{40 \text{ miles}}{? \text{ hours}}$$

Finding the unit rate by dividing 25 by 2.5, the bike rider can ride, on average, 10 miles per hour, so the number of hours to ride 40 miles can be found by dividing 40 by 10 = 4.

Using the scale factor strategy:

$$\frac{25 \text{ miles}}{2.5 \text{ hours}} = \frac{40 \text{ miles}}{? \text{ hours}}$$

Dividing 40 by 25 to determine the scale factor of 1.6, the student then multiplies 2.5 by 1.6 to determine the number of hours.

Conceptual Challenge

A number of common errors occur when students are learning to solve proportions. Students may set up the proportion without attention to the need for common units, such as with problems involving measurement. Students in a seventh grade science class are working to determine how much of a nutrient solution to put in the fish tank, based on the amount of water in the tank. The label on the bottle says to put in 15 drops for 2 quarts of water. They know they have a 10-gallon fish tank in their class, so they set up their proportion to determine how many drops to add as $\frac{15}{2} = \frac{?}{10}$, forgetting to change the quarts to gallons or vice-versa. Labeling the numbers in the proportion with the appropriate units helps to avoid this error and also assists students with recognizing they have placed the quantities appropriately in the proportion, using either *within* or *between* ratios. Connecting the answer to what it means in the problem is also important for students. As with other contextual problems, students may misinterpret their answer if not asked to relate what the x (or their chosen variable) is equal to as it relates to the question. A reliable solution to this problem is to ask students to use a variable in the proportion that represents what they are solving for. Using m to represent minutes and f for feet often keeps students connected to the meaning of the missing variable.

MP6
Precision

If only taught as an algorithm, students may be consistently challenged by the cross-multiplication procedure for solving a proportion. Assuring students' understanding of solving proportions using other strategies first and drawing upon what they know to learn the meaning behind cross-multiplying will encourage careful use of this method.

Relating the meaning of the cross product to the multiplication used to create equivalent fractions provides a greater meaning for these products. (See Figure 4.9.)

Figure 4.9 Use of Cross Products to Create Equivalent Fractions

Show steps to explain why cross-multiplication works: $$\frac{4}{5} = \frac{x}{60}$$	$$\frac{60}{60} \cdot \frac{4}{5} = \frac{x}{60} \cdot \frac{5}{5}$$ **Step 1:** Multiplying both sides by the equivalent of 1, using the denominators of the ratios as identities.

$$\frac{4 \cdot 60}{5 \cdot 60} = \frac{5x}{5 \cdot 60}$$

Step 2: As each numerator is being divided by the same denominator, the focus can be on the resulting multiplication in numerators, also know as the cross-products.

Knowing what the 5 × 60 means is challenging to students, as it is not obviously connected to the relationship between the two ratios, yet it provides equivalent denominators. This is not to say that teaching students the cross-multiplication strategy is not necessary, as it is an important strategy to use when the numbers in the proportion are too cumbersome. Using the cross-product method also provides students with an important strategy to use in the later grades, such as when they are solving rational equations in algebra.

Working with percent in this cluster extends to a variety of contexts, including complex situations involving percent of increase/decrease and percent of error (7.RP.3). Students must understand that percent increase and decrease problems represent the relative change in a value, often over time. It is common for students to write percent increase/decrease ratios as the new value/old value and then not understand the meaning of the percent they have calculated. Giving students many opportunities to express percent in a variety of situations is an important component of this domain.

For example, students in a grade 7 enrichment class have just finished reading *Alice in Wonderland* and are beginning a weeklong

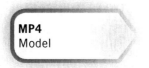

MP4
Model

project based on the mathematics they found in the book. They use the assignment as their guide for choosing the mathematics in which they are most interested.

Choice 1: Find 5 situations in which Alice could have used percent of increase in the book. Write problems for Alice and solve them.

Choice 2: Make your own video, creating a short clip showing how percent of error might be represented in the movie of Alice.

Assessment Note

As students progress through this domain, it is important to note, when students have difficulty calculating the unit rate or the missing number in a proportion. As the students are given assessment tasks, teachers should recognize if it is the concept of proportional reasoning or the calculations that are causing the difficulty. These challenges often stem back to their previous understandings of operations with whole numbers or fractions. The real-life nature of such problems should be emphasized and connections to other domains should be frequent.

Students challenged by what they perceive as the more abstract nature of ratio and proportional relationships should be given ample opportunity to represent these relationships in a visual context. Understanding their learning styles to know that visual representations are helpful to students allows teachers to provide assessment tasks where connecting the numbers to pictorial representations will assist students to more conceptually understand what they are solving for and how their answer relates to the situation. As previously mentioned, the use of technology is often an important tool for students in representing ratio and proportion. Having the diagrams drawn according to students' specifications will allow them to focus on the problem rather than the often-tedious nature of drawing a picture or relying upon whether or not the diagram was accurately drawn to scale.

Voice from the Classroom

As I begin to understand the ratio and proportional relationships domain, I am struck by the importance of relating these concepts to other domains. My colleagues and I made a list of all of the connections, including operations with whole numbers and fractions, graphing, slope and writing equations. I'm really glad that learning these concepts occurs over two years as there is so much packed into this domain. This is such a big idea and is obviously essential to students' understanding. We do feel as though the writers have provided a nice progression for students from fully understanding ratios in grade 6 to proportions in grade 7, transitioning between the two with a fuller understanding of unit rates at the beginning of grade 7. In our attempt to relate what we previously taught to these new standards, it took us awhile to figure out that rate is not explicitly taught in either of our grades. We had always taught what a rate is, often because we teach the formula distance = rate x time. So, we have had to adapt our teaching to focusing primarily on unit rate and helping our students connect the general idea of rate to this specific type. In talking with the grade 8 teachers about this, we have come to realize that this will help them when they teach the concept of slope. We also did not recognize, at first, that this domain is the only one in which percent is taught. We have had to look very carefully at how percent is first introduced in grade 6 and then expanded upon in grade 7 and figure out what to teach at each grade level.

In our "Looking at Student Work" session last week, the grade 7 teachers reported on the results of the pre-assessment they had done on unit rate.

We were pleased to hear that they did well overall. As grade 6 teachers, we are hoping that this is because we placed so much emphasis on students' understanding of the meaning of the ratios they were creating. The new standards seem to really emphasize the labels for the quantities and how the two units create one new unit when made into a ratio. We used to place more of a focus on ways to write the ratios with just the numbers. We had to really resist using the language that we used to, too quickly naming the ratio of 5 boys to 7 girls as "5 over 7". Maybe keeping the quantities in a context is what has helped them to remember this material as they moved to grade 7.

—6th-Grade Teacher

 ## Let's Think and Discuss

1. What issues have you encountered with respect to language with ratios? How would you assist your students with these issues?

2. What contexts do you think your students would be most interested in for learning about ratio and proportion?

3. Have you created any study groups in which you look at student work? Do you think that would be helpful to you in your teaching practice?

Chapter 5

The Number System

 **Snapshot**

As the sixth grade students enter their second period class, they notice a number of brightly colored index cards placed around the room. Each card has a letter on the front and Caleb peeks, as he moves toward his desk, to find a decimal multiplication problem on the back of one of the cards. The students have been practicing various operations, including solving problems in real-world contexts, with decimals. Today, it is the students' turn to write the word problems. Each pair of students is given a clipboard and a slip of paper with a letter written in the first box. The teacher directs the students to find the index card that has their assigned letter on it. When they find it, they are to turn the card over, write down the decimal problem on their paper and then leave the index card where they found it and return to their seats. Their directions are to create an interesting context for their given problem.

Zane and Ryder are to write a word problem involving $3.5 \div 0.7 =$ ____. Zane tries to convince Ryder that they should write their problem about money, but he changes his mind when he overhears another classmate saying that their story was going to be about buying something. He wants their story to be unique. Ryder eagerly comments, "Remember the measuring we did in science class the other day? Maybe we should write about the length of something." Zane reminds him that the best lengths to use would be metric because they are using decimals. After considering several different contexts, the two boys decide on the lengths of snakes, measured in meters. Their first attempts at thinking of a division context were challenging for the boys. They decided to draw a model to represent a snake that was 3.5 meters long and another one that was 0.7 meters long and started to write something about how much longer the really long snake was than the short one. But, they soon figured out that meant subtraction.

Several attempts later they settled on, "The Children's Zoo had a snake that was 3.5 meters long and another one that was 0.7 meters long. How many of the small snakes could fit inside the large snake?" It was hard for the boys not to share their problem right away, but the teacher asked everyone to keep their problems a secret. When they were ready, they were asked to put the slips with their problems on them into a bucket at the front of the room. A few students had finished earlier than others, so they were working on number puzzles with decimals until the teacher asked the class for their attention.

Once all the problems were placed in the bucket, each pair of students was asked to come up and take a problem out of the bucket. Luckily, no one got the problem they had written. The goal now was for the pairs to solve the student written problems and then find the card with the problem that matched it. The teacher was pleased with what she observed her students doing during this activity. Although several of the students, including Zane and Ryder, used their prior experience of drawing a model to begin their thinking, she heard her students discussing how the problem related to using decimals in real-life contexts and determining an appropriate situation for the operation they were given. She was able to gather some helpful informal assessment data regarding which students had difficulty distinguishing between multiplication and division in a context. She observed which students needed more work with the standard algorithm for division and took notes on possible groupings for the next day's activity. She concluded that having her students write their own word problems rather than just solve word problems that she had given them provided her with some interesting data about her students she may not otherwise have realized.

MP2
Reason

Big Picture

The Number System domain in grades 6–8 requires students to solidify their understanding of number as learned in the elementary grades, as is noted in the cluster descriptions in Figure 5.1. The number line is heavily relied upon in these standards as a visual model for students to relate fractions, decimals, negative numbers and, in grade 8, irrational numbers.

Figure 5.1 Clusters in the Number System Domain

Grade	Cluster
6	Apply and extend previous understandings of multiplication and division to divide fractions by fractions.
	Compute fluently with multi-digit numbers and find common factors and multiples.
	Apply and extend previous understandings of numbers to the system of rational numbers.
7	Apply and extend previous understandings of operations with fractions to add, subtract, multiply and divide rational numbers.
8	Know that there are numbers that are not rational, and approximate them by rational numbers.

Grade 6 students move from using concrete models to solve problems to using algorithmic approaches, now involving whole numbers, fractions and decimals. Prior to the adoption of the Standards, students were not required to use a standard algorithm for operations with whole numbers. However, the standards in this domain do require students to learn and use standard algorithms. Bill McCallum, a lead author of the CCSS, is quoted describing a standard algorithm as, "In mathematics, an algorithm is defined by its steps and not by the way those steps are recorded in writing. With this in mind, minor variations in methods of recording standard algorithms are acceptable" (Common Core Standards Writing Team 2013). So, while a standard algorithm is a necessity for all students, McCallum leaves the door open for students to work within a general structure, yet make their own adjustments based on their understanding of the algorithm. A more detailed discussion of what these student adjustments may look like is described in this chapter.

MP7
Structure

The standards for this topic begin in grade 5 with using concrete models to divide with unit fractions and continue in grade 6, with a focus on conceptual understanding of the algorithm rather than procedural fluency alone. A critical area in grades 6 and 7, students are called upon to use their knowledge of the properties of operations as they now apply to decimals and to negative numbers. As an example, students' understanding that multiplication and division are inverse operations has, prior to middle school, mainly been used with whole numbers to justify solving problems such as 12 ÷ 3 by thinking about the problem as 3 x _____ = 12. This relationship between the two operations can now be used to see that –12 ÷ 3 may be solved by 3 x _____ = –12.

Although the domain's standards do not fall within a critical area in grade 8, the properties of operations with all types of numbers in our number system are integrated into students' work, in particular, with solving linear equations. Understanding how a rational number differs from an irrational number is introduced in grade 8, with strong ties to the use of radicals, and standards related to the Pythagorean Theorem and geometry topics such as volume draw upon an understanding of our number system.

The Number System domain calls upon middle grade students to have a solid understanding of the connections between different types of numbers in our number system and to know how these numbers are used in real-life contexts. Students should be "computationally fluent" in the sense that they are able to solve problems flexibly, accurately and efficiently, understanding when it is appropriate to use mental math, paper and pencil, or another tool such as a calculator or a computer (Russell 2000). Drawing visual models are certainly an acceptable strategy for solving a problem as an initial step, yet students should work toward algorithms to solve problems, where appropriate, requiring them to be procedurally fluent with all operations. The challenge for teachers with this domain is keeping the focus on a conceptual understanding of number and not relying on rules too quickly.

MP5
Tools

Computation with Whole Numbers, Fractions, and Decimals

Division of Fractions

Fractions are a critical area in each of grades 3–5 with an introduction to division of fractions in grade 5, when students divide a unit fraction by a whole number or a whole number by a unit fraction. These two types of fraction division are initially conceptualized by extending students' understanding of whole number division and using visual models such as number line diagrams. Grade 5 students consider fraction division problems such as:

- ✏ Four students were given a bag of balloons to share. What portion of the bag of balloons will each student get? (Partitioning/sharing model)

- ✏ Four yards of shoelace material will be used to make shoelaces, each $\frac{1}{2}$ yard. How many shoelaces may be made? (Measurement model)

Sixth graders build on the understanding of these two models of division with more complex fractions, from which they then build procedural fluency (6.NS.1). Initially, students continue to use visual models often drawn from word problems such as, *Melba has to practice the piano for four and a half hours. It takes her an hour to practice each piece of music. How many pieces of music can she practice in that time?* Referring to the models used in grade 5, students choose either measurement or sharing to visualize this problem and must also recognize the result as a non-whole number answer. Interpreting the leftover amount provides for an interesting discussion, as some students may say that Melba can only practice 4 whole pieces of music and disregard the other $\frac{1}{2}$ piece, while others will say that she can practice $4\frac{1}{2}$ pieces. Understanding that the calculated answer is $4\frac{1}{2}$, then deciding how to interpret the numerical answer in the context of the story is a conversation worth having with your students.

Movement from reliance upon a visual model to solving a fraction division problem with an algorithm must be managed well if students are to make meaning for why numerical approaches work. The transition should involve finding patterns within the answers that students find when using a visual model, coupled with their understanding of the connection between multiplication and division of fractions. As an example, students may initially determine the answer to $4 \div \frac{1}{3}$ as 12 using a visual model, then recognize that there will be 3 for every 1 whole, so the answer may be found by multiplying 4 x 3 = 12. Related problems such as $4 \div \frac{2}{3}$ may be solved by recognizing that there are only half as many because the thirds are grouped by 2's. By doing many problems which demonstrate the relationship between the visual model and the numerical interpretation, the goal, in this model, is for students to recognize that multiplying the denominator by the first number tells you how many thirds you have and the numerator tells you the size of the thirds. So, the steps are to multiply by the denominator and divide by the numerator. The final step should be for students to recognize that they can invert and multiply (Van de Walle, Karp, and Bay-Williams 2013). Students can prove this answer with a visual model, an approach that they are more familiar with, until they see that this numerical approach works every time. Practice with many variations of a fraction divided by a fraction, recognizing that the same process leads to accurate results, can lead to consistent use of the invert-and-multiply method for dividing fractions (Flores 2002).

Teachers should make every effort to provide a conceptual understanding for why this method works. In a study by Liping Ma (1999) of U.S. teachers, it was determined that many teachers, at that time, could not provide a conceptual explanation for why the invert-and-multiply method worked and, in many cases, could only explain division of fractions with this method. The approach of relating division of fractions to a related multiplication problem most often leads students to discovering this efficient method of invert-and-multiply on their own. It should be noted that, while the invert-and-multiply method is efficient, it is not a direct requirement of the standards. Teachers and students often

MP8
Regularity

find other methods for dividing fractions efficiently. Teachers may choose to engage in activities with their students that employ strategies such as finding common denominators to divide, which relies on the measurement model for division (Van de Walle 2011).

For example, to solve $\frac{7}{5} \div \frac{1}{3} = \frac{21}{15} \div \frac{5}{15}$ with using common denominators, the problem may now be thought of as how many $\frac{5}{15}$'s there are in $\frac{21}{15}$'s. Using the measurement model, students can then think of the problem as $21 \div 5$ which is equal to $4\frac{1}{5}$ so there are $4\frac{1}{5}$ thirds in seven-fifths.

Conceptual Challenge

Teaching the division of fractions for meaning has traditionally been a challenging endeavor for students and for teachers (Flores 2002). A number of misconceptions often arise, especially if struggling students do not connect a general understanding of the division concept regardless of whether they are using whole numbers or fractions. Sometimes students:

☞ think that the quotient should always be smaller than the divisor. Estimation should be emphasized prior to solving the problem.

☞ invert the first fraction (the dividend) instead of the second (the divisor) when they use the invert-and-multiply algorithm. Returning to a visual representation of the problem or reminding students of the related multiplication problem often helps students to see why it is the second fraction that is inverted.

> ✏ determine that dividing *by* $\frac{1}{2}$ is the same as dividing *in* half (or any comparable problem). Discussion should center around dividing by $\frac{1}{2}$ as finding how many $\frac{1}{2}$'s there are in a quantity and dividing in half means breaking it into two parts (Kansas Association of Teachers of Mathematics 2012).

Divide Whole Numbers with the Standard Algorithm

Grade 6 students must learn to fluently use the standard algorithm to divide with whole numbers (6.NS.2). It should be noted that this is a change from many previous state standards, which stated that students should be able to divide fluently using *an* efficient algorithm, but now the shift has been in the CCSS to have students learn to use the U.S. standard algorithm. But, what does this shift entail? McCallum, Fuson, and Beckman (2012) articulated that there should be variations within a standard algorithm, as long as it is generalizable and is efficient. The foundation has been laid in earlier grades for students to conceptualize the standard algorithm as a result of using concrete models and invented strategies. As students have been introduced to the concept of division in grade 4, practiced this concept with more complex dividends and divisors in grade 5 through visual representations, the third year of study of division with whole numbers, in grade 6, culminates their understanding of this operation with the use of a standard algorithm.

MP7
Structure

Unfortunately, in the past, it has been all too common for students to struggle when asked to remember the steps to follow using the standard algorithm, in even such a short time as a few months after learning it. Oftentimes, in classrooms, the transition from visual models to an algorithm has not been a smooth one. The standards call for a greater focus on understanding the structure of our number system with a greater emphasis on conceptually understanding the meaning behind the standard algorithm.

MP7
Structure

For example, sixth-grader, Filipe, represented a division problem such as in fifth grade with a pictorial representation. He now learns to connect his visual model to a written record of what he is doing, as he draws the picture and then transitions to just using the numerical steps. Still based on an understanding of place value, Filipe, includes the zeros as he records each step. By the end of sixth grade, he may not need to write all of the zeros anymore, but he is still able to explain each step of his written algorithm, rather than just thinking of the steps as a memorized procedure.

If the standard algorithm is based on conceptual understanding, students will be more readily able to recall this algorithm when needed. They will be able to use it in other contexts, such as when dividing decimals or in algebra when they learn to use long division with polynomials using the same algorithm.

Operations with Decimals

In grade 5 the focus is on the conceptual understanding of operations with decimals. Based on an understanding of place value, students add, subtract, multiply and divide with decimals by employing the use of concrete models, pictorial representations, the properties of operations and strategies. In grade 6, students transition from models to the use of standard algorithms for all operations, also now including multi-digit decimals (6.NS.3).

Students' work with multi-digit decimal calculations should also be rooted in number sense and reasoning, as the standards again require students to compute with decimals fluently. Middle school students should be expected to employ a variety of strategies, drawing upon mental math, use of estimation, and a continued focus on the use of place value.

MP5
Model

As part of a unit on multiplication with decimals, one sixth grade teacher put the multiplication problem 62 x 57 = 3,534 on the board and then asked her students to create problems with products of:

0.3534   3.534   35.34   353.4

Several students in the class asked if they could use a calculator to solve the problems, to which the teacher replied, "I'd like you to think about the placement of the decimal point in the original problem to find an answer rather than relying upon manipulating the decimals with your calculator." Through discussion, most pairs of students soon recognized the connection between the product for the whole number problem and how it could be used to solve the other problems. Several groups were not convinced and so they chose to write out their problem and do the calculation, until someone said, "Oh, yeah, it's the same answer, it's just that the decimal point goes in a different place." This teacher does not always discuss all of the questions that she poses to the class as a whole group, as she finds that some students tune out when they know they have the right answers. However, she does often ask pairs of students to come together to discuss their findings. She found, as expected, that there were disagreements. Ben and Shiva had found an answer for the product 3.534 by multiplying 6.2 x 0.57 and Vera and Lopa multiplied 0.62 x 5.7. The students soon recognized that both answers were accurate and that, as long as there were three decimal places between the two factors, there would be 3 decimal places in the product. The teacher asked the students in this group to describe their conclusion to the class. The whole group discussion then continued by describing problems where that pattern is not readily noticeable, as is the case when the multiplied factors produce a result where the last digit is a zero. The teacher was pleased that the groups found this distinction themselves without her having to point it out.

MP8
Regularity

MP2
Reason

MP3
Construct

Greatest Common Factors and Least Common Multiples

Grade 6 students' initial introduction to greatest common factors and least common multiples should stem from providing students with problems where using such numbers to solve the problem is considered an efficient method (6.NS.4).

 Aided by prior knowledge of the definition of factors and multiples learned in prior grades, consider how students could solve the problem below:

> The student council needs to order school supplies for their upcoming fundraiser. They can order pencils in boxes of 12 and blue pens in boxes of 8. They ordered the same number of pencils as they did pens. If they did not order more than 200 pens and pencils combined, what's the greatest number of boxes of each they could have ordered? What is the smallest number of boxes of each that they could have ordered?

One way to solve the problem is by making a list of the multiples of 12 and 8:

12, 24, 36, 48, 60, 72, 84, **96**…..

8, 16, 24, 32, 40, 48, 56, 64, 72, 80, 88, **96**…..

This allows students to visualize the multiples of each number and that the greatest multiple, without going over 200 total, that is the same in each list is 96. Therefore, the solution to the problem is that the student council must have purchased 96 pens and 96 pencils. While past practice may have involved using prime factor trees to solve for the least common multiple, the authors of CCSS (Common Core Standards Writing Team 2013) are discouraging the use of this model. As the multiples are relatively small numbers, since they are found by using numbers less than or equal to 12, the list process provides for a better visual model of what students are actually looking for rather than reliance on the process of prime factorization, which often feels like a rote method to students.

In preparation for the study of expressions and equations, students in grade 6 also learn to represent the sum or difference of two numbers using the distributive property. Given the task of representing (40 + 60) in another way, students learn to find the greatest common factor of 40 and 60 as 20 and learn to write (40 + 60) as equal to 20(2 + 3). Again, visual models may first be used to give students the opportunity to represent the problem more concretely, such as the diagram shown in Figure 5.2.

Figure 5.2 Greatest Common Factor

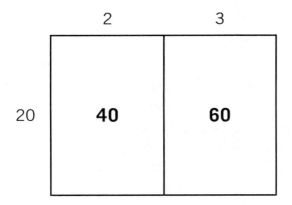

Introducing Integers

Contexts for Positive and Negative Numbers

The introduction of negative numbers in grade 6 is based on providing students with real-world contexts for their meaning. Initially, such numbers are usually integers, although students could engage in learning about negative numbers involving fractions and decimals as well (6.NS.5).

In this example, a grade 6 science class has been studying what sea level means. They were asked by their geography teacher to bring their data to her class where they would do some further study on various sea levels in different parts of the world. Not surprisingly, they found that their geography and math teachers decided to combine their classes that day, so they met in the library. The geography teacher introduced the task:

☞ Each group will be given a card listing the names of 5 places in the world.

☞ Groups should write the sea levels they found on the back of the cards.

☞ Once this task is completed, students will bring their cards to the front of the room and put the cards on the number line on the whiteboard, placed according to the sea levels.

☞ As a class, we will then discuss whether or not the numbers were placed appropriately, make guesses about which place is represented by the number shown, and answer some challenge questions such as which places had the highest/lowest sea levels.

Once the students agreed on the data to use, their attention turned to where they would place their cards on the number line. Students were overhead discussing whether -2.42 was to the left or the right of -2.3 on the number line, what it meant if the sea level was 0, and why one place could have a higher sea level than another. These students were engaging in an activity to place positive and negative numbers on a number line in order to visually represent the concept of a negative number as the opposite of a positive number. Other real-world contexts, such as reading temperatures on a thermometer, provide a visual introduction to the vertical number line, with teachers knowing that the next step is to introduce students to the coordinate system by representing a horizontal and vertical number line as intersecting lines (6.NS.6).

Representing negative numbers with a negative sign should be introduced as describing the opposite of 6 in its written form as −6. The negative sign is employed to tell what direction the student should move from 0 to place the number on the number line and 6 and −6 are seen as reflected images of each other as points an equal distance from 0. Students can also begin to think about what is the opposite of the opposite of a number, such as the opposite of 6 is −6, so the opposite of −6 is 6, represented by −(−6) = 6 (6.NS.6a).

Honoring Individual Differences

It is not uncommon for teachers to identify the number −6 as *minus 6*. However, as the work with negative numbers progresses to carrying out operations, this way of naming the number can cause confusion for students, especially those with auditory-processing challenges, thinking that *minus 6* always means to subtract. This will not be true if the problem is to subtract -6. Care should be taken to use correct terminology, referring to −6 as *negative 6*, so that students can relate the term negative as meaning to move to the left of 0 on the number line, providing the direction of the number, not as an operator.

Including Negative Numbers in the Coordinate Plane

As both horizontal and vertical number lines including negative numbers are introduced, the emphasis shifts from finding where just one number falls on the number line to where both parts of a coordinate pair are found within the coordinate system (6.NS.6b). The two number lines are now called axes, with the horizontal number line designated as the *x*-axis and the vertical number line as the *y*-axis. Students must also come to know the axes create quadrants in the system, with each quadrant given a Roman numeral representation as shown in Figure 5.3.

Figure 5.3 Quadrants of the Coordinate Plane

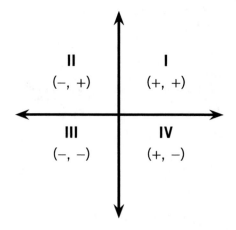

The standards require students to do more than memorize how to place a coordinate pair on the coordinate graph. To conceptualize what it means to change only the signs (+ and –) to find a related point, students should be asked to do tasks such as:

▷ Plot the points (3, 5) and (–3, 5) on the graph.

  • In what quadrants are the two points?

  • Over what axis are these two points reflected?

▷ Plot the point (–3, –5) and reflect it over the *y*-axis.

  • What coordinate pair names the reflected point?

▷ What point would represent the point (–5, 6) reflected over both axes?

Ordering and Absolute Value

Now that students have been introduced to negative numbers as part of the number system, ordering numbers is not as easy as when all of the numbers were positive (6.NS.7). As students compare numbers such as −12 and 8, providing a context will often spare students the confusion that is present at times, initially. If your piggy bank has a note in it saying that you owe $12 to your sister, this amount may be represented as −12. This amount certainly represents a lesser amount of money than having $8 in your piggy bank, represented as +8. Such models often help students as they learn to write −12 < 8 or 8 > −12 (6.NS.7b).

A common misinterpretation of the meaning of absolute value stems from describing a rule for what is "inside" the two vertical lines as "it just always comes out positive." The standards require students to understand that absolute value must be thought of as whatever number or expression is inside the absolute value bars, is representative of that distance from 0. Since distance itself is never represented as a negative number, absolute value always represents a positive value (6.NS.7c). Focusing on a real-world context for why absolute value is important, students can engage in applications such as:

In this situation, a perfectly packed box of cereal at the Crunchy Cereal Company weighs 26.0 ounces, however, it is acceptable for the weight to be "off by" 0.2 ounces.

1. If a box weighs 26.6 ounces, how would you represent, using absolute value, how far off it is from being a perfectly weighed box? (Solution: $|26.6 - 26.0| = |0.6| = 0.6$)

2. If a box weighs 25.8 ounces, how would you represent, using absolute value, how far off it is from being a perfectly weighed box? (Solution: $|25.8 - 26.0| = |-0.2| = 0.2$)

3. Are either of the cereal boxes an acceptable weight?

Representing the weights of the two cereal boxes to the weight of a perfect cereal box using absolute value allows students to focus on the distance that the weight is from a perfect weight rather than whether the number is negative or positive. Although $-0.2 < 0.6$, this is not as relevant as knowing that the absolute values of these numbers more purposefully represent the numbers needed in this situation (6.NS.7d). Some students may argue that they can just subtract to find the weights as acceptable or not and ignore whether the answers are positive or negative. However, it should be noted that future use of this concept requires students to represent absolute value using equations in algebra and this task presents itself as an introductory activity.

As students learn to represent coordinate pairs on x-y axes and are asked to find the distances between two points on the graph, they must incorporate their understanding of absolute value to this task (6.NS.8). The students in a sixth grade class enjoy practicing their new math skills by playing games. Today, they are playing a board game, by first choosing a card from a deck, which names a coordinate pair for them to place on a coordinate grid, overlaying a picture of an ocean. After each student of the pair places his or her rescue ships (pieces) in the correct place on the grid, they must determine which of their ships is closest to the sinking ship. For example, as shown in Figure 5.4, one student places his ship on (2, −7) and the sinking ship is on (2, 4). The distance between the two points should be represented as allowing students to practice, in a real-world context, the distances between two points using the true meaning of absolute value.

Figure 5.4 Coordinate Graph

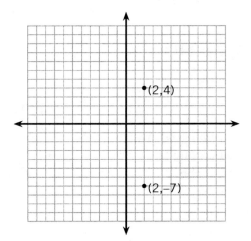

It is also quite common to see sixth and seventh grade students representing positive and negative numbers with colored chips. This model is often useful for students as they can visually represent properties, such as the commutative property, with chips, recognizing that the numbers can be added in any order. However, the standards focus primarily on the use of the number line model to provide a conceptual understanding for several reasons. The standards do not designate that students should only work with integers as they are learning about positive and negative numbers and the colored chips model does not traditionally involve more than whole numbers. Showing $-\frac{1}{2}$ is cumbersome and would require a good deal of effort to represent numbers using the chips for problems involving fractions and decimals. As well, the standards call for students to be able to represent all rational numbers on a number line for both locating and ordering points as well as representing operations. However, if students have difficulty with one model, teachers may want to introduce another model, such as the colored chips, providing students with another visual representation for working with these numbers.

MP5
Tools

Operations with Positive and Negative Numbers

Adding and Subtracting

MP4
Model

Grade 7 students apply their understanding of negative numbers to operations (7.NS.1). The standards call for students to represent, as they gain conceptual understanding of operations with integers, the addition and subtraction of positive and negative numbers on a number line diagram. Initial practice using this model involves students with the opportunity to learn how problems such as 4 + (−4) = 0 mean something different than just adding 4 + 4, as the negative sign attached to −4 represents a direction on the number line (7.NS.1a).

Figure 5.5 Number Line Example 1

Extending this model to problems such as 6 + −10 = −4, students represent this problem by moving to the right 6 on the number line and then moving to the left on the number line as the negative sign represents moving to the left, stopping at −4.

Figure 5.6 Number Line Example 2

Continuing with the number line diagram for subtracting negative numbers, students also connect their understanding of using missing addends to formulate the problem. For example, $6 - (-4) = $ _____ as $-4 + $ _____ $= 6$. In order to know that to get from -4 to 6 is 10 units, students must move to the right a certain amount from -4 to get to 6, finding the answer is $+10$ (7.NS.1d).

MP7
Structure

It should be noted that this model is intended to provide a conceptual understanding for students about why they get the answers that they do. One possible method for leading students toward developing a procedure for adding and subtracting positive and negative integers is by analyzing the answer patterns they found using the number lines.

One group of seventh grade students recorded a number of the subtraction problems solved by using the number line, and organized the problems by whether they were starting with a positive or a negative number.

$$7 - (-4) = 11 \qquad -5 - (-4) = -1$$

$$6 - (-9) = 15 \qquad -8 - (-3) = -5$$

$$13 - (-7) = 20 \qquad -3 - (-6) = 3$$

Asked to see if they could find a pattern, the students decided that every time they started with a positive number and subtracted a negative number, the answer was found by adding the two numbers together, always resulting in a positive number answer. The same situation occurred when they started with a negative number, as the students realized that they were still adding the numbers together, but this time, the addition involved starting with a negative number. This analysis of the problems eventually led the students to writing their own rules for adding and subtracting positive and negative numbers (7.NS.1c).

MP7
Structure

Multiplying and Dividing

The number line model is not called upon in the standards for teaching students to multiply and divide with positive and negative numbers. Rather, there is more of a reliance on the properties of operations, practiced repeatedly with other types of rational numbers, prior to doing so with positive and negative numbers, to find meaning (7.NS.2). Students may be introduced to solving problems such as 5 x (–2) = –10 by relating the problem to whole number multiplication as repeated addition, showing that 2 + 2 + 2 + 2 + 2 = 10 or as 5 groups of –2 is the same as –10. Determining (3) x 6 = 18 may be thought of as the same as 6 x (3) = 18, as the commutative property is applied (7.NS.2a) (7.NS.2c).

A conceptual representation for –5 x (–3) = 15 has consistently plagued many teachers and students, often because it is a challenge to devise a real-life context for situations involving (–5) groups of (–3). However, there are several different representations for 5 x 3 = 15 that may be useful to teachers when exploring this type of problem with their students:

☞ Use of the word opposite is often helpful, thinking of –5 x –3 as the opposite of 5 groups of –3 (Kansas Association of Teachers of Mathematics 2012).

☞ An interesting model for depicting 5 x (3) relies upon the distributive property to provide an explanation (Khan 2013): First consider 5 (3 + –3) = 0 written as (–5 x 3) + (–5 x 3) = 0, and if 5 x 3 = 15 then 5 x 3 must equal 15 if the two expressions added together must equal 0.

As students learned to relate multiplication and division with other rational numbers, so, too they can do so with positive and negative numbers. Creating fact families such as: 5 x (–3) = –15 and –3 x (5) = –15 leads to –15 ÷ 3 = –5 and –15 ÷ 5 = –3 (7.NS.2b). An often overlooked representation for division of positive and negative numbers is when students write division as a fraction, such as when they write –8 ÷ 4 as $\frac{-8}{4}$. Again, using fact families to assist students with understanding what the standards call for, students should know that –8/4 may also be written as $\frac{8}{-4}$ or as $\frac{-8}{4}$ as each division representation results in a negative number for an answer.

Almost all of the standards in this seventh grade cluster call upon students to relate the operations with positive and negative numbers to real-world contexts (7.NS.3).

A seventh-grade teacher engaged her students in solving word problems involving positive and negative numbers by having them first do some research on ways in which negative numbers are used. Students were asked to interview their family members as to how they used negative numbers in their jobs, they looked online and found numerous science resources mentioning the use of negative numbers and those students who were interested in sports found interesting references to negative numbers in that area as well. Once students chose a topic to pursue further, they wrote scenarios describing what they learned and had a choice to depict their real-world context by:

1. Making a video, acting as news reporters.

2. Creating a rap, portraying rock stars.

3. Writing a poem.

4. Making an illustration.

One group created an illustration of going on a shopping spree showing how they spent their money throughout the trip by marking their expenditures as adding negative numbers on a number line.

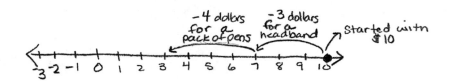

Moving Beyond Rational numbers

Students in grade 7 learn to compute the decimal equivalent of a fraction (7.NS.2d). An understanding of the difference between terminating and repeating decimals occurs primarily through long division calculation. Using the standard division algorithm to represent $\frac{5}{8}$ as a decimal using only whole number division, a first attempt may be to equate $\frac{5}{8}$ as $\frac{x}{10}$, then $\frac{x}{100}$. As grade

7 students have learned to solve proportion problems, they will equate these problems as dividing 50 by 8, 500 by 8, etc. until eventually a denominator including a power of 10 is found the result of which produces a zero remainder.

Division of 8 divided into base-ten unit

$$
\begin{array}{r}
6 \\
8\overline{)50} \\
-48 \\
\hline
2
\end{array}
\qquad
\begin{array}{r}
62 \\
8\overline{)500} \\
-480 \\
\hline
20 \\
-16 \\
\hline
4
\end{array}
\qquad
\begin{array}{r}
625 \\
8\overline{)5000} \\
-4800 \\
\hline
200 \\
-160 \\
\hline
40 \\
-40 \\
\hline
0
\end{array}
$$

Notice that it is not necessary to restart the division for each new base-ten unit, since the steps from the previous calculation carry over to the next.

MP7
Structure

As students learn that not all decimals terminate, they will benefit from using the strategy described above to look for patterns with fractions involving thirds, sixths, sevenths, and ninths.

$$
\begin{array}{r}
3 \\
3\overline{)10} \\
-9 \\
\hline
1
\end{array}
\qquad
\begin{array}{r}
33 \\
3\overline{)100} \\
-9 \\
\hline
10 \\
-9 \\
\hline
1
\end{array}
\qquad
\begin{array}{r}
333 \\
3\overline{)1000} \\
-9 \\
\hline
10 \\
-9 \\
\hline
10 \\
-9 \\
\hline
1
\end{array}
$$

Grade 8 students continue to explore the decimal equivalence of a fraction and consider in-depth the patterns found when decimals repeat (8.NS.1). Exploration activities give students the opportunity to conceptualize:

- what fraction denominators will result in a terminating decimal,

- why certain fractions produce a repeating decimal and when the repetition will occur, and

- the notion that a repeating decimal will do so infinitely.

Using the whole number long division strategy to find the decimal equivalent, grade 8 students interpret the related long division problems and find exactly where the repetition occurs.

A natural extension of finding a decimal equivalent for a fraction is to engage grade 8 students in finding a fraction for a repeating decimal. Regular exploration with some common repeating decimals will often result in students essentially knowing that such decimals as $.\overline{3} = \frac{1}{3}$ and pattern exploration reveals such fraction equivalents as those with a 9 in the denominator as $.\overline{4} = \frac{4}{9}$ and $.\overline{5} = \frac{5}{9}$, etc. However, if students do not remember the equivalence or if they need to find the equivalent fraction for a more complex repeating decimal, other methods must be employed. A traditional strategy for finding fraction equivalents for repeating decimals involves an understanding that equations may be subtracted from one another as with solving a system of linear equations as shown in Figure 5.7.

Figure 5.7 Changing to a Fraction

To change 0 to a fraction:

Step 1: Let $x = 0.\overline{36}$

Step 2: Let $100x = 36.\overline{36}$

Step 3: Subtract the two equations: $100x = 36.\overline{36}$

$$x = 0.\overline{36}$$

Result: $99x = \overline{36}$

Step 4: Solve for x by dividing both sides by 99: $\frac{99x}{99} = \frac{36}{99}$

Step 5: If $x = \frac{36}{99}$, then in simplified form $x = \frac{4}{11}$.

If students who are learning this method have not yet learned the elimination method for solving a system of linear equations, they may not conceptually understand why you can subtract the two equations. An alternative explanation for Step 3 may look like this:

If $x = 0.\overline{36}$ and we know that there is a property that says we can add (or subtract) the same amount to both sides of an equation, then we can subtract x from the left side and $0.\overline{36}$ from the right side to make the equation: $100x - x = 36.\overline{36} - 0.\overline{36}$. Because x is the same as $0.\overline{36}$, we can subtract x from one side and $0.\overline{36}$ from the other side of the equation, thereby subtracting the same amount from both sides.

Students come to know that all fractions either terminate or repeat and have given a name to this type of number as rational. As the conceptual understanding of infinitely repeating decimals is solidified, students begin the exploration of infinite decimals that do not repeat. There must be an understanding that these decimals cannot be found by changing a fraction to a decimal.

One teacher introduced the set of irrational numbers by giving each group of students in her classroom a set of cards, as in Figure 5.8.

Figure 5.8 Irrational Numbers

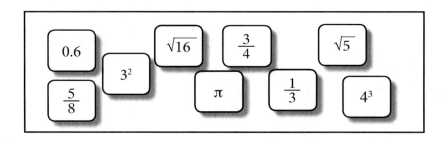

She asked the students to group the cards any way that they wanted to, although they had to be able to justify why they grouped them the way they did. Some of the students grouped them by fractions and whole numbers; some grouped them by whole numbers and decimals, and some further delineated the cards as terminating or repeating decimals. Each of the student groups had a lively discussion about how to group the cards with π and √5. The students recognized that these numbers did not terminate or repeat and could not be represented as a fraction. This led the teacher to introduce this new set of numbers, named irrationals, defining them as numbers that were not rational.

As irrational numbers are introduced, students come to know that these two sets of numbers, rational and irrational, are part of a larger set of our number system, known as real numbers. A pictorial representation of our number system is often helpful, now including the irrational numbers as a subset of real numbers.

Figure 5.9 Real Numbers

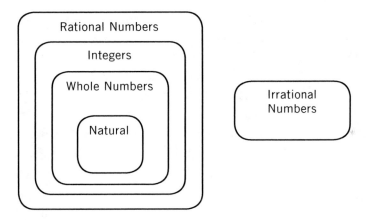

Although it is reasonable to have students use a calculator to determine an approximation for irrational numbers such as √5, it is important for them to recognize that the result is a rounded answer, as the calculator will produce a finite set of digits, despite the fact that the number continues infinitely. In order to solidify their understanding of the fact that the calculator's result is an approximation, it is beneficial to have students square this result, as in √5 = 2.2360679775, noting that the calculator does not use dots to show that the number continues. They will see that $(2.2360679775)^2 = 5.00000000000094050625$, only a very close approximation of 5.

MP6
Precision

 129

Conceptual Challenge

MP1
Making Sense

The task described above gives students practice with understanding the relationship between the square root of a number and its square. This is an important connection for students as there is sometimes confusion between representations. Now that irrational numbers have been introduced, working with numbers such as $4^2 = 16$ and the relationship $\sqrt{16} = 4$, some students will need to be reminded of these inverse relationships (8.NS.2).

MP2
Reason

Students experience a more in-depth analysis of irrational number approximations when they complete tasks such as creating a table to see how close they can get to $\sqrt{5}$ without the use of a calculator. Considering what two perfect squares the $\sqrt{5}$ is between gives students benchmark numbers with which to work. Students recognize that $\sqrt{5}$ falls between $\sqrt{4}$ which equals 2 and the $\sqrt{9}$ which equals 3, so the $\sqrt{5}$ is between 2 and 3. Then, creating tables with the squares of numbers between 2 and 3 to get closer to $\sqrt{5}$ becomes an interesting mathematical task. Recognizing that $\sqrt{5}$ is closer to 2 gives students a narrower range of numbers with which to work. It is the student's choice as to what approximation of $\sqrt{5}$ with which she is satisfied. The student's work below shows how she used multiple attempts to determine that the $\sqrt{5}$ is between 2.23 and 2.25.

Figure 5.10 Student Work Showing $\sqrt{5}$ is Between 2.23 and 2.25

Attempt 1

x	x^2
2.1	4.41
2.2	4.84
2.3	5.29

Attempt 2

x	x^2
2.2	4.84
2.25	5.0625
2.3	5.29

Attempt 3

x	x^2
2.2	4.84
2.23	4.9729
2.25	5.0625

Students also benefit from representing an approximation for the $\sqrt{5}$ on number line diagrams. Plotting $\sqrt{4}$, $\sqrt{5}$, and $\sqrt{9}$ allows students to compare the proximity of these numbers and to create benchmarks from which to determine what decimal number $\sqrt{5}$ is close to. Students see a reason for finding an approximation for an irrational number when solving application problems such as:

> You are about to take a walk with your friends at a local state park, which is 4 miles long and 2.5 miles wide. You have decided that you don't want to walk the perimeter of the park, so you suggest that you should cut across the park instead. How long a walk is it to walk directly across the park? (Round your answer to the nearest tenth.)

Using the Pythagorean Theorem to find the solution to this problem, students must then determine the approximation of $\sqrt{22.25}$ to the nearest tenth.

MP6
Precision

Assessment Note

Getting a read on how well your students understood the day's topic may be assessed by giving students what is commonly known as a "Ticket to Leave" or a TTL. Allowing 5–7 minutes at the end of class, students are asked anywhere from 1–3 questions such as:

☞ Show a number line representation for $-6 + 4 = -2$.

☞ Explain why you did it the way you did.

☞ What two whole numbers is $\sqrt{60}$ between?

Students may also be asked questions that refer to their level of understanding of the day's concepts such as:

☞ What topic did you best understand today?

☞ If you had a chance to ask more questions about one of today's topics, which one would it be?

☞ What would you like to ask about ...?

☞ If you had a test tomorrow on a topic, which one would you prefer it to be?

Students may be asked to write their responses in a journal, jot them on a slip of paper or a sticky note and hand them to the teacher as they are leaving. Alternatively, students may be asked to verbally share their responses with a peer or their teacher prior to leaving the class.

The results of a "Ticket to Leave" are often used to determine what the next day's instruction might look like. For example, a teacher might group the TTL's in one class by all of the students who did/did not answer one question correctly. The students who got the question right would work on something different the next day, while the group who needed more work would have further instruction or more practice before moving on. Teachers find this formative assessment practice to be quite helpful as they learn a good deal of information about their students in a short period of time that they might otherwise not have learned. Students often think of this type of informal assessment as a reality check for their understanding of a topic and appreciate being given the opportunity to do further practice if necessary or to not have to revisit the topic if they already understand it.

As a number of the standards in this domain represent a culmination of students' work with number and operations, it is expected that standardized assessments will focus on students' fluency and ability to use standard algorithms. There is also a good deal of emphasis placed on the use of number line diagrams to represent meaning for operations with integers. A task on a standardized test might ask students to answer the following questions:

MP2
Reason

Rikke thinks that $-5 - (-3) = -8$ and Meg thinks that $-5 - (-3) = -2$.

☞ Tell which student is correct in solving the problem.

☞ Explain your answer by showing a model on the number line. (Note: Students will likely be asked to create this model using a number line applet on a computer, so practice with such applets prior to testing is helpful.)

Voice from the Classroom

I was originally trained to be a high school teacher and moved to teaching middle school about 8 years ago. I had never learned anything about using visual models to teach my students to conceptually understand the math they were learning. So, when I found out that I had to teach my students why $3 \times -4 = -12$, I was worried. I didn't necessarily know myself why that statement was true, never mind know how to teach it to my students. I was fine explaining the rules, but I was not ready to give an explanation as to why they worked. Thankfully, this year we are spending a good deal of time during our weekly math meetings doing some great professional development work on the standards. Our math coordinator usually joins us and so I told her ahead of time that I'd like to spend some time focusing on how to explain the rules for operations with integers. We had such a great meeting that day. First we started with looking at different kinds of models such as number lines, colored chips and even some applets that we found online. Then, we looked at how to transition from the models to the rules. This was the trickiest part, but it felt so good to finally figure out that I should not just draw a model and then say, "Now, this is really how you do it with the rule." The next week, I tried the number line model to do some addition of negative numbers with a small group of students. They practiced a fair number of problems that way, and then, a few days later, we looked at how to not have to use the number line anymore to solve some similar problems. What was fascinating was that the students themselves found a pattern and then we turned their pattern into a rule that they stated using their own words. I felt like it was a great success, especially because a few weeks later, well after the test, they still remembered the rule. I'm starting to figure out that the less that I tell my students and the more that we figure things out together the better they remember what we learn!

—7th-Grade Teacher

Let's Think and Discuss

1. How well do you think you understand why the invert-and-multiply rule for dividing fractions works?

2. The CCSSM requires students to engage in more problems using real-world contexts for learning about integers. What contexts can you think of that use positive and negative numbers, keeping in mind that the topics should be relevant to what your students are interested in?

3. Consider doing some further research on computational fluency for middle level students. What might incorporating these ideas into your curriculum mean for your teaching?

Expressions and Equations

 **Snapshot**

There's always an interesting twist when the students in Mr. Fernandez's seventh-grade class practice what they have been learning. Today, they are sitting in groups of three, surrounded by square puzzle pieces, glue sticks, paper and pencils. Each group of students has been given a different puzzle (Figure 6.1) to put together, chosen for them by the complexity of multi-step equation they need to practice solving. At the end of class the day before, Mr. Fernandez had given each student several linear equations to solve. Based on the results of the "Ticket to Leave", students were then assigned a group to work with, during this day's class, to put together a linear equations puzzle. Each group was busily working to complete their own puzzle, matching the equation with the solution. When all of the pieces are correctly placed, a 5 x 5 grid of puzzle pieces will fit together. As Mr. Fernandez circulates around the classroom, he notices each group strategizing somewhat differently to solve their puzzle. Harry, Gavin and Nairob have decided to solve each problem separately, compare their answers and then decide how to place each puzzle piece.

Marko, Elena, and Saul are solving each problem together, sharing strategies about what step to take next in the problem and what to do if they make a mistake. Mr. Fernandez stops to listen at one table where Tara, Beth and Gabe are working, as they are disagreeing as to the final answer for the equation: $3 - 5(x - 2) = 15$. Tara got the answer $x = \frac{-2}{5}$ and Gabe found the answer to be $x = \frac{-11}{2}$. Beth says, "Well, looking at the puzzle for the correct solution doesn't help because both of your answers are there." Mr. Fernandez, while he doesn't want to step in and solve the entire problem with them, does suggest a possible strategy. He asks the students to exchange papers and each look at their first step. Because his students have learned that showing their work when solving a problem helps for when they need to go back and review their steps, they were able to see they each started the problem a different way. Tara says, "Gabe subtracted $3 - 5$ first and got -2" while Gabe says, "It looks like Tara multiplied -5 by x and by -2 first." They know that Mr. Fernandez won't just tell them who's right, rather he will ask them to think about their recent work with solving problems like these. Beth pipes up with an idea, "How about if you both put your answers back into the equation and see which one works." As it turns out, Tara's answer is correct so now Gabe must go about figuring out why his answer is not. As he was substituting his possible answer into the equation, he recognizes that he is supposed to multiply in an equation before he adds or subtracts. "Oh, you're right, Tara, I subtracted first, that's not right. I was supposed to multiply first." All three students go about finding where the puzzle piece fits, pleased that they found a solution and are anxious to move on to the next piece.

Figure 6.1 Puzzle Pieces

$3 - 5(x - 2) = 15$

$x = \dfrac{4}{5}$ · $5x - \dfrac{2}{5} = 8$

$X = -12$

$X = -\dfrac{2}{5}$

$X = \dfrac{9}{10}$ · $-12x = 0$

$4x - 3(x + 5) = 20$

$3 - (x + 2) = 10$

$\dfrac{-6x}{7} = 21$ · $5x - 12 = -10$

$X = -\dfrac{3}{4}$

$X = -6$

$X = \dfrac{-11}{2}$ · $\dfrac{3x}{5} = 7$

$3x - 5 = 2x + 7$

Big Picture

The content of the Expressions and Equations domain is seen as a stepping stone from the work that students have been doing since kindergarten with numbers to the work of algebra in the middle grades and in high school. The Operations and Algebraic Thinking domain of the elementary grades sets the stage for the Expressions and Equations domain by teaching students about how operations work, not only to manipulate numbers but also to create a foundation for the related work with algebra. For example, recognizing that multiplication and division are inverse operations or that subtraction may be thought of as addition with a missing addend leads students to relate these operations algebraically in the Expressions and Equations domain (McCallum 2011). Thought of as "Gathering Momentum for Algebra", students' work in elementary school with numbers may be seen as a "rehearsal" for the work they do with variables in this domain. Students' conceptual understanding of how expressions are interpreted, written and eventually used to solve algebraic equations, provides essential building blocks for the work of high school mathematics.

For this reason, the work of this domain is a critical area within each of the middle grades. Sixth grade students generalize their knowledge of arithmetic and begin to use the properties of operations, learned previously, with variables. Students use algebraic approaches to solving problems by writing expressions and solving one-step equations involving whole numbers.

Seventh graders must apply their fluent knowledge of operations with rational numbers to write expressions and to solve multi-step equations that now involve rational coefficients. The application problems at this grade level lead students to writing and solving one-variable equations in a variety of real-life contexts. As eighth grade students work toward meeting the standards of this domain, they complete their understanding of solving one-variable linear equations, integrate their work with proportional relationships and draw upon the content in the Functions domain to solve a wide variety of problems involving two-variable linear equations.

Transitioning from Arithmetic to Algebraic Expressions

Students have been working with expressions since kindergarten. In the early grades, students come to know a mathematical expression as a symbolic way to describe a calculation such as 3 x 6 + 3 x 4. By grade 5, students are interpreting expressions with parentheses, brackets, or braces and learn to recognize that expressions written differently may represent the same quantity. Students learn to write simple expressions by translating words such as "Add 2 and 5, then multiply by 3" into mathematical representations written as "3 x (2 + 5)." Often the expressions involve whole number exponents to represent numbers in powers of ten such as 20 square inches to represent the area of a square whose sides are each 20 inches (6.EE.1). Grade 6 students are interpreting numerical expressions with greater complexity, and are learning to interpret vocabulary such as terms, factors, and coefficients. Division is more frequently represented with a bar as $\frac{1}{7}$ rather than 1 ÷ 7 and multiplication problems are written with a dot rather than an x. Preparation for representing multiplication with variables, students learn to write 4 · 6 rather than 4 x 6. Work with exponents involves including a base number of increasing complexity, moving from powers of 10 in grade 5 to any whole number, decimal, or fraction in grade 6, such as $2 \cdot 5^2$.

Understanding how to appropriately apply the order of operations is of great importance in the transition from arithmetic to algebra, as the same properties apply in algebra as with numbers. It has long been accepted for students to memorize the rules of the order of operations with acronyms such as PEMDAS, or a variation, to give students an easy way to remember what order to follow. However, equating an order for carrying out calculations to the age-old "Please Excuse My Dear Aunt Sally" is fraught with challenges. While following a set of rules for calculating complex expressions is necessary, the focus on conceptual understanding requires students to contemplate each problem individually, rather than universally relying on a memorized phrase.

Conceptual Challenge

Some common misconceptions of PEMDAS include:

- ✏ Seeing M and D first together in the phrase implies that multiplication must be done before division (and before addition/subtraction). This works with problems like 6 + 3 x 5 but not with 6 ÷ 3 x 5. The same is true of the A and S in the phrase and the true meaning of the order of operations in which addition and subtraction are of equal importance is not revealed.

- ✏ Students' lack of understanding of the left/right rule of the order of operations is not helped by using PEMDAS.

- ✏ The P in the acronym implies to students that just the expressions within parentheses must be done first, ignoring other grouping symbols such as the division bar, brackets or braces.

- ✏ There is no reference to the square root as a grouping symbol or where factorial (!) fits into the order of operations.

If PEMDAS or other such acronyms do not lead to a true understanding of the order of operations, how should students learn these rules? Students can certainly relate to the fact that there are rules for playing board games or sports and the same holds true for simplifying expressions. Students learn that there must be a set of rules to follow or there may be, inaccurately, multiple representations for the same expression. Once they learn the rules they must practice them in varied contexts, with complex expressions, so they can be used in multiple situations, not just memorized.

MP7
Structure

Sixth graders play games such as Krypto© to practice order of operations in the context of a logical reasoning activity. A set of numbers is provided such as 3, 5, 1, 2, 8 and players must use order of operations to find a target number (the solution) such as 3. Each number may only be used once yet there is no limit to the number of times an operation or another mathematical symbol may be used. There are often many possible solutions, allowing for a wide range of strategies, using various arithmetic properties and applications of the order of operations.

The popular 24® Game provides another context for practicing order of operations. Given a card with four numbers on it, students must use operation rules to create an expression that results in an answer of 24. One such Level 3 card, shows the numbers 5, 8, 2 and 2. Students in a sixth-grade classroom found this problem to be quite challenging. Rather than revealing the answer too quickly, the teacher allowed this card to remain on the board for several weeks until, one day, working in a problem-solving group, several students found a solution (one solution: $2 \cdot (5 + 8) - 2 = 24$).

Figure 6.2 Game for Practicing Order of Operations

Cards: 3, 5, 1, 2, 8   **Target Number**: 3

One solution: $\frac{3+5}{8} + \frac{2}{1} = 3$

Learning to use appropriate mathematical vocabulary, applying the properties of our number system, and understanding the use of mathematical symbols prepares students to transition from using numerical expressions to algebraic expressions in a variety of contexts (7.EE.3).

Understanding Algebraic Expressions

Students have been representing various problems by using a symbol for an unknown number since grade 2, with such equations as $13 + \square = 22$. Middle grade students develop an understanding of how to incorporate variables into numerical expressions and equations. Students find purpose for variable expressions as they engage in tasks in which doing repeated numerical calculations would be more cumbersome than using an arithmetic expression. Grade 6 students write algebraic expressions from given verbal descriptions and begin to apply the subtleties of symbolic representation. Examples include such verbal descriptions as those in Figure 6.3 (6.EE.2).

Figure 6.3 Verbal Descriptions to Algebraic Expressions

Verbal Description	Algebraic Expression	Notes
Six times a number	$6n$	Students may initially write the expression as 6 x n or as $n6$
Subtract 12 from b	$b - 12$	Students may reverse the order and write $12 - b$
A number m divided by 8	$\frac{m}{8}$	Although m ÷ 8 is not incorrect, students should learn to write division with the fraction bar
Fives times the sum of y and 7	$5(y + 7)$	Students may, incorrectly, write $5y + 7$, not recognizing the need to see $y + 7$ as a quantity

As students become more familiar with writing algebraic expressions, use of the distributive property should be a critical part of their study. As described in the previous section, students' understanding that 6(8 + 5) may be simplified as 6 × 13 or as 6 × 8 + 6 × 5, leads to a much clearer understanding of how to simplify expressions such as 6(b + 2) and then 6b + 12. Another important application of the distributive property is seen as students learn that b(4 + 2) is the same as 4b + 2b and its inverse shows that collecting like terms is justified by the distributive property, representing 4b + 2b as (4 + 2)b is 6b (6.EE.3).

Students are also asked to write algebraic expressions from contextual situations such as:

Kellian brought $15 to the carnival, where it costs $1.25 per ride.

1. Show in a table how much money Kellian has left after each ride.

2. Write an algebraic expression to determine how much money he has left after any amount of rides.

Solutions:

Number of rides	1	2	3	4
Money he has left	15 – 1.25	15 – 2(1.25)	15 – 3(1.25)	15 – 4(1.25)

15 – 1.25r where r stands for the number of rides Kellian went on at the carnival.

It should be noted that writing the expression with 1.25r might initially challenge students rather than r(1.25) as this is the way the table is constructed. However, students should learn it is convention to write the coefficient, 1.25 first and then the variable. This task is extended by having students use their expression to solve for how much money Kellian would have left after 7 rides or 10 rides, learning to input a number for the variable and simplify the expression. The ability to substitute a number for a variable in an expression is further practiced with students being given tasks to evaluate expressions that come from using such formulas as P = 4s, by which the perimeter of a square may be found efficiently.

MP7
Structure

As grade 7 students further their work with algebraic expressions, they incorporate more operations, including those with negative numbers, and use complex rational numbers as coefficients (7.EE.1). Teachers engage their students in activities in which they interpret and write equivalent expressions involving combining like terms, factoring, and the distributive property.

 One whole class activity engages students in working as a team to simplify expressions through a Team Rally, described to students as a game like Pass the Baton that they play in P.E. Desks are lined up in rows and the first student in the row is given an expression. This student must carry out the first step in simplifying the expression. She then hands the expression to the student behind her in the row, who carries out the second step. The handing-off of the expression continues, until it is fully simplified by the last student in the row. This student brings the simplified expression to the teacher, who confirms that the answer is correct. The team who correctly simplifies the expression first wins a point for their team. A sample round of the game is shown in the figure below.

This activity as shown in Figure 6.4, gives students the opportunity to discuss various strategies and to practice flexibility in how the expression may be simplified, recognizing that different steps will lead to the same answer, while at the same time recognizing that some steps may be more efficient than others. Students must fully simplify the expression by the time it gets to the last student in the row, so how the steps are carried out must be thought out strategically.

> **MP8**
> Reasoning

Figure 6.4 Activity to Discuss How an Expression Can Be Simplified

Student 1 receives a card with the expression: $-\frac{1}{2}(b + 3) - 5(3b + 3^2)$

Student 2 simplifies the expression to: $-\frac{b}{2} - \frac{3}{2} - 5(3b + 3^2)$

Student 3 confers with Student 2, asking if $-\frac{b}{2}$ is the same as $-\frac{1}{2}b$?

The two students discuss how $-\frac{1}{2} \cdot \frac{b}{1}$ is equal to $-\frac{b}{2}$ and play continues.

Student 3 then simplifies the expression to: $-\frac{b}{2} - \frac{3}{2} - 15b - 5 \cdot 3^2$

The expression is further simplified until it reaches the end of the row when Student 6 turns in the card, showing the fully simplified expression as: $-\frac{31}{2}b - \frac{93}{2} = -31b - 93$

In preparation for solving application problems with algebraic equations, grade 7 students also learn to write expressions from a given context, recognizing that expressions may be varied depending upon how they are viewed in the context, yet that the expressions are equivalent (7.EE.2). As an example, a group of students is posed the "border" problem:

> Myra and Jolina are in charge of making the border from 1-square inch tiles for the 7th grade class mural. They know that the mural is a square, with each side length measuring 15 inches. Write an expression that represents the number of border pieces (b) that will be needed and make a diagram to show the relationship between the expression and the border number of tiles needed.

Students may write different expressions depending on how they visualize the problem:

- One student may choose to write the expression as $4(15b) + 4$ explaining that each side needs 15 tiles and there are 4 sides. The + 4 represents the need for a tile in each corner.

- Another student may choose to write the expression as $2(15b + 2) + 2(15b)$ explaining that two sides have $15b + 2$ (one for each corner) and the other two sides have $15b$.

- A third student may choose to write expression as $60b + 4$, explaining that she found the perimeter of the mural first and knew that each inch of the perimeter would need a tile and then added in the four corners.

There are certainly many other possible representations for this problem and students should engage in comparing their expressions, determining if the expressions are each equivalent and considering which expression might be the most efficient for solving the problem.

MP3
Construct

As students in grade 8 learn the rules for operating on same base numbers with integer exponents, they incorporate these rules while working with algebraic expressions (8.EE.1). Students must also come to know how the distributive property may be used when the exponent is the same but not the base. The rules are summarized as algebraic expressions in Figure 6.5.

Figure 6.5 Rules for Operating on Same Base Numbers with Integer Exponent

Operation	Example	Rule
multiplication	$4^2 \cdot 4^3 = 4^5$	$a^m \cdot a^n = a^{m+n}$
division	$\frac{4^5}{4^2} = 4^3$	$\frac{a^m}{a^n} = a^{m-n}$
raising a power to a power	$(4^3)^2 = 4^6$	$(a^m)^n = a^{mn}$
zero as an exponent	$4^0 = 1$	$a^0 = 1$
negative exponents	$4^{-3} = \frac{1}{4^3}$	$a^{-m} = \frac{1}{a^m}$
distributing an exponent	$4^3 \cdot 6^3 = (4 \cdot 6)^3$	$a^m \cdot b^m = (a \cdot b)^m$

While it is tempting to teach students the rules for working with exponents, the focus of the standards requires a conceptual understanding of how and why these rules work, as they are continuously applied in many different contexts.

MP2
Reason

The work with understanding the rules of exponents is also extended to explorations with very large and small numbers by writing these numbers in scientific notation (8.EE.3). While it is not a new concept for students to learn how to write numbers in scientific notation, the focus has traditionally been to teach students the rules of translating from one form to the other. The standards call for an emphasis on estimating with numbers in this form, so first connecting the exponent rules to how these numbers are formed provides a foundation. With a focus on multiplication rather than on moving the decimal point, as is traditionally taught, students come to understand that multiplying by a power of 10 with a positive exponent creates a larger number such as in the example of:

$6.9 \times 10^3 = 6.9 \times 1000 = 6,900$

And that multiplying by a power of 10 with a negative exponent creates a smaller number such as in the example of:

$6.9 \times 10^{-3} = 6.9 \times \frac{1}{10^3} = 6.9 \times \frac{1}{1,000} = 6.9 \times 0.001 = 0.0069$

Comparing then the thickness of a grain of pepper as inches to the thickness of a grain of sand as inches, students will be better equipped to conceptualize that the grain of sand is 10 times smaller than the grain of pepper.

Unfortunately, it is not uncommon for students to be asked problems such as the following, and to find them willing to calculate with these very large numbers in their current form, even if the problem asks for the answer to be provided in scientific notation.

> Pluto's distance from the Sun is 3,600,000,000 miles and the Earth's distance from the Sun is 93,000,000 miles. How many times longer is the distance from Pluto to the Sun as it is from the Earth to the Sun? Express your answer in scientific notation.

MP5
Tools

Students will often attempt the calculation, using many zeros and then change the final answer to scientific notation. The goal with grade 8 students should be to help students come to understand that scientific notation can be advantageous to them while calculating, making the steps of the problem easier to carry out (8.EE.4).

Solving Equations and Inequalities

The grade 6 standards, represented in the cluster on solving equations, involves students in a deeper study of the processes involved both in writing and solving equations. Special attention is paid to the relationship between arithmetic and the algebraic methods for solving the equation. Students must first come to know what finding the solution to an equation means. While finding an answer such as $x = 5$ does provide students with the satisfaction that the problem is solved, students must also understand that solving an equation means finding a number to make the equation true (6.EE.5). For grade 6 students, this may involve reasoning about finding the solutions to the equation by focusing on the meaning of the equation, such as in the example of $10p - 4p = 20 - 4p$. To understand that the addition or subtraction of the $4p$ on both sides of the equation may essentially be skipped as students are finding the final answer necessitates a deeper understanding of what solving the equation means rather than just following a set of rules. At this point, it is also important for students to come to know that each occurrence of the variable in the equation represents the same number, so the $-4p$ is superfluous. Students can solidify this understanding by substituting 2 into the equation for p will prove that $p = 2$ satisfies the equation.

Solving equations in grade 6 involves developing effective reasoning strategies and drawing upon prior knowledge, such as using fact families and inverse operations. In the example below, a student is being asked to solve the following problem:

> The softball team needed to purchase some new softballs, so they started getting donations. On Monday, they had collected $14.25 and by Wednesday they had enough money to buy the softballs, which cost $68.75. How much money did they collect between Monday and Wednesday?

As students represent the unknown as a variable within real-life contexts, it is important for them to provide meaning for the variables that they use. Many teachers require students to define the variables as a regular practice as they solve word problems. As in the problem above, students may learn to first write: m = the amount of money collected between Monday and Wednesday. While it may seem unnecessary to some students, learning to clarify what the variable represents will prepare students for a better understanding of the solution once it is found. As they prepare to write an equation, students may then choose to represent the situation using a bar model as in Figure 6.6 to visualize that the $14.25 and the unknown amount together equal $68.75.

MP4
Model

Figure 6.6 Bar Model

$68.75	
$14.25	m

Other strategies may involve knowing that the equation may be written as $14.25 + m = 68.75$ and students use their knowledge of fact families to determine that $68.75 - m = 14.25$ and that $68.75 - 14.25 = m$. This strategy may then be extended to use inverse operations to solve the equation, knowing that subtraction is the inverse of addition, so 14.25 may be subtracted from 68.75 to get m (6.EE.6). At this grade level, students may still then compare the solutions they found arithmetically to those found algebraically, thereby assuring that their algebraic solution is correct and vice-versa. It may be a challenge to get some grade 6 students to be willing to write an algebraic equation to solve problems such as the one written above. However, students at this age must come to know that learning to write algebraic representations, despite the fact that it is a fairly straight forward problem to solve arithmetically, will provide them with the foundation for much more complex representations in their future study (6.EE.7).

Defining the variable students are solving for in a real-life context also extends their thinking about whether the solution is one number or a range of numbers (6.EE.8). For example, students are asked to write an equation or an inequality to represent each of the following situations and then represent the answer on a number line diagram:

▭ Kayden earned less than $75 when he was dog-sitting last week.

▭ Gail wants to make 24 muffins for the bake sale tomorrow.

▭ Femi planted more than 25 tomato plants in her garden.

As students represent the solution, they can visualize the infinite solution as shown in Figure 6.7.

Figure 6.7 Visualize the Infinite Solution

Students often demonstrate initial difficulty with using an open circle to depict the verbal description of "more than" or "less than" on the number line. Clearly delineating that the reference number in the problem is not included as a part of the solution on the number line may help and provide an important step toward conceptualizing more complex inequalities later on.

The grade 7 cluster focusing on expressions and equations involves students solving equations that include numbers in any form. It is expected that students will continue to compare their arithmetic solutions to those found algebraically. The problems, however, should become increasingly complex so that students will recognize that solving the problem algebraically is the most effective and efficient way to solve it (7.EE.4a). McCallum (2011) suggests that seventh-grade students should be given problems to solve where the "cognitive load" is lessened when developing an algebraic method for solving the problem.

One teacher asked her students to solve the following problem:

> A seventh-grade team held a coin drive to collect money for a local charity. Told that they could only donate dimes and quarters, the students found out they collected $71.45. If the total numbers of coins was 337, how many quarters did the team collect?

As students set out to solve this problem, they initially tried to guess and check to find the number of each type of coin. Some of the students set about making a table to represent the possible combinations that make 337 coins and checked to see if the combination produced $71.45. Even though it is certainly possible to solve the problem in this manner, most students recognized early on that this solution method was taking a long time and that an algebraic method may be more efficient because they could solve the problem more quickly this way. Choosing the letter d for the number of dimes and q for the number of quarters initially proved to be problematic as these students did not know how to solve an equation with two variables.

Several students soon recognized that the number of quarters could be represented by the variable expression $337 - d$ or, conversely, the number of dimes could be represented by the expression $337 - q$. Determining an equation to represent the total value of the coins may also be represented in several different ways, such as $.25(337 - d) + .1(d) = 71.45$ or $25(337 - d) + 10d = 7145$. This problem also lent itself to variety of ways to represent the equation. Being able to think flexibly about the numbers they chose also indicated students' ability to reason about the quantities, as indicated in the standards.

MP3
Reasoning

The related standard in this cluster requires grade 7 students to connect their understanding of solving equations to solving inequalities (7.EE.4b). Although not referenced in the standard, the progression document for this domain states that students should, at this level, also work with inequalities that involve "less than or equal to" and "greater than or equal to" symbolized as ≤ and ≥. Solving problems such as the one below pose a new situation, not before encountered.

> Devon has $22.00 to spend at the local school supply store. She buys a binder for $2.50 and spends some of the money on packages of mechanical pencils (p) that each cost $3.50. She'd like to have at least $2.00 left to buy a snack on the way home. Write and solve an inequality to show how many packages of mechanical pencils she can buy and still have money for a snack.

One way students may set up the inequality is as $22 - (2.5 + 3.5p) \geq 2$, showing that the money she has left must be greater than or equal to $2.00. It is soon recognized that students must now divide by a negative number when solving this inequality. While students are comfortable with dividing by negative numbers at this point, they do not always initially recognize that the symbol used in the problem is no longer correct, when they carry out this calculation. The authors of the standards suggest that students should be asked to reason about which symbol should be used, rather than, at this level, being taught the rules for reversing the symbol when multiplying or dividing by a negative number. In solving the problem above, recognizing that writing the answer as $p \geq 5$, implying that she can purchase any amount more than 5 pencils is incorrect, students will reason that the answer must be $p \leq 5$. As the Standards state that students should also graph the solution to an inequality, their need to visualize the inequality will help them to interpret if their solution is correct or not, as using any number in the range greater than 5 will not work.

Honoring Individual Differences

Some students find that writing equations and inequalities from a word problem is extremely difficult. Providing these students with a set of tools for translating from the verbal description to the algebraic model may include:

1. Practice in finding the important information in the problem without the need to solve the problem.

2. Use of manipulatives to represent the situation prior to writing an equation.

3. Create drawings such as the bar model, mentioned previously, including the given information and the variable(s).

4. Avoid looking for key words, such as thinking that finding the total always means to add, as students may try to memorize when to these words rather than attempting to conceptually represent the problem. The standards ask students to learn to interpret the problem and the solution rather than to just memorize how to set it up and solve it.

MP1
Make Sense

The work of solving one-variable linear equations culminates in grade 8, solving problems that include any rational coefficients (8.EE.7). Problems such as the one below that an eighth grade teacher posed to her class as a warm-up led students to write equations with variables on both sides.

These types of problems give students further opportunities to recognize that it is easier to solve the problem algebraically than to find it arithmetically.

> Carina and Jayron are both growing sunflower plants for their science projects. When Carina bought her plant it was 3 inches tall and it is growing 1.5 inches per week. Jayron's plant, when he bought it, was 2 inches tall and it is growing 1.75 inches per week. When will both plants be the same height?

Students learn to recognize the expressions to solve this problem may initially be set up as Carina's sunflower growth: $1.5w + 3$ and Jayron's sunflower growth: $1.75w + 2$, then make the two expressions equal as $1.5w + 3 = 1.75w + 2$ to find what week (w) the plants are the same height.

Students at this grade level must also determine the number of solutions that the equation will have: one, infinitely many, or none as summarized in Figure 6.8.

Figure 6.8 Number of Solutions to an Equation

Example:	Students learn:
$-3(x + 5) = 30$	$x = -15$ is the only value for x that will work in the equation.
$-5(6x + 2) = 2(-15x - 5)$	When the equation is simplified, both sides of the equation are equivalent, so the value of x can be any number. Students may initially see the solutions as: $-10 = -10$ or $-30x = -30x$

$6x - 5 = 3(2x - 15)$	When the equation is simplified, the two sides of the equation are not equivalent, so there is no value for x that will work to make the equation true.
	Students may initially see the solution as:
	$-5 = -45$ or $0x = -40$

The grade 8 cluster involving solving linear equations requires students to use radicals involving square and cube roots in their solutions (8.EE.2). Grade 8 students need only to learn to solve equations with variables that are raised to the second or the third power, such as $9x^2 = 81$ or $2x^3 = 16$. Solving such equations involves learning to work with the square and cube root symbols, such as $\sqrt{9}$ and $\sqrt[3]{8}$. Students must also learn that the answer to these equations involves including the $\pm$ symbols, writing their answers as $x = \pm 3$ because either a positive 3 or a -3 may be squared to get 9 in the first equation.

MP6
Precision

Conceptual Challenge

Students are often challenged by the difference between knowing that $\sqrt{64} = 8$, yet that the answer to $x^2 = 64$ is $x = \pm 8$. Students must come to know that finding the $\sqrt{64}$ means finding its principal square root, which is always a positive number. As well, students may need to consistently substitute both $+8$ and -8 back into the equation $x^2 = 64$, to recognize that both $+8$ and -8 when squared, result in 64.

Solving simultaneous linear equations, also known as solving systems of equations, involves grade 8 students with finding the solution to more than one two-variable equation where the solutions are the same (8.EE.8) as shown in Figure 6.9. The standards clearly state that students should learn to solve a system by graphing. Students must learn that the point of intersection of the two graphed equations produces the same solution to each of the equations. Students will learn to make sense of these solutions as they make connections between the graphical and the algebraic solutions to the system (8.EE.8c).

MP4
Model

Figure 6.9 Student Work Showing Systems of Linear Equations

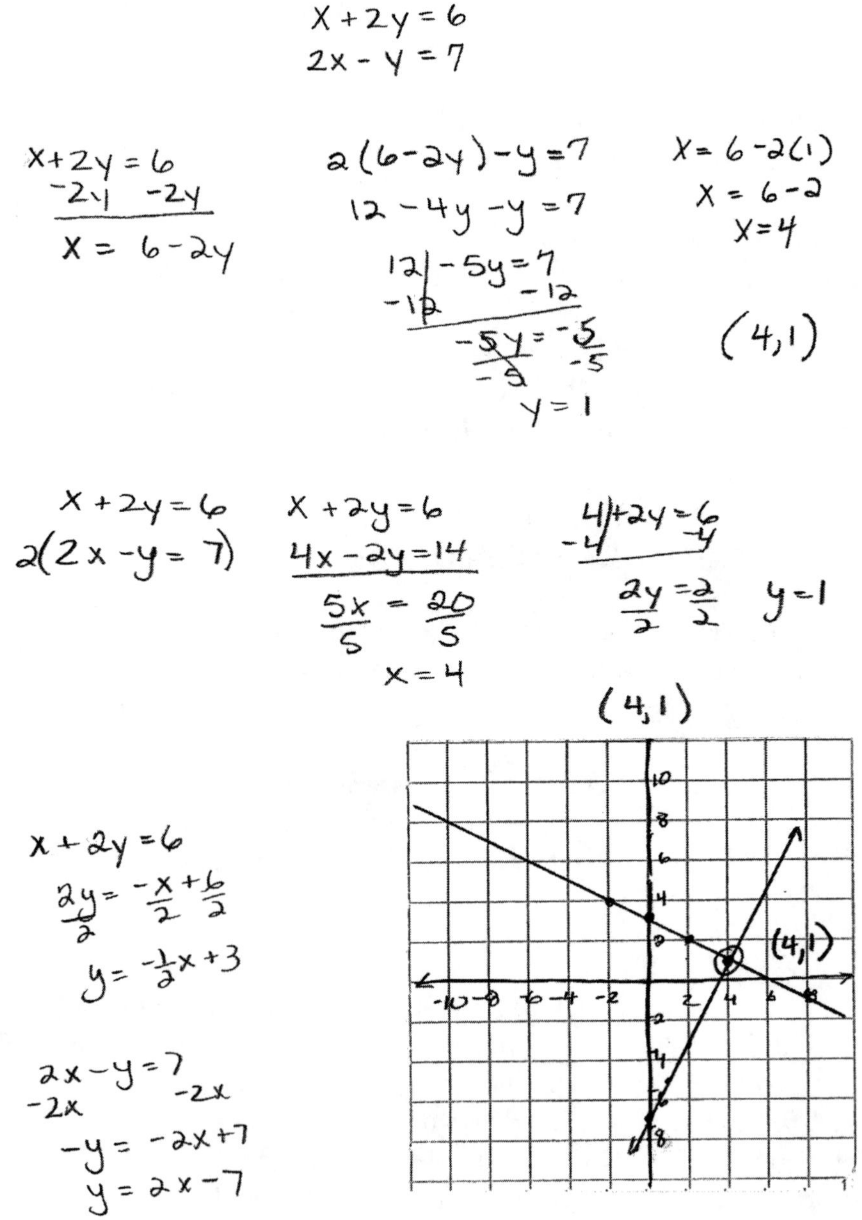

$$X + 2y = 6$$
$$2x - y = 7$$

$X + 2y = 6$
$\underline{-2y \quad -2y}$
$X = 6 - 2y$

$2(6 - 2y) - y = 7$
$12 - 4y - y = 7$
$12 - 5y = 7$
$\underline{-12 \qquad -12}$
$\dfrac{-5y}{-5} = \dfrac{-5}{-5}$
$y = 1$

$X = 6 - 2(1)$
$X = 6 - 2$
$X = 4$

$(4, 1)$

$X + 2y = 6$
$2(2x - y = 7)$

$X + 2y = 6$
$\underline{4x - 2y = 14}$
$\dfrac{5x}{5} = \dfrac{20}{5}$
$x = 4$

$\dfrac{4 + 2y = 6}{-4 \qquad -4}$
$\dfrac{2y}{2} = \dfrac{2}{2} \quad y = 1$

$(4, 1)$

$X + 2y = 6$
$\dfrac{2y}{2} = \dfrac{-x}{2} + \dfrac{6}{2}$
$y = -\tfrac{1}{2}x + 3$

$2x - y = 7$
$-2x \qquad -2x$
$-y = -2x + 7$
$y = 2x - 7$

$(4, 1)$

154

Representing Relationships with Algebraic Equations

As sixth-grade students become adept with writing and solving one-variable equations, they also learn to write algebraic equations to represent the relationship between independent and dependent variables in real-life contexts (6.EE.9). Explorations should provide students with experience in analyzing how one quantity changes based on another. Determining which is the independent variable and which is the dependent variable may initially be challenging. Asking students to verbally discuss and to provide written descriptions of the relationship builds understanding about these two types of variables. For example, two students were discussing a situation relating the time they studied for a test and how well they did. They filled in the blanks in this sentence _____ causes _____ in two ways to determine which variable was the independent variable and which was the dependent variable. The statement "Studying for a test longer caused a higher test score" made more sense to the students than "A higher test score caused a longer study time." Understanding the causality allows students to give meaning to the variables so students should be given ample opportunity to practice which variable is independent and which is dependent in a variety of situations.

Multiple representations for the relationship between the two variables should be explored by learning to write a verbal description, make a table, create an equation or represent the relationship on a coordinate graph. A focus on analyzing how these different forms each show the same relationship provides a foundational understanding for students' work in the grade 8 Functions domain and in high school.

One sixth-grade teacher, in preparation for the next day's class, asked his students to tell him something interesting about themselves that they could do. He took the information and wrote statements such as the following on index cards:

- ✐ Marissa can do 15 sit-ups in 1 minute.
- ✐ Zach works at the local farm stand and earns $7 per hour.
- ✐ Elena rides her bike an average of 10 miles per hour.

The next day the students were asked to draw a card from the pile and to represent an extension of the situation on the card by a graph, a table, and an equation. For example, the students displaying the information about Zach, first determined that the independent variable was the number of hours he works and the dependent variable is how much money he earns. They then showed a relationship between the hours he works and the money he earns in a table, with an equation and on a graph. The students were given large sheets of paper on which to display their work. Once they were done displaying the information, they were asked to return the card to the pile. The cards were shuffled and then redistributed. Students had to find the displayed data that represented the information on their cards. This type of activity gives students the opportunity to interpret data given in various forms where the focus is on analysis of the data by relating the two variables.

It is interesting to note that there is little to no emphasis on expressing relationships between two variables in the seventh grade Expressions and Equations domain. Rather, these connections for seventh grade students lies primarily within the Ratios and Proportional Relationships domain, which provides a heavy emphasis on developing a deep understanding of proportionality. This work ties back into the Expressions and Equations domain in grade 8, as students connect the work from previous grades regarding proportionality as it relates to slope. It should be noted that there is a perceived overlap between this standard and the standards regarding slope and rate of change in the Functions domain. However, the focus within the Expressions and Equations domain in grade 8 lies primarily with connecting the unit rate in a proportional relationship from an algebraic perspective (8.EE.6). Students learn why linear equations have a constant slope from interpreting similar triangles on a graph, drawn from connecting two different sets of points on the graph. Drawing upon their understanding of ratios, students learn that if the ratio of the rise to the run with each similar triangle is the same, then the slopes are the same. When the line on the graph goes through the origin, the connection may then be made between the points that create the hypotenuse of one of the triangles to deriving the linear equation. One way for students to understand the equation $y = mx$ is to then draw an algebraic comparison between the points on the graph and the two ratios as shown in Figure 6.10:

Figure 6.10 Understanding the Equation $y = mx$

If the two points are:

(0, 0) and (x, y) and then the point (x, y) is described as $(1, m)$ then:

$$\frac{rise}{run} = \frac{y - 0}{x - 0} = \frac{m - 0}{1 - 0}$$

Simplifying this proportion will result in:

$$\frac{y}{x} = \frac{m}{1}$$

If the line on the graph goes through a point other than the origin, the point may be labeled as (0, b) and the equation may be derived as $y = mx + b$.

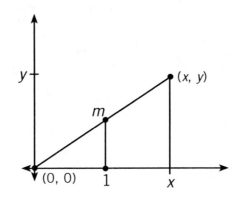

The progression document for Expressions and Equations outlines several topics for grade 8 students to tie together as they prepare to study functions.

1. A one-variable expression describes a calculation where the variable represents the input and the calculation represents the output.

2. As a variable is chosen to represent the output, a two-variable equation is created and the relationship between the two quantities may be described.

3. Creating a table of values for the two quantities allows for the creation of solution pairs for the equation.

4. These solution pairs may then be plotted on a coordinate graph, allowing for a visual representation of the situation.

Assessment Note

The topics covered in this domain are numerous and have many connections to the standards of other domains. If a student is showing difficulty with the work of the standards in the domain, it may not always be readily apparent as to where the confusion lies. Informal assessments, such as Do Now problems, thumbs up/thumbs down responses, or individual questioning, should be conducted where an attempt is made to clarify as to whether the student is struggling with such individual concepts as the following:

- Carrying out the arithmetic operations
- Interpreting the situation due to reading comprehension difficulties
- Using mathematical symbols accurately
- Drawing an accurate graph

After conducting an assessment, teachers may want to ask students to reflect on their own work, asking such questions as:

- ✏ **Relating to graphs**: Was your scale accurate on each axis?

- ✏ **Relating to tables**: Did you accurately choose the right independent and dependent variables when you made your table?

- ✏ **Relating to equations**: Did you accurately distribute the negative sign when necessary in the equation? Did you use the appropriate symbols to describe the inequality?

As students become more familiar with reflecting on their work by answering questions the teacher asks, they may then be asked to freely describe their own reasons for misinterpretation of a question. Self-reflection is a powerful tool for more clearly understanding the topic and leads to greater accuracy when the same type of problem is seen in another context in the future.

MP6
Precision

Standardized test questions focusing on the work of this domain are likely to draw upon the connections between various representations of real-life contexts with a focus on reading/writing a verbal description, creating a table, drawing a graph and writing an equation. As described in detail throughout this chapter, emphasis should be placed on helping students to understand how to relate these various representations so that any one of the models may be used to create another.

Voice from the Classroom

As a sixth-grade teacher, I was astonished when I first saw the amount of algebra written into the sixth-grade standards that I was going to have to teach my students. Prior to this year, I had taught my students very little about writing algebraic expressions, never mind having to solve equations from word problems. When I was studying to be a teacher, I never had any formal courses on teaching these topics, as most of my work was on learning to teach elementary level mathematics. Until now, I focused primarily on teaching students about operations with whole numbers, fractions and decimals. I hadn't studied these algebraic concepts myself since high school, or maybe a course in college. But, I don't remember those courses helping me figure out how to teach this material. This was a whole new world for me. I wasn't really sure what to do to bring myself up to speed and neither was the other sixth-grade teacher.

So we started researching online for how to teach topics such as translating from a verbal description to writing an algebraic equation. The material that we found that made the most sense to us focused a lot on having students first draw pictures to interpret the problem. The pictures looked a lot like the bar models we were using when we learned about teaching ratios and we started to make some connections. We thought that if these bar models helped us to understand the material better, perhaps it would help our students too. So, we spent this year having all of our students first interpret the situation by drawing a picture. Sometimes our students drew pictures and had their partners write situations to represent the models. Our students got really good at making these models and most of them agreed that it really helped them to understand the problem better. After awhile, some of them said that they started to just see a picture in their head and they didn't think that they needed to draw the pictures anymore. That's when we knew that they were ready to move on to another stage in their learning of how to write the equations. Not all of our sixth graders were ready at the end of the school year to write an equation directly from the story problem, but many of them were able to and they all agreed that making a picture first was a great tool that they would keep in their math toolbox.

—6th-Grade Teacher

Let's Think and Discuss

1. Have you found particular manipulative materials that are helpful to your students in learning to solve algebraic equations?

2. Do you find that your students are challenged by using mnemonics such as PEMDAS to remember rules for concepts such as the order of operations? If so, what difficulties do they often have?

3. How much of a shift do you see in what you have been teaching about the topics in this domain at your grade level? What kind of professional development do you think that you need in order to best be prepared to teach these topics?

Chapter 7

Functions

Snapshot

Ahmet and Cecilia are seated with their small group, working on their warm-up problem. Their eighth-grade teacher has just given each group a card with an equation on it; in their case they have been given the equation $y = x^3$. They must determine whether or not the equation represents a function. One person in their group is in charge of graphing the equation on the graphing calculator while another is making a table of values, or an input-output table. Cecilia is responsible for making a visual representation of the inputs and outputs that her classmate making the table has determined. She has chosen to use toothpicks to make the representation and is conferring with Ahmet to see if he thinks that her visual model shows an appropriate pattern for the equation. Cecilia thinks her job is the hardest, but she is glad she picked it because she likes working with her hands to make the model. Once each member of the group has made a different representation, they will confer about whether or not they think that $y = x^3$ is a function. Ahmet will represent the group when they share their results with the class and wants to get everyone's results before he presents. As the teacher moves to each group asking them if they are ready to present, he asks Cecilia how she sees that each input has a one, unique output.

She tells her teacher that she has confirmed this data with the Table feature on the graphing calculator. As Ahmet shares the group's findings, he must refer to all of the models made by his group members to present his case. Each person in the group must also be prepared to answer questions if asked by anyone in the class. The group concludes that yes, $y = x^3$ is a function because it fits all of the criteria for functions. The teacher finds this way of learning about functions to be successful as each student is actively involved and is able to choose how to represent the equation. Drawing upon individual learning styles and yet working toward a common goal always seems to work well.

Big Picture

The Functions domain is one of three critical areas in grade 8. Well connected to concepts taught prior to grade 8, within the grade and far-reaching into high school mathematics, teaching middle grade students the concept of a function now has a place of its own in the standards. Past curriculum standards found the function definition embedded into early algebra units, however the Standards have included a set of standards which focus directly on learning what a function is, how to recognize a function and how to represent functions in a variety of ways.

Students begin learning function concepts as early as grade 3 by identifying and describing patterns. By grade 5, students are forming pairs of numbers by observing a pattern and are graphing those pairs on a coordinate system. Grade 6 students are learning about dependent and independent variables and learn to represent the relationship between those variables in a variety of ways. The work in grade 7 on forming proportional relationships and writing equations provides many opportunities for students to recognize how two quantities may be related and how to represent these relationships in an algebraic form. With a strong foundation from the earlier grades, the stage is set for the formal introduction to a function in grade 8.

MP7
Structure

The first three standards within this domain focus on students' ability to make sense of what a function is by understanding its definition as well as to interpret and compare functions. Although the formal notation f(x), described as "ƒof x", is not introduced until high school, students do learn that function equations are usually written as $y =$ where y represents the dependent variable. While the primary focus lies with linear functions, students in grade 8 are asked, as well, to determine whether or not the function could be non-linear. Represented in a variety of ways, students work to describe functions by what is often referred to as a "rule of four" format (Hughes-Hallett 2010).

Figure 7.1 Rule of Four Format

Verbal Description	Graphical Representation
Algebraic Model (Equation)	Bivariate Data (Table)

Recognizing the characteristics of a function in these different formats allows grade 8 students to learn to reason quantitatively as they must represent the function with different models and must be able to flexibly move within these models to make connections.

MP2
Reason

The last two standards in the domain give particular attention to modeling with functions. It is within these standards that students solidify their understanding of linear functions, with a focus on slope as rate of change and the y-intercept as an initial value. Each of these important aspects of function must be explained through various representations (table, graph, equation, or context). Modeling with functions also takes on the form of conceptualizing relationships without the use of numbers. Opportunities are given for students to explore the qualitative aspect of a function, primarily through interpreting graphs that do

MP4
Model

not have a scale on the axes. This standard provides students with a unique opportunity to describe the relationship between the independent and dependent variable without reliance on the use of numbers to tell the story.

As students in grade 8 move to high school, their initial understandings of function are built upon with a formal introduction to function notation and by exploring non-linear functions in much greater depth. Students are introduced at the middle level to functions as a general mathematics concept and then high school mathematics coursework exposes students to the connections between different types of functions, rather than seeing each type of function as a completely separate entity. Building upon their understanding of linearity, high school students will see the connections between linear functions represented by a variable with a degree of 1 and subsequent functions increasing in degree (such as quadratic and polynomial).

What Is a Function?

Four students are seated at the front of an eighth grade mathematics class, each wearing a different t-shirt. Each student is holding a sign identifying himself as a coordinate pair. The pair is described by first the student's name and second the name of the sports team on the student's t-shirt. Brent is identified by (Brent, Blues) and his classmate next to him is holding a sign that says (Gavin, Hurricanes). Brent and Gavin's classmates are to determine whether the representation of these students' pairings represent a function. According to the *definition of a function, described as a rule whereby each input has exactly one output,* these students do represent a function. The class agrees that each person's name, representing the input, produces only one output, the name of the sports team on his T-shirt. Another group of students move to the front of the room, this time all wearing the same T-shirts, holding signs, again stating their names and the sports team on their shirt.

Only this time, the pairing is reversed. Jarva's sign states (Aces, Jarva) and her classmates' sign reads (Aces, Seth). This eighth-grade class again applies the definition of function to this representation of the students and their shirts. The class determines that this way of representing the relationship between the students' name and t-shirt worn does not represent a function. In this situation, each input does not have a unique output. One student reflects on why this is true by stating, "Hey, if I wanted to ask the kid who was wearing the Aces shirt a question, there would be too many choices." Students in this class are learning to understand the definition of a function by first focusing on the relationship between the input and the output of a relationship devoid of numbers. Figure 7.2 further emphasize the definition of function as having one unique output. Students learn to recognize the input must always produce the same output each time it is chosen.

Figure 7.2 Table with Input and Output

Name	T-Shirt
Brent	Blues
Gavin	Hurricanes
Naira	Reds
Bart	Diamonds

T-Shirt	Name
Aces	Jarva
Aces	Seth
Aces	Mikey
Aces	Aylin

As demonstrated in the example above, it is advantageous to focus on the conceptual meaning of a function prior to creating detailed representations (8.F.1). As another example, students are given a set of cards to choose from (Figure 7.3) and must choose one card from Set A and one from Set B. Once the cards are chosen the students must write a sentence describing a function. Students write sentences such as "The hours the turkey is in the oven is a function of its weight" and determine the input as the weight of the turkey and the output as the hours the turkey must be cooked in the oven.

It is also important for students to recognize when it is possible for the input and output values to be reversed and a function may still result. For example, a function representing the relationship between the width and length of a rectangle with an area of 32 square units may be described with the width as the input values and the length as the output values or vice-versa.

Figure 7.3 Input and Output

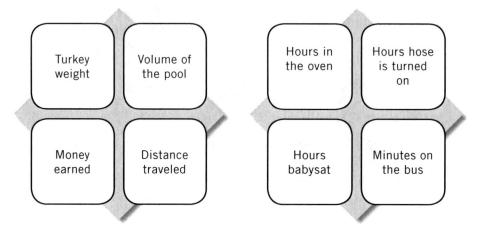

As functions involving numerical relationships are studied, explorations with a function machine give students the opportunity to build input-output tables. The resulting data should then be written as ordered pairs and eventually graphed. Once students think they know the rule, they determine the output values from given inputs. The related input-output tables are then written as ordered pairs and graphed as shown in Figure 7.4.

Figure 7.4 Input-Output Table

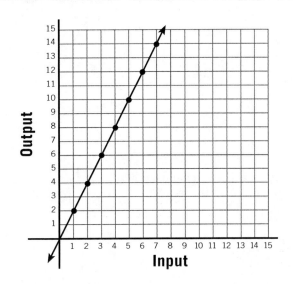

Rule = 2x

In	Out
1	2
2	4
3	6
4	8
5	10
6	12
7	14

It is advantageous for students to create function graphs by hand prior to using a graphing calculator or another tool in order to practice such aspects of graphing as how to label the axes and what scale to use. As well, the physical experience of plotting the points is often quite useful to students as they focus on the pattern and the relationship between the points as they are drawing the graph.

MP2
Reason

Prior to the introduction of the Common Core, it was commonplace to analyze the graph as a function through the use of a vertical line test as a determination that there is only one input for each output. Used as a way to know if there is more than one *y* for each *x*, an invisible line is drawn through each part of the graph. If the line goes through more than one part of the graph, it does not represent a function. This "test" is now discouraged as it often leads to a narrow view of a function, often used without thinking about the meaning behind its use. Rather, students should be encouraged to view the graph more broadly as *y* graphed as a function of *x*. It is also important to keep in mind that the Standards do not require students to consider the domain and the range of the function from a graph in the eighth grade, rather this vocabulary and the related concepts are reserved for study in high school.

As previously introduced in this chapter, functions may be represented in four ways:

1. the context which this is the story of the function

2. the table of data

3. the graph of the ordered pairs

4. the symbolic representation known as the equation

Students should be familiar with all four ways of representing any function and should learn to be flexible in thinking about how those ways are connected (Van de Walle, Karp, and Bay-Williams 2013). The tasks students are presented with must require students to consider which representation(s) best leads to a solution and how the various representations give a different view of the story.

Consider the following task: Joseph and Amy have spent two class periods playing the online game, *The Lemonade Game.* Their teacher has asked them to model some of the numerical relationships they have found while playing the game by using several representations. They start by gathering some data. They remember they were given $20.00 to spend at the beginning of the game to get started with their lemonade stand. Although the lemonade can cost them different amounts to make depending on their recipe, they like the recipe that costs them $.40/cup. On sunny days, they find they can sell their lemonade for $.90/cup.

Joseph gets them started on their task by deciding they should write a function rule to represent their profit. He writes a short paragraph telling the story and follows it with a sentence describing the function as, "Our profit is a function of the number of glasses of lemonade that we sell." This sentence helps Amy, as she is responsible for determining the dependent and the independent variables and including them in a table. She has had difficulty in the past with knowing which variable is which, so first writing the function sentence has made it much clearer for her. The students work together, based on their experience with playing the game, to choose appropriate cups of lemonade sold as their input values and determine their associated profit as their output values. Joseph recognizes the recursive pattern, how the profit changes by selling one more glass of lemonade. Both students know that the equation must represent the explicit formula, one that connects the two variables directly. As the function is described by an equation, they are able to use it to determine how much profit they will make if they sell 100 cups of lemonade (an input value) or if they have $200.00 to spend (an output value). It helps them to see the functional relationship in the form of a graph as well, for they are able to visualize how the two variables are related "quickly" without having to use numbers to see the constant rate of change. Their teacher has said that they may use a graphing calculator to make their graph and, although initially pleased they did not have to graph it by hand, they did find it to be a challenge to determine how to set their window settings to see a good portion of the graph (8.F.2).

MP5
Tools

Other students in the class have been working on the same task. As they present their results to the class, the teacher asks the students to take notes on several different aspects of the task.

Choose two groups whose results have:

1. the same rate of change

2. the same rate of change with a different starting amount

3. one rate of change that is double the other

Several classmates noticed that Ashlyn and Ruben presented a graph that showed only dots for the ordered pairs and did not connect their dots to make a straight line. Ruben explained that he wasn't going to sell only part of a cup of lemonade so he didn't think he should make a line on his graph by connecting the points, as this would imply he could sell 4.5 cups of lemonade. This is a common question among middle level students when they are graphing and should be addressed. However, there is no one right answer. The standards do not specify whether students should connect the points when the graph represents data that is discontinuous. Understanding why the points may be connected with some data and not with others does give students the opportunity to more fully consider what the independent variable means in the function and what values are appropriate.

MP7
Structure

More fully, the standards do not address continuous and discontinuous functions at the eighth-grade level. However, these situations do provide for interesting conversation at this level and provide an initial context for further study in high school. It is common for middle level students to connect the points in order to create a graph that allows students to better visualize the relationship between the two variables.

The standards require students at this level to focus primarily on recognizing a linear function and to interpret the slope-intercept form ($y = mx + b$) of this type of function. However, attention is also given to asking students to compare linear functions to those that are not linear and to distinguish between the two. For example, students may be given tables of data where they must determine the recursive pattern in order to determine whether or not the functions are linear. If students are familiar with the use of a spreadsheet, they may be asked to continue the pattern of a linear function by writing an equation that is then inserted into the spreadsheet in order to continue the data.

Figure 7.5 Linear Function

x		y	
7	+2	10	+5
9	+2	15	+5
11	+2	20	+5
13	+2	25	+5
15	+2	30	+5
17		35	

x		y	
3	+2	10	+2
5	+2	12	+4
7	+2	16	+6
9	+2	22	+8
11	+2	30	+10
13		40	

While it is not necessary to derive the formulas for non-linear functions, each of the four representations for functions described earlier in this chapter should be provided, then ask students to state whether or not the function is linear and to describe why.

Figure 7.6 Is It Linear?

Students are given a set of 10 cards on which there are different representations for functions. They must determine whether each situation represents a linear or non-linear function and place it in the appropriate column on their handout.

Sample cards are shown below:

Card 1:

x	−1	1	3	5
y	10	20	30	40

Card 2:

Suppose you threw an object up to a friend who is waiting in a window 20 feet high off the ground. You described the distance from the ground as a function of time.

Card 3:

$y = -3x + 5$

Card 4:

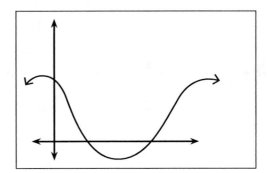

There are many formulas used in geometry and in science that teachers may refer to, providing students experience with identifying, in particular, non-linear functions.

For example:

- recognize that the growth of mold is not a linear function
- compare different side lengths of squares to their areas
- understand the half-life of a radioactive substance as a function
- measure the height of a bouncing ball as related to the number of bounces

The children's story *One Grain of Rice* (Demi 1997) provides an interesting context for students to explore exponential functions. The storyline involves a young girl attempting to find a way to feed her village by outsmarting the village's leader. She tricks the leader into providing more than enough rice by agreeing to double the amount of rice provided each day for 30 days. Engaging students in a graphical representation of this data, provided in the book, provides yet another context for seeing why some functions are non-linear.

Modeling with Function Equations

The study of linear functions in grade 8 is primarily focused on the meaning of the variables in the equation $y = mx + b$. What does the m mean? What does the b mean?

Using the "rule of four", students should recognize the b value, seen as the initial value or the value of y when $x = 0$, in all contexts. As well, the slope m should be interpreted as the rate of change (8.F.4).

Experiences with slope should connect rate of change for a linear function to its numeric value. Conceptually, slope represents the change in y when x increases by 1. A solid foundation in proportional reasoning, developed in grade 7, will allow students to also connect the concept of slope to unit rate. Slope may be presented to students through various visual representations, including the use of a slope triangle.

Recognizing that the distance between the x values and the y values of any two points on the line will produce the same ratio allows students to connect this visual representation with the concept that the same slope of the line is created no matter which two points are chosen. There is also value in having students see the triangles drawn on the coordinate graph as similar, thereby creating equal ratios.

This visual representation may then lead to the formulaic representation of slope as:

$$m = \frac{change\ in\ the\ y\text{-}values}{change\ in\ the\ x\text{-}values} = \frac{y_2 - y_1}{x_2 - x_1}$$

Students should be given many opportunities to find the slope of a linear function, as a number of misconceptions often result as they first explore this concept. Often students ask if it matters which (x, y) pair is considered (x_1, y_1) and (x_2, y_2). Practice with finding the slope using each pair as (x_1, y_1) and recognizing that it is the change in the values that matters will assist students in their thinking about this issue.

> **MP2**
> Reason

Figure 7.7 Slope

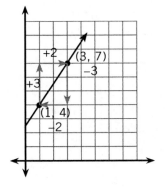

if $(3, 7)$ is (x_1, y_1)

then $m = \frac{4 - 7}{1 - 3} = \frac{-3}{-2} = \frac{3}{2}$

if $(1, 4)$ is (x_1, y_1)

then $m = \frac{7 - 4}{3 - 1} = \frac{3}{2}$

The concept of rate of change is explored as students relate the slope of a linear equation in a context. Knowing that the procedure of adding $0.75 each time x is increased by 1 means, in context, that $0.75 is spent for each mechanical pencil purchased. Representing this change by $0.75x$ not $x + 0.75$ is critical to students' understanding of slope and rate of change. Recognizing the verbal description within the equation assists students with this representation.

Verbal description:

Each time I buy one more mechanical pencil I spend another $0.75.

If required to use the unit labels when including the rate of change in the equation, students may see yet another representation of why the slope is being multiplied by x.

Figure 7.8 Using Unit Labels

$$\frac{\$0.75}{1 \; \cancel{\text{pencil}}} \qquad \frac{4 \; \cancel{\text{pencils}}}{1}$$

Understanding when the slope is zero or when it is undefined is best understood in context. Representing a slope of zero as the x-value continuing to change while the y-value stays the same may be explored by having a student walk toward the whiteboard, stop for several seconds and then continue on. Students should recognize that time (the x-value) will continue while the distance from the whiteboard (y-value) stays the same during that time will be represented as a horizontal line. An undefined slope, represented by a vertical line, would mean that time stopped passing and yet the student kept getting closer to the whiteboard.

Students also become familiar with b as the value of y when $x = 0$, represented by the point $(0, b)$. If the function describes a real-life context it is often thought of as the initial value. Situations, as in the example below, allow students to connect the verbal description of the initial value to its related representations.

Describe the initial value(s) in each situation below:

1. Gabriel and Makayla are competing in a road race. Gabriel runs about 4 mph, however, because he is younger, he is allowed to get a 20-yard head start.

2. A water amusement park charges $10.00 to enter the park and $2.00 for each ride.

Honoring Individual Differences

English language learners are likely to be more comfortable with using the metric system to do these problems involving kilometers/hour or liters/second since that may be a measurement system more familiarly used at home.

Students will, most likely, recognize that the examples above do not necessitate any values of x that are less than 0. In such cases where x may be represented as less than 0, the b value in the related equation actually represents the place where the line crosses the y-axis and should be thought of as the constant in the equation. As well, connecting their prior knowledge of proportional relationships from their work in grade 7 to these representations on a graph should emphasize the y-intercept is also the origin.

Figure 7.9 Y-Intercept

The table below shows the data for a linear function. Provide a possible context for this data, draw a graph and write an equation.

x	1	5	7	10	15
y	5	13	17	23	33

What is the slope in your equation? What does it mean for this problem?

What is the y-intercept in your equation? What does it represent in this problem?

Culminating experiences with linear functions and the associated equation $y = mx + b$ should involve students with providing any one of the four representations for the function and asking students to complete the picture with the other three representations. As well, a comprehensive understanding of the slope, or rate of change, and the initial value, or the y-intercept, should be emphasized.

It should be noted that students may be challenged by determining the y-intercept from a table when the related value for $x = 0$ is not provided. They may, at first, choose to graph the equation, by plotting points, to see the y-intercept or they may determine the slope from the table and use the slope to subtract from another x-value, to determine what y is when $x = 0$. Eventually, students should be able to determine the y-intercept algebraically by determining, or being given, the slope and one point. They should learn to use the slope-intercept form (Figure 7.10) to substitute in the known values then compute b.

MP1
Make Sense

Figure 7.10 Slope-Intercept Form

Leo asked Van how much he paid to belong to his local gym. When Van looked it up, he was able to tell Leo that he paid $110 for 5 months. But, he also found a receipt showing that he paid $70 for 4 months. Write an equation for Leo so that he can calculate the cost for any amount of months at Van's gym.

Points (3, 70) and (5, 110) $\qquad m = \frac{110 - 70}{5 - 3} = \frac{40}{2} = 20$

Using $y = mx + b$, substitute $m = 20$, $x = 3$ and $y = 70$ to solve for b.

The last standard within the Functions domain gives students experience with determining relationships between two quantities through qualitative reasoning (8.F.5). Students learn to provide a verbal description of what they see on a graph where there may be a label for the axes but no numerical scale. As well, they may be given a verbal description from which to draw a graph, again with labels for the axes but without using numbers. Such tasks reinforce for students the relative nature of slope as more or less steep on a graph while also emphasizing what that steepness means in a real-life context. Initial tasks may involve students choosing an appropriate graph for one related event, as shown in the example in Figure 7.11.

Figure 7.11 Choosing an Appropriate Graph

Saige is walking from her house to her grandmother's house. As she walks in the city, she has to walk at different rates depending upon traffic or if she is walking on a side street.

Relate each scenario to the appropriate graph of Saige's walk.

1. Saige initially walks at a steady pace until she gets to downtown traffic where she must stop every block for 5 blocks to wait for the pedestrian light to show she can cross.

2. Saige decides to take the side roads, but slows down when she sees several stores that she likes to peek in while she is walking.

3. While she is walking to her grandmother's house, Saige stops once to tie her shoes and a second time to get a drink of water, otherwise, she walks at a steady pace.

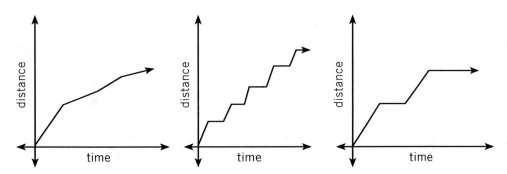

Students in one eighth grade classroom are studying qualitative graphs. Today, they are working in small groups to create their own graphs. Each group is given a card stating a scenario that they must graph about something changing over a 1 hour time period, without using numbers. Each card is held secret by the group so that the other groups do not know what they are graphing. One card says, "Graph the relationship between time and height of a cake as it rises in the oven" while another card states, "Graph the relationship between time and your energy level during soccer practice." Students work together to create graphs, without any numbers on the axes, on large sheets of coordinate grid paper.

When each group is ready, they hang their graphs around the room and hand their cards back to the teacher. She then mixes up the cards and displays them on the whiteboard in a list. Students move around the room observing the graphs, also holding clipboards with the student handout. Each student must write down what graph they think matches the given scenario. As the class comes together to discuss their findings, it is interesting to listen to the students describing why they think each graph matches the chosen scenario. Reyna responds to one student's comment about a graph with a steep slope, by saying, "That's too steep a slope to represent someone running. I don't think that's possible." Another student responds, "But doesn't it make a difference as to what the scale would be? Maybe it is about running."

As students master these initial tasks relating a verbal description and a graph, more complex ones may be provided. Students may be asked to draw graphs for a number of situations given sophisticated pictorial representations, such as comparing the time that it takes to fill a variety of differently shaped watering cans.

MP3
Construct

The focus should continue to be on the relationships between the two quantities as shown in the graph, rather than between two sets of numbers. Relating steepness, how rapidly or gradually the quantity changes and whether or not there is a part of the graph where there is no change, requires students to focus on the characteristics of the graph to see the change rather than rely on the numerical data (Van de Walle, Karp, Bay-Williams 2013).

Assessment Note

The Functions domain requires students to be able to recognize linear and non-linear functions and to fully interpret all components of a linear function. The "rule of four" should be fully utilized and students should be able to work flexibly between each of these representations. The template for the "rule of four", depicted earlier, should be made available whenever students are asked to provide multiple representations of a function or to compare two or more functions. Standardized testing will likely ask students comparison questions such as *Which graph shows the greater rate of change and why?* rather than "Is this a linear or non-linear function?" A sample question, provided on the Smarter Balanced website demonstrates the level of conceptual understanding required, "Fill in each x-value and y-value in the table below to create a relation that is not a function." (www.smarterbalanced.org 2013). Providing students with numerous experiences to relate slope and y-intercept as observed in an equation, table, graph or verbal description provides them with opportunities to understand the general concept of function as well as the specifics of a linear function.

MP2
Reason

MP8
Regularity

Voice from the Classroom

I've been teaching eighth-grade math for about 10 years and have always done some work with my students on graphing linear equations. I've mostly focused on teaching them how to find the slope from two points using the slope formula and to find the y-intercept from a graph. But, the Functions domain is asking me to teach these concepts much more deeply. I agree that students do need to really understand what a function is before they study lots of different kinds of functions in high school. It's actually been a lot of fun doing problems with my students that ask them to determine whether or not a situation is linear without telling them to put the change in y over the change in x or that the line doesn't always have to be straight. We can just pay attention to what the graph is telling us rather than always relying on the numbers. This has really helped my students who are not as strong with number relationships.

They like figuring out whether one line shows something increasing faster than another line by just looking at the steepness of the line.

I know that I must also teach them about slope and y-intercepts, but it seemed to go better this year when I related the slope to a visual model with the slope triangles. Their work in grade 7 with ratios and proportions also seemed to help them to conceptually understand slope this year. They seemed to better understand as to why they can write the slope as a fraction or just with a 1 in the denominator. Several students said, "Oh, yeah, I remember when I learned last year about unit rates. Is that the same thing?" I thought that I would also have to teach my students about the standard form and the point-slope form but these standards don't require those forms. The primary focus on the slope-intercept form allows me to have my students truly understand how the rate of change and the initial value are related and where they are found in a real-life context without having to think about relating to other forms.

I've also taught a full algebra course in eighth grade and I think that these students could really have benefitted from the standards in this domain as well. I've often thought that the work that students did in that course bounced them from one function to another without an introductory unit on functions in general. Linear, exponential, quadratic and absolute value functions all seemed to blend together and my students didn't always connect that they were all functions that related two quantities, just differently.

—8th-Grade Teacher

Let's Think and Discuss

1. How much of a change have you seen in what you now teach with the new standards regarding function from what you taught before?

2. Consider making a list of function topics from which your students could create graphs.

3. Have a discussion with your colleagues about your students' use of a graphing calculator as they work within this domain. What do you think that the role of the calculator should be?

Chapter

Geometry

 **Snapshot**

The seventh-grade team teachers are working together to plan their students' upcoming interdisciplinary project. This year, the teachers have decided to have all of the students choose a book to read in which they will learn some of the geometric concepts required in the new standards. The teachers have given the students a list of book choices, providing for a wide variety of interests and reading levels. Ten of the students on the team have chosen to read the book, *The Wright 3* (Balliett and Helquist 2006), which is part of a series of three mystery books integrating mathematics and art. The language arts teachers made a plan to meet in literature circles with the students who are reading this book, discussing the plots' twists and the relationships among the characters. The social studies teachers are enjoying working with the students to learn more about the history of Frank Lloyd Wright, the famous architect featured in the book and the Robie House, designed by Wright in 1908. The math teachers have given students a choice as to what aspect of the math they have found in the book they would like to learn more about.

- ✏ Mark and Nastia are making a scale drawing of one room in the Robie House using an architect software program they found online.

- ✏ Several students have developed an interest in the Fibonacci sequence, introduced in the book through observations of the patterns found in the stained glass windows.

- ✏ Saya and Grace made three-dimensional models of the pentominoes used in the book to do the puzzles and are making buildings out of them, observing the top, side and front views of the buildings.

- ✏ Gabe and Drew are interested in looking at an online tour of the Robie House so they can observe the various shapes found throughout the structure.

This interdisciplinary project gives students the opportunity to explore the standards in this domain through real-life contexts with a focus on exploration of the concepts and the formulas for area, surface area and volume of the two- and three-dimensional objects found in the novel. This teacher knows that the study of two-dimensional polygons and three-dimensional figures is a major focus of the standards in the Geometry domain. He also believes that working on interdisciplinary projects provides students with opportunities to delve into something that is of particular interest to them, while learning how to plan for open-ended tasks.

MP4
Model

Big Picture

Study of two-dimensional polygons and three-dimensional figures is a major focus of the standards of this domain. The clusters in this domain are highlighted in Figure 8.1 below:

Figure 8.1 Clusters in the Geometry Domain

Grade Level	Clusters
6	• Solve real-world and mathematical problems involving area, surface area, and volume.
7	• Draw, construct, and describe geometrical figures and describe the relationships between them. • Solve real-life and mathematical problems involving angle measure, area, surface area, and volume.
8	• Understand congruence and similarity using physical models, transparencies, or geometry software. • Understand and apply the Pythagorean Theorem. • Solve real-world and mathematical problems involving volume of cylinders, cones, and spheres.

Standards in the Geometry domain are critical areas in grades 7 and 8. Connections to other domains include students' work with multiplication in the elementary grades as it leads to their understanding of the formula for the area of a rectangle in grade 6. The study of scale factor in grade 7 is developed for future work in similarity and congruence in grade 8. The use of physical models as well as composition and decomposition of shapes are used to develop formulas for area, surface area, and volume, allowing for a clearer understanding of the formulas for these attributes of two- and three-dimensional figures.

MP5
Tools

In grade 7, students expand their understanding of area to circles, and surface area of three-dimensional figures. The study of circles also includes circumference. Further study, in grade 7, of three-dimensional figures involves examining cross-sections and relating them to two-dimensional figures. In preparation for study of congruence and similarity in grade 8, grade 7 students study the relationships between angles formed by non-parallel, intersecting lines.

A critical area in grade 8, the study of rigid motions and dilations, familiarly known as transformational geometry, leads students to the concepts of congruence and similarity. Development of the Pythagorean Theorem comes

MP8
Regularity

from exploration with a variety of models, forming a conceptual understanding of the theorem and its converse. Students also use the theorem to find distances between points in the coordinate plane. Students in grade 8 complete the middle grades study of volume by developing formulas for cones, cylinders, and spheres.

While prior geometry standards focused on primarily using prescribed formulas, the CCSS standards rely on student exploration to develop the formulas, with an effort toward allowing students to recall the formulas as a result of conceptual understanding rather than memorization. The strong focus on an intuitive understanding of congruence and similarity in grade 8 provides the opportunity for a seamless transition to high school geometry through the study of transformations. In this domain, transformational geometry is explored as a means for learning geometric topics and not just seen as useful for connecting art appreciation and mathematics (Wu 2012).

Middle grade students extend their understanding of area and volume from the elementary grades and students are introduced to surface area as part of a critical area in grade 7. Figure 8.2 shows how the standards outline what aspects of each of these topics are covered at each grade level (Figure 8.2).

Figure 8.2 Topics Covered at Each Grade Level

Grade	Area	Surface Area	Volume
Six	Triangles Special Quadrilaterals Polygons	Three-dimensional figures made from triangles and rectangles	Right rectangular prisms
Seven	Triangles Quadrilaterals Circles Other polygons	Cubes Right prisms	Cubes Right prisms
Eight			Cones Cylinders Spheres

Area

Relating previous experiences with composing and decomposing shapes, students in grade 6 learn to find the area of various polygons by identifying triangles and rectangles within the polygons (6.G.1).

For example, one-sixth grade student found the area of a parallelogram by decomposing the triangles on either end of the parallelogram and composing them to form a rectangle, then using the area of a rectangle formula, learned previously.

Figure 8.3 Finding the Area of a Parallelogram

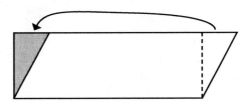

Another sixth grade student found the area of a trapezoid by a similar method, decomposing the trapezoid into triangles and rectangles, then adding the areas to find the total area.

Polygons drawn in a coordinate plane may be used to determine the area of figure (6.G.3). Students can plot the vertices of the polygon, seeing the length of each side of the polygon as the absolute value of the difference between the coordinate points, and the formula for the area of the polygon is applied.

Figure 8.4 Polygon Graph

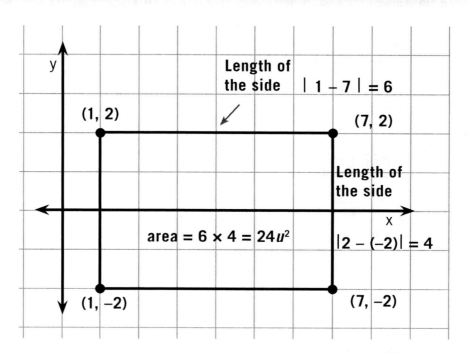

The final standard for finding the area of two-dimensional figures is found in grade 7, as students focus on the formulas for area and circumference of a circle (7.G.4). Explorations with circles may involve students with activities such as folding different-sized circles in half in various locations on the circle, leading to conclusions about the relationship between the radius and the diameter of the circle by measuring each to find that the radius is always half of the diameter. Students may then use string to investigate the length of the perimeter of the circle, also known as the circumference. The length of the yarn may then be measured (in inches or centimeters) and compared with the length of the diameter, using a consistent form of measurement.

> **MP6**
> Precision

Figure 8.5 Exploration with Circles

Diameter (cm)	9	12	14	15
Circumference (cm)	19.5	36.5	40.5	46

Students may also find an approximate area of a circle by drawing it on grid paper and counting the squares that are included in the circle. As with the circumference, students can experiment with the relationship between the area and the diameter of the circle. Although students are only able to use approximations, students should be initially exposed to these relationships by experimentally relating the diameter, the circumference, and the area of the circle. Then, as a rule is created, it should lead to a discussion about using an approximation for pi in the rule. The number to multiply the diameter by may be determined by using a ratio, dividing the circumference by the diameter. Students in the middle grades may not be required to use pi as an exact number and are often allowed to use 3.14 for pi. Interesting discussions may result about how pi is an infinite number, and that 3.14 is only an approximation for pi, used for convenience. If technological tools are used, students may be encouraged to use a closer approximation for pi rather than 3.14. Explorations may include having students see that they will find a more exact answer, using pi.

> **MP6**
> Precision

Another useful method for determining the area of a circle demonstrates that the circle may be cut into equal pieces and rearranged into a parallelogram. The base of the parallelogram is determined to be $\frac{1}{2}$ the circumference and the height is r as shown in Figure 8.6.

Figure 8.6 Circle Into a Parallelogram

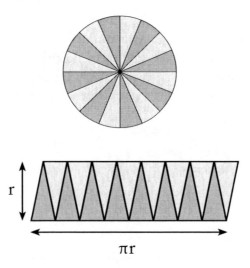

As the above figure shows, the circle has taken the form of a parallelogram. The formula for the area of a parallelogram may be used to determine the area of the circle, as $l \times w = \pi r \times r = \pi r^2$. This model provides a conceptual understanding for the formula and can help students to retrieve it, if necessary.

Surface Area

As grade 6 students consider three-dimensional figures, they develop a model for a right rectangular prism and explore the surface area and volume of this figure. A right rectangular prism is composed of rectangular sides and bases. A right prism distinguishes itself from an oblique prism by the fact that its bases are directly above one another in space. Grade 6 students learn the structure of three-dimensional figures by describing the shapes of the faces and determining the number of faces, edges, and vertices (6.G.4). As it may be challenging to visualize all faces of a three-dimensional figure by looking at a two-dimensional representation, students learn to draw nets of the figure. In this way, they learn that the figures' faces make up the outer surface and the surface area may be determined by finding the area of each of the faces.

Conceptual Challenge

While it may be tempting to teach students formulas for finding the surface area of various three-dimensional figures early on in the learning process, these formulas are easily misconstrued. If you first provide explorations with how the surface areas are determined, students may then construct their own formulas and then use it in context. Students challenged by making and using nets to find surface area formulas may be assisted by the following:

- ✏ Using enlarged graph paper to make the nets

- ✏ Using three-dimensional models to make the figures and then the nets

- ✏ Tracing each of the faces of a three-dimensional figure onto graph paper

- ✏ Using dynamic geometry software to visualize the nets of the figures

Seventh grade students extend their understanding of surface area, begun in grade 6 with right rectangular prisms, by exploring cubes, pyramids and other prisms, with triangle, quadrilateral, and other polygon faces. As with previous explorations, students may initially find drawing nets for the three-dimensional figure to be an effective way to find the surface area (7.G.6). As three-dimensional objects such as cylinders are introduced, students may be asked to apply their understanding of surface area to real-life contexts, such as making a label for a soup can or designing the packaging for a tennis ball can.

MP4
Model

Volume

A class of grade 6 students convinced their science teacher to set up a fish tank in their science class. The students learned that, in order to determine the correct number and size of the fish for the tank, they needed to, first, determine the volume of the fish tank their science teacher had in storage. Their mathematics teacher assisted them by setting up an exploration activity. First putting a layer of unit cubes (each 1 cubic inch) in the bottom, they determined the first layer of cubes was 10 x 8, therefore the base of the tank held 80 unit cubes. Realizing that each subsequent layer would hold the same number of cubes and that there were 9 layers, the students were able to determine there were 80 x 9 unit cubes for a total of 720 cubic inches. Conducting this task helped students visualize that the base of the prism is the same as finding the length times the width of the prism, equating l x w as equal to b, the area of the base, in volume formulas. In both cases, students needed to multiply the base units by the height to determine the final volume (6.G.2). Subsequent problems involved finding the volumes of right rectangular prisms where the length, width, and height were not whole numbers. As an example, one sixth grader wanted to find the volume of the box of his favorite cereal. He measured to find that the dimensions of the cereal box were 9.5 x 3.5 x 22.5 cm. Recognizing that he could figuratively break a cm cube in half, he was able to determine the base layer and then again, break a cm cube in half as he found the height. The student then measured the volume of the cereal, by using a cubic centimeter beaker, and was surprised to find how much of the box was not filled with cereal. Through these types of explorations, students learn that any length x width x height will result in the volume of the figure, whether or not the dimensions are whole numbers.

Seventh- and eighth-grade students extend their understanding of volume begun in grade 6, to cones, cylinders and spheres (8.G.9). Students may initially explore their understanding of volume of these three-dimensional figures using materials such as water or rice to fill the objects, measuring the volume of the material with a known model, such as a measuring cup. Once intuitions have been established, formulas may be derived, drawing upon previous knowledge, such as knowing the volume of a right rectangular prism is found by multiplying the area of the base times the height. Students learn to recognize that same concept is used to find the volume of a cylinder, finding the base to be the area of a circle and then multiplying that area times the height. The volume of a cone may be determined by using a physical model to fit three cones inside a cylinder, so the formula for the volume of a cone is $\frac{1}{3}$ x (volume of a cylinder). Spheres may be explored by using a clay model of a sphere pushed inside a cylinder to determine that the volume of the sphere is $\frac{2}{3}$ the volume of the cylinder. Students may only be able to see this as an approximation, however, Euclid determined that it is exactly a 2:3 ratio.

Figure 8.7 Volume of a Cylinder

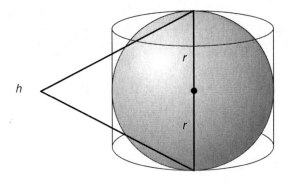

The formula for the volume of a cylinder is then used to determine the formula for the volume of a sphere as:

$$V_{cylinder} = \pi r^2 h \quad \text{replace } h \text{ with } 2r \quad \rightarrow \quad V_{sphere} = \frac{2}{3}\pi r^2 2r \quad \rightarrow \quad V_{sphere} = \frac{4}{3}\pi r^3$$

As is true with other standards, the geometry standards ask students to use their knowledge of area, surface area, and volume to solve real-life tasks. Examples may include:

- ✏ Members of the after-school garden club must fill their raised beds with organic soil. How much soil should they buy?

- ✏ Students in the seventh-grade art class need to paint their mural with a blue background. How much paint will they need?

- ✏ A group of eighth-grade students wants to fill cylindrical vases with colored sand to sell at a school fundraiser. How much sand should they buy?

Honoring Individual Differences

As the United States has now become the only country that does not solely use the metric system, students who come to our country to study mathematics are often challenged by our U.S. customary system of measurement. English language learners may have difficulty understanding the relationship between their familiar system of measurement, primarily using decimals, to unfamiliar terms and the use of fractions frequently used in our system. In-class activities for ELLs could focus first on estimating areas and volume and then providing conversion charts for students to reference. Practice with common conversions such as the width of one's thumb is about an inch will allow students to gain familiarity. Be sure to include tasks that involve metric units so that these students will also be able to work with a more familiar system of measurement.

Geometrical Figures

As one of the critical areas in grade 7, students solve problems in which they visualize various attributes of two- and three-dimensional geometric figures. The first standard within this cluster requires students to solve problems involving scale, relating proportional reasoning to geometry (7.G.1). A first step involves students understanding scale factor as the number of times you multiply one side length of an object to find the side length of a similar object. Concrete representations may include the use of pattern blocks or multi-link cubes to make an original shape, then make the next-sized shape, using the same blocks. Students recognize the subsequent iterations of the figure involve scaling up (or down) the side lengths depending on whether you want a larger or smaller figure. Students come to know the scaling down of the figure as multiplying by a fraction rather than dividing.

MP5
Tools

As the area of each of the figures is measured, students are often intrigued by how the areas of the figures do not follow the same scale factor as the side lengths. The use of concrete models, once again, helps students to visualize why the scale factor for area is the scale factor for side length squared. Practice with models such as those shown in the figure below allow students to explore with why it is that the scale factor for area is always the square of the scale factor for side length. Scale factor is further explored with fraction and decimal side lengths.

MP8
Structure

Figure 8.8 Finding Scale Factors

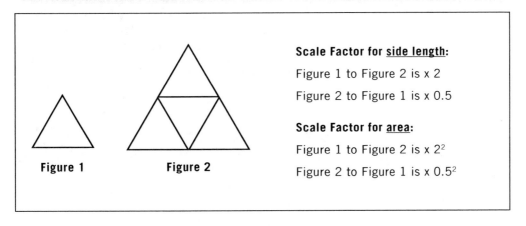

Scale Factor for <u>side length</u>:

Figure 1 to Figure 2 is x 2

Figure 2 to Figure 1 is x 0.5

Scale Factor for <u>area</u>:

Figure 1 to Figure 2 is x 2^2

Figure 2 to Figure 1 is x 0.5^2

Figure 1   Figure 2

Working with scale drawings used in practical situations such as road maps or models of buildings or structures studied in other coursework such as the Great Pyramids, provides students with opportunities to use scale factor for real-life purposes.

One such example involves students in the drama club. One of the students began researching designs for the sets for the school play and discovered just what he wanted for one particular scene in a book he found. In order to make a slightly larger model for the scene, he decided to make a copy of the one he found in the book and then scale it up to fit on a larger piece of paper. He soon realized this involved changing the scale drawing from an original scale factor to a new one to allow it a better fit on the paper.

Conceptual Challenge

Students are often challenged by scale factor problems in which they must change the units. For example, they may be given a scale drawing in which every 2.5 cm on the drawing equals 1.5 meters in real-life, necessitating a change in the units from cm to m, or, further still, the 2.5 cm on the drawing may be equal to 6 feet. Consideration should be given to having students initially change the cm to meters or vice-versa, prior to scaling up the figure to determine the new dimensions.

In this example, there are four stations set up in the seventh-grade classroom, each of which includes geometric tools for students to use (7.G.2).

- The tasks at station 1 ask students to draw sketches, using just pencils and rulers, of various triangles or quadrilaterals, such as an acute scalene triangle or an isosceles trapezoid.

- Station 2 tasks require students to use a protractor to draw triangles with acute, obtuse, and right angles, including accurate angle measures with their drawings. One such question asked students to draw a triangle with angle measures of 50 and 80 degrees.

MP5
Tools

- The computers at station 3 are set up for students to use geometry software to explore various side lengths in making triangles. Although not stated as such, students are given several problems in which the side lengths do not make a triangle. Students investigate and must explain why the side lengths do not form a triangle.

Through this standard, students learn a good deal more about various geometric figures by drawing the figures given certain conditions. Asking students to draw a figure that has two parallel sides and one right angle leads to a greater understanding of the attributes of a trapezoid than simply being shown a trapezoid and measuring it. This standard requires students to focus primarily on the construction of triangles. Activities such as those described by the station work give students the opportunity to explore when various measurements produce one triangle, no triangle or, given angle measures alone, that many triangles may be produced. Knowing there can be many triangles drawn with angle measures of 50° and 80° sets the stage for understanding the concepts of similarity and congruence in grade 8.

Students should be given many opportunities to explore with various side lengths to determine whether any three lengths can be used to form a triangle. While students may initially state that there are side lengths that do not form triangles, such as $1 - 1 - 2$, they may not yet be able to articulate why. Explorations with particular side lengths should focus on looking for patterns within the data (Figure 8.9). Many more data points can be collected by having students use dynamic geometry software to test various side lengths, as a focus on accuracy is important in leading to a conclusion. Although it is not stated as a requirement of this standard, students should be able to articulate an understanding of the conditions that make up the Triangle Inequality Theorem, which states that, in order for three side lengths to make a triangle, the sum of any two side lengths must be greater than the length of the third side. Students should also be given opportunities to recognize that the longest side of the triangle is always opposite the greatest angle in the triangle, and likewise, the shortest side is always opposite the smallest angle.

MP6
Precision

Figure 8.9 Sides of a Triangle

Side Length	Side Length	Side Length	Do they make a triangle?
1	1	2	No
2	4	6	No
4	5	9	No

The standards in this cluster conclude with explorations in finding two-dimensional figures by slicing through, or making cross-sections of, three-dimensional figures (7.G.3). Students learn to recognize that a slice made parallel to the base of the figure produces a different shape than a slice made perpendicular to the base. Slices made at an angle through the figure will produce different two-dimensional shapes altogether. Initial experiences with the content of this standard should be concrete. In order to concretely model finding the cross-sections, one teacher had seventh grade students make right rectangular prisms and pyramids from clay and use thin wire to cut through the figures. Students were then asked to describe what two-dimensional figure resulted when the figures were cut. Figure 8.10 describes the results.

Figure 8.10 The Results of Slicing Through Three-Dimensional Figures

Figure	Slice made parallel to the base	Slice made perpendicular to the base	Slice made diagonally through the base
Right rectangular prism	Same shape as the base	Same shape as the lateral (side) face	Parallelogram
Right rectangular pyramid	Square	Triangle	Trapezoid

The students liked working with the clay models as they could put them back together easily to make the next slice and many different sizes and bases of prisms and pyramids could be explored. Further explorations may involve students determining what cross-sections are created from various three-dimensional figures, asking questions such as:

1. What three-dimensional figure will create a slice in the shape of a hexagon?

2. What two-dimensional figure does making a diagonal slice from one corner of a right rectangular prism to the opposite corner create?

Congruence and Similarity

Although not explicitly described as such in the eighth-grade standards, the focus of congruence and similarity of two-dimensional figures is explored through the study of rigid motions, often referred to as transformational geometry. As described by Wu (2012), the Common Core Standards in this cluster use this study to provide a "seamless transition" from middle school to high school geometry (8.G.1). The basic rigid motions, also known as translations, rotations, and reflections, are the means by which grade 8 students conceptualize congruence and similarity among two-dimensional figures. Students begin their study by using physical models and tools such as mirrors, Miras, or transparent paper to visually represent the motion of a two-dimensional figure. The pre-image, is rotated, reflected or translated, thereby creating an image of the figure. When both the pre-image and the image are congruent, students come to know this transformation as an isometry or a rigid transformation. As students first study each transformation independently, they learn the physicality and attributes of each transformation as in Figure 8.11.

Figure 8.11 Transformations

Transformation	Pre-Image Action	Result
Translation	Slide along a vector line	Each point on the pre-image moves in the same direction and the same distance
Rotation	Turn around a center of rotation	Distance from the center to any point on the image remains the same
Reflection	Flip over a line of reflection	Distance from the line of reflection to any point on the pre-image or the image is the same

Through these experiences, students learn there are three basic properties of rigid motions:

- ▷ when they are transformed, lines, rays and segments remain as such.

- ▷ when distance is preserved, as when a segment is transformed, the length of the segment remains the same.

✏️ when degrees are preserved, as when an angle is transformed, the degree of the angle remains the same.

As these properties of rigid motion are understood, so, too, is the concept of congruence, as students visualize the image of the figure as congruent to the pre-image (8.G.2). Activities such as those in Figure 8.12 require students to demonstrate congruence of two figures by describing the transformations necessary to map one of the shapes onto the other.

Figure 8.12 Sample Congruence and Transformation Activities

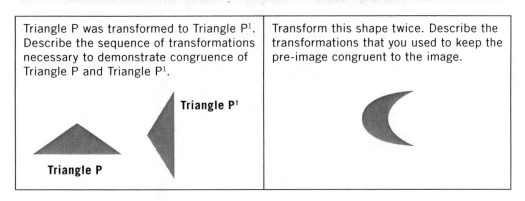

| Triangle P was transformed to Triangle P¹. Describe the sequence of transformations necessary to demonstrate congruence of Triangle P and Triangle P¹. | Transform this shape twice. Describe the transformations that you used to keep the pre-image congruent to the image. |

Creating tessellations is an engaging interdisciplinary activity, with a focus on transformations within the visual arts. Carrying out a series of transformations with the same shape, infinitely, to cover a space without any gaps or overlaps, creates a tessellation. Students in an eighth grade art class were instructed to make a tessellation by choosing either one of the regular or distorted polygons that tessellates. A number of students chose to make their tessellations using dynamic geometry software or applets that create tessellations. Upon completion, students were asked to describe what polygons they used and why, identify the transformations they performed, and to show how the shapes remained congruent. An example of a regular tessellation is shown in Figure 8.13.

Figure 8.13 Sample Tessellation

Although not a rigid motion, dilations of a pre-image are considered another aspect of transformational geometry, as the action transforms the pre-image, by scaling it up or down, to create a similar image. The similar image has congruent angles and sides that are proportional based on the scale factor of the dilation. Frieze patterns, horizontal or vertical repetitions of the same shape, often use dilations in the pattern (8.G.4).

The next step in students' study of congruence and similarity involves performing transformations on the coordinate plane (8.G.3). Students learn to carry out transformations and, subsequently, identify the coordinates of the image as in the next figure.

Translation: The pre-image is moved so that every point moves in the same direction for the same distance.

Described as: Translate triangle BCD to the right 4 units and up 2 units.

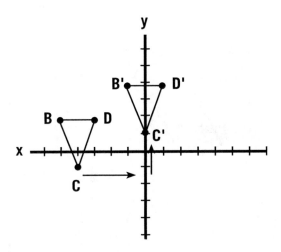

Reflection: Every point of the pre-image is flipped across a line of reflection (either the *x*- or the *y*-axis) where every point of the pre-image and the image is equidistant from the line of reflection.

Described as: Reflect triangle BCD over the *x*-axis.

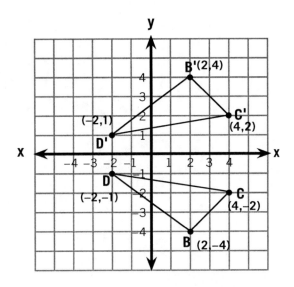

Dilation: The pre-image is dilated from a center by mutiplying by a scale factor.

Described as: Dilate triangle ABC from center p with a scale factor of 2.

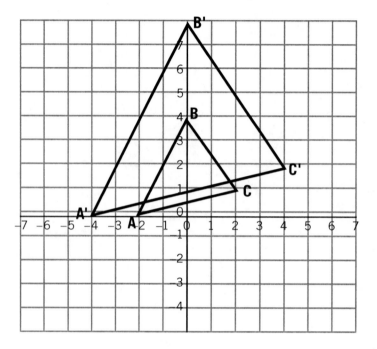

Rotation: The pre-image is rotated around a center of rotation up to 360 degrees.

Described as: Rotate rectangle ABCD 180 degrees clockwise about the origin.

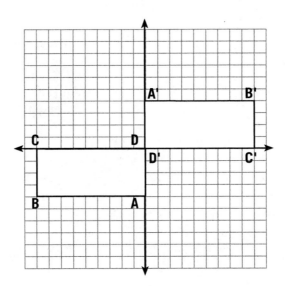

As an extension of this topic, although not articulated in the standards, students may learn the rules for transformations as described in Figure 8.14.

Figure 8.14 Transformation Rules

Transformation	Rules
Translation	$T_{ab}(x, y) = (x + a, y + b)$
Reflection	$r_{x\text{-axis}}(x, y) = (x, -y)$ $r_{y\text{-axis}}(x, y) = (-x, y)$
Rotation	$R_{90°}(x, y) = (-y, x)$ $R_{180°}(x, y) = (-x, -y)$ $R_{270°}(x, y) = (y, -x)$
Dilation	$D_k(x, y) = (kx, ky)$

Related tasks focusing on congruence and similarity may include:

- showing both the pre-image and the image, whereby students must describe the transformation(s) carried out to create the image.

- showing two images on a coordinate plane and asking if one figure is similar to the other.

- given vertices and a description of the transformation, students provide the new vertices.

- asking students to determine which of several possibilities create a similar figure, such as: $(3x, 2y)$, $(x + 4, y - 7)$, $(4x, y + 5)$.

The last standard in this cluster continues the focus on congruence and similarity, at this point, as related to angles made by parallel lines and angles within triangles (8.G.5). As two (or more) parallel lines intersect a transversal, corresponding, alternative interior, and alternate exterior angles are congruent. The relationship between these angles leads to informal proofs of the sum of the measures of the angles of a triangle and of triangle congruence and similarity. One group of students is asked to informally prove that the measures of a triangle are equal to 180°. These students know that angles 1, 2 and 3 equal 180° because they are supplementary, as learned in grade 7 (7.G.5). These students can also use their knowledge of corresponding angles to show that angles 1 and 5 are congruent, and that angles 2 and 4 are congruent because they are alternative interior angles. Substituting angles 3, 4, and 5 with angles 1, 2, and 3, the students are able to show that the angle measures of a triangle are 180° (Kansas Association of Teachers of Mathematics 2012). Other informal proofs may involve proving the measure of an exterior angle of a triangle as congruent to the two interior angles opposite to the exterior angle and that the sum of the exterior angles of a triangle is 360° or show three copies of a triangle lined up with each different angle along a straight line to show that the sum of the angles is 180°.

Triangle similarity is explored with the angle-angle criterion by recognition that, if two angles of one triangle are congruent to the corresponding angles of another triangle, students know the following:

☞ The third angle is congruent in each of the two triangles because the sum of the angles of a triangle is equal to 180°.

☞ The two triangles are similar.

Students may further explore the similarity of the two triangles by determining that the sides of the triangle are in proportion. Further study of triangle congruence and similarity is explored in high school.

The Pythagorean Theorem

Asked to recall their experiences with middle school geometry, many adults will provide some recollection of a formula resembling $a^2 + b^2 = c^2$. Further probing often reveals that the formula has something to do with triangles. Less often, the name of the theorem is cited, often pronounced incorrectly, and very rarely, an explanation is provided as to what the formula means or that the mathematician and philosopher, Pythagoras, developed the formula (8.G.6). Grade 8 students draw upon prior knowledge of the properties of triangles and the area of squares to derive the Pythagorean Theorem.

As an example, one eighth grade class is working in groups, gathering data about various right triangles as shown below in Figure 8.15, with several such triangles provided on another sheet of paper.

After the data has been collected on the triangles provided, students create their own right triangles to test their theories. Some of the students are using sets of four geoboards grouped together and rubber bands to find the lengths and areas while others are comfortable using grid paper to draw their triangles and squares, recognizing that accuracy in their drawing is important in this activity. Although the students have prior experience with finding the area of a square, finding the area of the squares that are drawn from the hypotenuse, as they are on the diagonal, challenges some.

MP6
Precision

Figure 8.15 Template for Data

Triangle	Length of Leg 1	Length of Leg 2	Area of square on Leg 1	Area of square on Leg 2	Area of square on Hypotenuse

Once the data is collected, the groups are asked to reflect on what they found and to prepare conclusions to share with the rest of the class. One student, referencing her data from her table, articulates, "Well, I can see that the area of the first square and the second square, when you add them together, equals the area of the third square." Another student chimes in, "I think that the third square always has to be the square that is made from the hypotenuse." Once the students in the class were able to accurately describe the relationship as the first two students did, the teacher put a picture of a triangle on the board, with given side lengths, asking the students to collect the same data without creating the triangle on the geoboard or drawing it on

MP3
Construct

grid paper. As the teacher recognizes that some students are finding the area of the squares by calculating 4 x 4 rather than 4^2 she asks, "If you know the length of the side of the triangle, what is the most efficient way to find the area of the square drawn from that side?" The teacher wants the students to begin thinking of 4 x 4 as 4^2 as she knows this is the notation used in the theorem. As the students move from stating their conclusions about the relationship in words to writing it as an equation, they found they had a solid understanding of what the Pythagorean Theorem meant, rather than just being asked to recite $a^2 + b^2 = c^2$ without a conceptual understanding of what the variables represent. The text in the figure below shows the students' thinking as they moved through this process.

As identified by Huang (2005), this discovery approach has proven to be a highly effective way for students to visualize the meaning behind the Pythagorean Theorem. There are myriad of other approaches for students to make meaning for this theorem, including, but not limited to the ideas that follow.

✏️ Have students conduct an investigation by which they cut out the squares drawn from the two legs and fit them into the square drawn from the hypotenuse, proving that the areas are the same.

Figure 8.16 Pythagorean Theorem Diagram

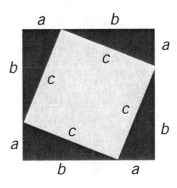

✏ Use technology-based applets to carry out similar experiments, thereby removing the difficulties some students may have with the cutting and fitting of the squares. Using applets also allows students to manipulate many examples of right triangles without having to make all of them by hand.

✏ For those students who have greater access to the algebra skills necessary to use this proof, it is theorized that the process of drawing right triangles around a square can be effective in visualizing the theorem. (http://www.mathsisfun.com/geometry/pythagorean-theorem-proof.html)

Figure 8.17 Development of the Pythagorean Theorem

I know that:

The area of the square drawn from one leg of the triangle + the area of the square drawn from the other leg of the triangle = the area of the square drawn from the hypotenuse of the triangle.

Area from leg 1 + Area from leg 2 = Area from hypotenuse

Area from a + Area from b = Area from c

$$a^2 \;+\; b^2 \;=\; c^2$$

✏ Students may also be intrigued by experimenting with drawing other shapes off of the sides of the triangles, such as semi-circles or triangles and find that the theorem still holds true, as it is the squaring that is important not necessarily the need for a square (Flores 2002).

As the use of the Pythagorean Theorem quite often necessitates finding the square root of a number to complete the solution, teachers should pay close attention to the curriculum sequence in which the theorem is introduced, before, after, or as a part of a unit on square numbers and square roots.

$$3^2 + 6^2 = c^2$$

$$45 = c^2$$

$$c = \pm \sqrt{45}$$

Students must recognize that the value of c is either positive or negative $\sqrt{45}$, however only positive values of c are relevant in this problem as we are finding length.

As well, leaving the answer as $\sqrt{45}$ or finding an approximate answer as between 6 and 7 is dependent upon the required answer for the situation.

As the focus of the standards is to engage students in applying the Pythagorean Theorem to determine various side lengths of a right triangle, every effort should be made to give students relevant, engaging problems to solve (8.G.7). Through exploration, students learn to recognize using the Pythagorean Theorem is an efficient formula for solving problems.

After a short practice session with finding various side lengths of right triangles, one eighth grade teacher challenged her students to solve the following problem:

> Malik is standing on a deck 2.5 m above the water. He is pulling in a raft that is attached to the end of a 7.2 m rope. If he pulls in 2.1 m of rope, how far did he move the raft?

The students worked in groups, many first creating a sketch. Some of the students did not immediately recognize that this was a multi-step problem, necessitating the use of the Pythagorean Theorem twice in order to reach a final solution. The teacher recognized it was important to allow the students to make the drawings themselves, as she found it was their own drawings that led them to better understand the problem.

MP4
Model

Figure 8.18 Student Drawing

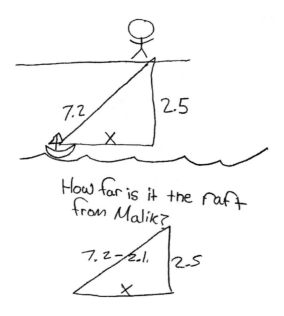

Varying the types of problems students solve will expose students to situations in which they learn about Pythagorean Triples, in which there are three integers such as 3, 4, 5 that make up the lengths of the sides of the triangles. Students learn to recognize the multiples of these numbers are considered triples as well. It is also important for students to try using the Pythagorean Theorem with non-right triangles, informally proving that the theorem only works with a special set of triangles.

Although grade 8 students do not formally learn the distance formula, using the Pythagorean Theorem to find the distance between two points on a coordinate graph sets the stage for constructing this formula in high school (8.G.8).

Again, the focus on the use of the theorem in a context is a key element in the standards, as is evident in the following problem, posed to some eighth graders:

Graph points A (3, 7) and B (–2, 5) on a coordinate graph. Write a real-life scenario as to why you would want to know the distance between these two points and then find the distance.

The students wrote about such situations as finding how far their house was from two other points or needing to know the distance so they could design an aspect of a videogame they were programming. This application of the Pythagorean Theorem leads students to conceptualize its use in a variety of contexts, including the recognition that the diagonal segment drawn between the two points may be seen as the hypotenuse of a right triangle. Students who are interested in history may also be encouraged to learn more about how Pythagoras discovered the theorem or to research which U.S. president discovered a new proof for the theorem.

Assessment Note

One aspect of this domain centers around the use of formulas to carry out real-life tasks. Open-ended tasks allow for students to demonstrate knowledge of the use of formulas rather than just memorizing the formula and applying it to isolated questions. As an example, the teachers and students in one middle school found themselves in the midst of a real-life situation when presented with the task of determining the size of a display that would hold at least 1.5 million pennies. The mathematics teachers in the school presented the task to all of their students, leaving the task open-ended by allowing students to determine the necessary formulas and steps to determine an appropriate size for the display.

Rubrics for open-ended tasks such as this one may include:

Figure 8.19 Sample Rubric

Part I: Understanding the task

2 Complete understanding of the task
1 One or more aspects of the task misunderstood or misinterpreted
0 Complete misunderstanding of the task

Part II: Explaining your solution strategy

2 Solution strategy is clearly explained
1 Partially correct solution strategy
0 No attempt, or totally inappropriate solution strategy

Part III: Justifying the answer

2 Correct answer and label and answer is justified
1 Computational errors or partial correct answer for the task and partially justified
0 No answer, or wrong answer or answer is not justified

Standardized test questions are likely to focus on conceptual understanding of developed formulas and proper use of the formulas in real-life tasks. Performance tasks will likely incorporate several concepts, asking questions such as:

- Design a cylindrical container that will hold at least three regulation tennis balls with a surface area less than 100 cm^2.

- How does the surface area of a right rectangular prism relate to its volume?

Voice from the Classroom

I used to think that teaching my students to understand how best to use the formulas for area, surface area, and volume was enough. Although we discussed, as a math department, that we wanted our students to memorize the formulas, we soon realized that the materials that accompanied state tests included a reference sheet that provided my students with all of the formulas they would need to answer the test questions. So much for having my students memorize them as they didn't see the need to since a reference sheet was provided. The problem was that once my students used the formulas for the unit tests and the state tests at the end of the year, they didn't seem to have the least idea about how to recall even the simplest of formulas the following year. Many of our eighth graders couldn't even remember the formula for the area of a triangle. Not knowing even the basic geometry formulas seemed to impede my students when they were asked to use them in more complex situations. They weren't even sure which formulas to use. The new geometry standards in the middle grades are much more focused on students' conceptual understanding of the formulas, rather than just memorization. I particularly like how students also learn to relate the formulas. I was so surprised when I, myself, learned to relate the formulas for the circumference and the area of a circle. I'm beginning to see that my students are now better able to reconstruct a formula if they don't remember it, rather than always feeling as though they have to go look it up, or more often they would just ask me. They also seem to be able to figure out what formulas to use when they are engaged in tasks that ask them to relate these concepts to real-life situations. My students may not all become architects and engineers, but I think that they will have a better understanding of how to use formulas in their daily lives.

—8th-Grade Teacher

Let's Think and Discuss

1. What real-life tasks can you think of in which you use geometric formulas in your daily life?

2. How could you turn them into open-ended tasks for your students?

3. How do you see these standards in this domain as different than the previous geometry standards?

Chapter

Statistics and Probability

 **Snapshot**

Students in Mr. Robbins' and Ms. Samos' sixth grade math class are learning to create boxplots to summarize a set of data. These students have struggled with conceptualizing mathematics in the earlier grades, so they have been placed in this small group class, totaling eleven students. Mr. Robbins has been teaching this class for several years now and is pleased to be able to share the responsibilities with his co-teacher, who specializes in teaching special education students. Together, they have planned a lesson to engage their students in a task to demonstrate how boxplots are constructed. The students in this class, according to their individualized education plans, respond well when they are kept active, so the teachers knew the best way to engage their students in the task would be to rely upon a kinesthetic model.

Each student is given a 9" x 12" piece of paper and a marker. Recalling the data from a previous lesson on data collection, the students are instructed to write the number of small cherry tomatoes, picked from the school garden, they were able to hold in one hand. As they write their numbers on the large sheet of paper, they are overheard disagreeing about how many each was able to hold.

Mr. Robbins was pleased that his co-teacher had asked one of the students to keep an accurate record, thus ending the disagreement. He appreciates that his co-teacher empowers their students to be responsible for their work and to keep organized notes in their binders. The student who held the accurate data felt accomplished as she contributed positively to the lesson. After each student finished writing their number, the co-teacher Ms. Samos, tells the students that they are going to learn a new way to look at the data. In their prior lesson, they had just made a list of the data and it was not in any particular order. Today, she tells them that this way of viewing the data would go beyond list making, and would help them learn more about their data than they could with a random list. She asks the students to come to the front of the room, the student with the least number stands on the left side of the room and the student with the greatest number on the right side. The remainder of the students realize they must fall in line between the least and the greatest numbers, as they had done before when they made number lines. Their teachers are able to view the students holding their cards.

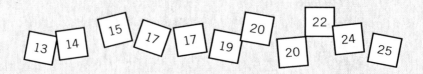

Mr. Robbins asks the student who is holding the card with the median of the data set to step forward. As students have previously studied what a median is, Sampson, holding number 19, knows he has the median number and moves forward. He is now given special status and is handed a star with the word *median* written on it to add to his paper.

Ms. Samos now turns her attention to the five students to the left of Sampson and Mr. Robbins stands in front of the five students to the right. At the same time, each teacher asks their group to step out if they hold the number that is the median of these new groups. Sylvia, who holds the number 15, is pleased she is deemed special and is given a star labeled quartile 1, while Tian, holding number 22, is given a star labeled quartile 3. Ms. Samos, cognizant that the remaining students in each group need to be recognized, asks for their assistance in making a box around the lowest number in the range, 13, to the number before the median and, again, around the number after the median to the highest number in the range, 25. The students use brightly colored duct tape, placed on the floor to make a box around the appropriate numbers, then all students step into place, as if choreographed to be on stage.

Although they do not yet recognize the entire picture of what they have created, the students are pleased to each be part of the activity. Mr. Robbins takes a picture of the students and then attaches his camera to his overhead projector. He shows the students the results of their hard work and they are initially abuzz with conversation about how they look in the picture. Mr. Robbins then asks his group to join him at one table and Ms. Samos instructs her students to join her at another table on the other side of the room. The teachers find that working in smaller groups allows the students to better concentrate on their work. The students are instructed in their small groups on how to transfer their human representation of a boxplot to paper. As the class nears an end, students are provided with another set of data, collected by another class of students, and are asked to make a boxplot of this new data for homework. They are told they will be using the second boxplot to compare to their data the next day and it will be interesting to see which class, as a group, holds more cherry tomatoes. The students know they will need to complete their homework or they will not be able to compare the groups. This "hook", set up by the teachers, encourages these students to see their homework as purposeful and necessary to the next day's lesson.

The Statistics and Probability domain calls upon grade 6 teachers to teach standards previously taught, using prior state standards, in the higher grades. This task engages lower level learners in these new, rigorous sixth-grade standards while drawing upon their teachers' recognition that they have particular academic needs, making the lesson as actively engaging and physical as possible. The co-teachers will spend the year focusing on how they can best deliver the content of these new standards in the context of active engagement. Regular classroom teachers would argue that this active, engaging task would be appropriate for their students as well.

Big Picture

While the formal study of Statistics and Probability does not begin until grade 6, the concepts necessary to understand the standards in this domain begin in the elementary grades. Through the grades K-5 Measurement and Data domain, students learn to organize, represent, and interpret data categorically. They primarily use statistical tools such as picture graphs and bar graphs with single-scales as well as use line plots to solve problems, with a focus in grades 4 and 5 on measurement data sets involving fractions.

The representation and interpretation of data has been a supporting rather than critical area in the elementary grades. However, in the middle grades, students begin to learn what it means to think statistically. A summary of the statistics and probability clusters are provided in Figure 9.1.

Figure 9.1 Summary Clusters

Level	Summary Clusters
Grade 6	• Develop understanding of statistical variability • Summarize and describe distributions
Grade 7	• Use random sampling to draw inferences about a population • Draw informal comparative inferences about two sample populations • Investigate chance processes and develop, use, and evaluate probability models
Grade 8	• Investigate patterns of association in bivariate data

A critical area in grade 6, students begin to view statistical thinking as a process by which they can investigate a relevant question. According to the Statistics and Probability Progression Document, this four-step process involves:

1. Formulating questions to be answered by using collected data

2. Designing and using a plan to collect the data

3. Analyzing the data using appropriate methods

4. Interpreting the results and learning to make conclusions relevant to the questions that were asked (McCallum 2011).

Tasks in grade 6 begin with identifying symmetry in the data as viewed primarily on histograms and line plots. Also looking for clusters of data and peaks as well as gaps in the data, they learn to see the data with a holistic view rather than a focus on numerical data to determine how many more there may be of one aspect of categorical data than another, such as "Do more of us like cats or dogs?" While grade 6 students are primarily learning informally what it means to find the center of the data, they also learn that there can be more than one center depending on how it is measured, using either the median or the mean. They explore what is termed as a "measure of variability" through study of interquartile range and mean absolute deviation. These are new concepts to teach for most grade 6 teachers as well as for students to learn and will require a good deal of practice to obtain a conceptual understanding.

MP3
Construct

A critical area in grade 7 as well, students learn more specifically about making inferences about data sets based on collecting sample data. Students in this grade learn what makes for an appropriate random sample size based on what they want to find out about the population. Tasks also involve making comparisons about two populations of data and choosing which measure of center or variability most appropriately represents their data. Students may engage in discussions to simulate how politicians or advertising agencies make compelling arguments to persuade their audience by using one particular measure of center or variability over another. Students in this grade begin the study of probability by investigating chance and learn to use probability models. Although not explicitly connected to the statistics standards, students should see the relationship between what they learn about asking statistical questions and drawing statistical conclusions to doing the same with probability models. Students create these models to simulate all possible outcomes for a situation, such as how many possible combinations there are when a number cube is thrown and a coin is tossed.

The statistics standards in grade 8 are closely tied with the work that they do with functions and the study of linear equations. As students in this grade study what is termed bivariate data, that which compares two variables, they primarily learn to graph this data on a scatterplot and analyze the data by describing the shape as a group of points on the scatterplot. As well, students learn to connect their understanding of linear regression to statistical study. They conclude their work with bivariate data by creating and analyzing two-way tables in which they look for associations within categorical data.

MP4
Model

There are numerous opportunities for students in the middle grades to find practical uses for the standards in this domain. Teachers may choose to connect with teachers of other subjects in these grades to create interdisciplinary tasks involving data collected in a science class or in social studies. Learning to see how analysis of data assists them to learn more about their world is a strong focus in these grades. Providing a real-world context is an important aspect of learning these standards, giving students the opportunity to feel as though they are doing statistics as a model for using mathematics with purpose

(Selmer, Bolyard, and Rye 2011). By relying on a deeper study of data with one variable, a student's work with these standards provide a smoother transition from elementary grades to the middle grades. As middle grade students also begin their study of functions, high schoolers further associate their understandings of bivariate data to functions, which allow them to move beyond thinking of bivariate data as always having a linear relationship.

Statistics

Analyzing Data

Statistical thinking begins with knowing the right questions to ask. Grade 6 students learn the importance of asking good questions with the goal of understanding how a population varies (6.SP.1). As students come to know what makes for a good statistical question, they learn to anticipate that the data they collect to answer the question will hold variability. For example, asking a friend if he attends any extracurricular activities after school is not a statistical question because there is no possibility for change in the answer. In contrast, asking a group of friends how much time they each spend doing an extracurricular activity after school on various days of the week allows for a variety of numerical responses. Grade 6 students are transitioning from collecting data, in earlier grades, that is primarily categorical, to that which is numerical. Survey questions should anticipate numerical responses, such as 1, 2 or 3 hours, restricted at first to a whole number of hours, of extracurricular activity after school. As students interpret their results, they learn to determine whether the variability in the data is large or small and if the variability is appropriate. Understanding variability means for students to know that it is common to have a wide range in the cost of baseball bats yet not in students' ages in their grade.

Students learn to interpret the distribution of data by primarily describing its center and spread (6.SP.2). They interpret clusters found in the graphical representations of the data, the peaks and the gaps, while looking for common shapes and patterns in the displays. In contrast with previous standards, in which students primarily looked for one numerical answer, resulting in conclusions such as "Most kids like oranges," they now learn to interpret the data by looking at a picture of the data as a whole. Descriptions of the shape of the data may come from asking questions such as:

- Is the data spread out or is it mostly clumped together around a few values?

- Are there any holes in the data where there is no data for some values?

- What does the overall shape of the data look like? Does the data seem symmetrical or skewed to one side?

As described by Kazak and Confrey (2006), students should learn to use language that makes sense to them regarding the qualitative nature of the data. Their descriptions may be informal, using terms such as "all jammed together," "bunched up," or "spaced out." In turn, students begin to see patterns in the data as they compare the qualitative (the overall view of the data) and the quantitative ("more than" or "less than") views.

MP7
Structure

A group of sixth grade students is given a line plot representing data collected from their classmates about how many hours they exercise in a week (Figure 9.2). They are asked to describe what they notice. One student says, "I see that a lot of the kids exercise between 2 and 3 hours a week" while another comments, "There is a hole between 7 and 9 hours a week and only one person exercises 10 hours a week." Another student described the data as skewed to the left, because most of the data was on the left side of the plot. This common misconception was corrected by another student by stating that skewing should be described as where the tail of the graph is. If the tail comes from the right then the graph is skewed to the right and vice-versa. These students went on to make conjectures about why there was one person who exercised much more than the others and why most of the students' hours of exercise centered around a clump of data. They were encouraged to discuss the shape of the data as a whole and then interpret its shape, rather than to discuss individual data points.

Figure 9.2 Dot Plot

Exercise per week

Number of Hours

As grade 6 students learn to interpret the data numerically, they understand one interpretation of center as the median, found by counting to the middle number in an ordered set of data points. Students learn that, when the set of numbers is odd, the median is the middle number and when it is even, it is the average of the two middle numbers.

Conceptual Challenge

Two common misconceptions students make about finding the median are:

➫ Students may not understand that the data needs to be ordered. Students often better understand why it needs to be in order if the data is placed on a number line and then the middle number is found.

☞ If the data is presented in a frequency table, rather than in an individual list of data points, students often misinterpret what the middle number is. For example, the data in the table below summarizes the number of tigers found in zoos around the country. Students may incorrectly state that the median is 4.5, as it is the middle number of the number of tigers recorded. However, the actual median is found by interpreting the data in the table as 17=0's, 12=1's, 14=2's, etc., and counting to find the middle number of the list as the median. While it may be impractical to record all of these numbers, students should do this at least once to fully comprehend the reason why they cannot just use the middle of the number of tigers as the median.

Number of tigers	0	1	2	3	4	5	6	7	8	9
Number of zoos	17	12	14	23	6	34	20	14	3	10

A second interpretation of center is the mean. Students in grade 6 have learned previously to consider what would happen if all of the data points were "evened out" or "leveled off" but have not yet determined the leveled off amount. Students should practice finding the mean as center by physically moving data points.

One class of students each made towers with multi-link cubes of the number of apples they had eaten the week before. They had to figure out what to do when a student did not have an apple that week, deciding to represent this data as a sticky note rather than a tower. Asked to find the mean number of apples eaten, they put all of their towers on the table in the front of the room and moved the cubes from one tower to the next until the towers were even. They had to keep in mind that they needed to use the sticky notes, representing zero apples, as a part of their data as well. Each of the 22 towers had 3 cubes representing 3 apples. Students should transition from finding mean with a physical model to a drawing for finding the mean, and eventually recognizing that the number of original sets divides the total number of objects. When there are remainders in the data, students must learn to interpret these parts of another object as often unrealistic, as in 1.5 dogs per family, however this interpretation of the mean is statistically accurate and should not be rounded off for ease of use.

MP6
Precision

Students in grade 6 recognize that a measure of center, as median or mean, represents the data set with one number. Measures of variation are ways to measure how spread out the data is and describe how the data points vary in a set (6.SP.3). There are a number of measures of variation, two of which students study in the middle grades: the range and the mean absolute deviation. The range of the data is the simplest to compute, finding the difference between the greatest and the least values. Students learn that the range does not take into account the way in which the data are distributed, yet is extremely sensitive to outliers as it only uses the minimum and the maximum data points. Two sets of data may have the same median and mean, yet have a vastly different range.

Figure 9.3 Sets of Data

Tree	Height (feet)
Japanese Maple	7.5
Maple	8
Crabapple	8
Dogwood	9.5
Cypress	12

Tree	Height (feet)
Japanese Maple	3
Cypress	7
Maple	8
Redwood	12
Dogwood	15

Although not explicitly described in the CCSSM, the Statistics and Probability Progression Document clearly articulates the mean absolute deviation (MAD) as a component of measures of variation for grade 6 students (McCallum 2011). Intended to lead students to a deeper understanding of variability, it is arguably a fairly complex concept for this grade level. Many grade 6 teachers will need to spend time working on understanding this concept themselves prior to teaching it to their students. This measure of variation describes how far the data values deviate from the mean. Exploring this concept in grade 6 leads to study of standard deviation, a more robust version of MAD, in high school. Calculation of the MAD is carried out by:

Step 1: Finding how far each value is above or below the mean.

Step 2: Finding the absolute value of these differences. (The reason for finding the absolute value is that the actual differences added together would result in a sum total of zero. Exploring why this is true is an interesting activity for students.)

Step 3: Finding the mean of the numbers found in Step 2.

An exploration of this concept should include interpreting various MAD results to recognize how a small number demonstrates a narrow variability in the data while a greater number shows a wider variability. As an example, students recorded how many jumping jacks they could do in a minute in physical education class and recorded it in a table. (While not common to find the MAD with only four data points, it is often unwieldy for students to learn this concept with large data sets, so initial explorations may work best if small data sets are used.) They calculated the mean and recorded it as 16. The students found the total of the absolute deviations from the mean as 12 then divided it by the number of values (4) to find the MAD of the data set as 3. It was easier for students to interpret the MAD when they compared it to another data set.

MP3
Arguments

Figure 9.4 Interpreting MAD When Compared to Other Data

Name	Number of jumping jacks	Deviation from the mean	Absolute deviation from the mean
Gabe	14	−2	2
Pat	12	−4	4
Ben	20	4	4
Fran	18	2	2

MAD = 3

Name	Number of jumping jacks	Deviation from the mean	Absolute deviation from the mean
Mark	14	−2	2
Ric	17	1	1
Tan	16	0	0
Kit	17	1	1

MAD = 1

The mean of this data set is also 16, yet the MAD is 1. Although the mean of the two data sets is the same, students can now compare the two measures of MAD and can interpret the second set of data as having less variability.

Honoring Individual Differences

English language learners are often quite challenged by the vocabulary embedded into the mathematics they are learning. The standards in this domain are no exception when it comes to needing to understand the meaning behind terms such as measures of variability and Mean Absolute Deviation (MAD). One strategy that has proven useful to English language learners involves the use of sentence frames such as "The mean in this problem is _____ because _____." Participating in classroom discussions also gives English language learners the opportunity to use the vocabulary while talking about the mathematics integral to the lesson (Bresser, Melanese, and Sphar 2008).

While students in grade 6 have had previous experience with creating and analyzing plots on number lines by creating dot plots and histograms, using a number line diagram to create a box plot is a very new concept (6.SP.4). Box plots are utilized as pictorial representations of a five number summary of the data consisting of the minimum, quartiles (there are 3 marked quartiles) and the maximum. The quartiles divide the data into four quadrants by dividing each half of the data in half again.

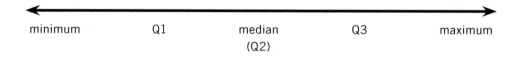

minimum   Q1   median   Q3   maximum
                              (Q2)

Students see yet another context for the range of the data and also now consider the interquartile range of the data by finding the difference between the Q3 and Q1. This interpretation of the data is another measure of variation, or the spread of the data, where a small value represents data that is narrowly distributed and a larger value represents data with a wider distribution. Students may once again consider the data collected by doing jumping jacks for a minute. Put in order, the data for 8 students is shown as:

12	14	14	16	17	17	18	20
Min		Q1		Q2		Q3		Max

Minimum: 12

Maximum: 20

Range: 8

First Quartile (Q1): 14

Median (Q2): 16.5

Third Quartile (Q3): 17.5

Interquartile Range: 17.5 − 14 = 3.5

Jumping Jack Data

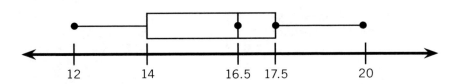

Students must understand that quartiles divide the data into fourths, and learn to interpret that 25% of the data falls within each quartile. Students may mistakenly include the median of the data set when finding the upper and lower quartiles in box plots. Instead, they must know to use the data point to the left of the median to find the lower quartile and the data point to the right of the median to find the upper quartile. Learning to compare this set of data and the measures of variation to another set gives students the opportunity to more fully interpret the data as to its relative variability.

Snake Data from Snakeville

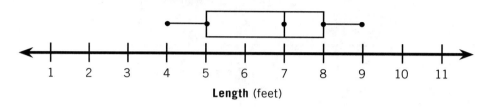

Length (feet)

Snake Data from Slippery Snakes

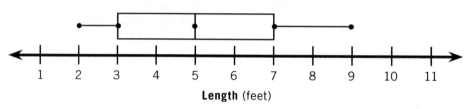

Length (feet)

As students learn to analyze data sets by looking at the overall shape of the data and calculating various data points, they culminate these experiences by summarizing what they have learned about a particular data set. Summarizing a distribution of data may be accomplished by interpreting the data set (6.SP.5).

Research has shown that, in general, students have had difficulty with reading beyond the graph (Friel, Curcio, and Bright 2001). In this domain, students learn to evaluate the data, interpret relationships that require a further assessment than that which is provided in a graph, draw inferences, and make connections.

Figure 9.5 Summary of Tasks

Standard	Tasks
6.SP.5a Reporting the number of observations.	Students may choose to use histograms and must determine the number of values in each interval.
6.SP.5b Describing the nature of the attribute under investigation, including how it was measured and its units of measurement.	Students may include in their summary an explanation of how the data was collected. Knowing the method by which the data was obtained may provide an explanation for some of the data points, such as outliers. For example, students may raise questions about the accuracy of data collected on the speed of cars outside their school found by using a stopwatch.
6.SP.5c Giving quantitative measures of center (median and/ or mean) and variability (interquartile range and/or mean absolute deviation), as well as describing any overall pattern and any striking deviations from the overall pattern with reference to the context in which the data were gathered.	As students have learned to calculate measures of center and variability, they include in their summary of the data how these measures relate to the overall pattern of the data. Students explain how including or excluding outliers in the data set affects the picture of the data as it relates to the described measures.
6.SP.5d Relating the choice of measures of center and variability to the shape of the data distribution and the context in which the data were gathered.	Choosing which measure of center or variability best describes the data, students learn to interpret these measures as related to one another. Relating these data points, students realize such ideas as, when the median and the mean are close to one another the graph is fairly symmetric and the MAD is a reasonable measure of variation.

Producing Data

"What percent of people in our town will go to the parade?"

Students in grade 7 move from using data that was provided to paying close attention to how the data is collected. They understand that it would be unreasonable to ask each person in their town if they will go to the parade. Instead, students determine a method by which they could ask a random sample of the town's population if they will go. Recognizing that a sample will not produce the exact same results as if they did ask everyone in the town, students also determine that, depending upon the size of the sample, they will find a slightly different estimate (7.SP.1). Students may choose to take a random sample of 100 people in their town to estimate the percent of townspeople who will attend the parade. To determine if this is an appropriate number of people to sample, they study how variability in the size of the samples will affect the validity. If it seems likely that 20% of the townspeople will attend the parade, a simulation of these results may be constructed, by using simulation software or a manipulative, a population of 500 in which 20% of the chips in a bag of 100 chips is green, to represent those who will attend and the other 80% is represented with red chips to show those who will not attend. Students then draw 100 circles from the population and record the results in a dot plot.

Changing the percent of green to 10% and 30%, they conduct the simulation a second and third time. Students then compile their individual results into one data set, recognizing that a random sample of 100 will produce the same amount of variation from the intended percent, regardless of the percentage chosen (7.SP.2). An interesting extension of this task would be for students to determine how changing the sample size by doubling the size of their sample population or cutting it in half would affect the results.

Comparing Data Sets

Students have learned to use measures of center and variability to make inferences on single populations. In grade 7, they are given tasks to make comparisons, based on their inferences, on two populations. Students in one class were provided with data regarding two populations of students and were asked to make compelling arguments about whether grade 7 or grade 8 students had more hours of homework on a particular night of the week, in this case, Monday. They thought it was likely the data would show more hours of homework for 8th graders, but they weren't sure how much more (7.SP.3). Initially, they viewed the data informally, graphing each of the data sets on line plots, using the same scale for each plot.

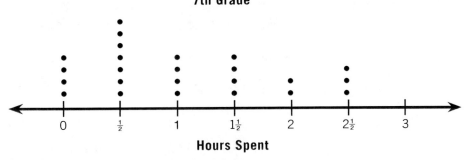

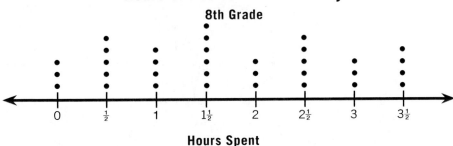

The students realized they needed to learn more about the data, so they calculated the measures of center and variability. Using the mean and the MAD to compare the data sets, they recognized that there was variability in each set, but there was slightly more variability in the grade 7 students' homework hours.

These calculated values allowed the students to provide a compelling argument on either side. With less variability in the data for grade 8 students, they could state that the mean number of homework hours for these students was greater, however, with more variability in the data for grade 7 students, they could state that this variability allows for an argument that an absolute conclusion that grade 8 students have more homework cannot be made (7.SP.4). Giving students tasks to compare sets of data allows them to see a practical use for the measures of center and variability and to construct arguments based on the data to support their arguments.

MP3
Arguments

Constructing and Analyzing Bivariate Data

The grade 8 standards in this domain are closely associated with students' understanding of the standards in other domains in grade 8 and across grade levels. The standards in this domain heavily rely on standards such as:

👉 Understanding of proportions and percent from grades 6 and 7

👉 Interpretation of one form of a linear equation $y = mx + b$ (8.F.3)

👉 Conceptual understanding of rates of change and initial values of functions (8.F.4)

👉 Qualitative descriptions of functional relationships between two quantities (8.F.5)

As a result of the experiences grade 8 students have had with linear functions, they can analyze the relationships formed between two variables by viewing the results through statistical modeling of what is termed as bivariate data. Finding the relationship between two variables, graphed in a coordinate plane, may be represented on a scatter plot, where students then learn to determine whether the patterns in the data are viewed as linear or non-linear. If the relationship is viewed as linear, then a closer look determines whether the trend is positive, negative, or if there is no association between the two variables (8.SP.1).

MP4
Model

One group of grade 8 students was learning, in their anatomy unit in science class, that one could predict the height of an individual based on the length of several bones in one's body. They decided to test out this relationship using data collected in their mathematics class.

They decided to measure the length of their femur bones, the large bone from the hip socket to the kneecap, and their height.

Figure 9.6 Scatterplot Comparing Femur Length to Height

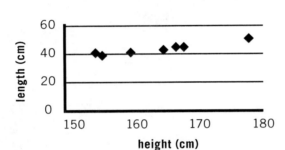

The students determined informally, from observing the scatterplot, that there was a linear positive correlation between the femur length and the person's height for the students in their class. While the use of linear regression is not expected in grade 8, students do informally create a straight line through the scatter plot of data where the associations are deemed to be linear (8.SP.2). Considered a *line of best fit*, students learn to draw a line through the data, where about half of the points are above the line and the other half of the points are below the line. Of course, some of the points could actually fall on the line as well. Drawing this trend line, known as conducting linear regression, allows students to make predictions about the femur lengths for people's heights for whom they did not collect data. Recognizing that the point (162, 40) is

MP3
Tools

a point on the line of best fit, students can state that a person who is 162 cm tall would have a femur length of about 40 cm as seen in Figure 9.7.

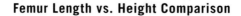

Figure 9.7 Scatterplot Including Line of Best Fit

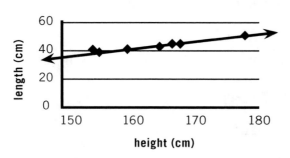

Femur Length vs. Height Comparison

Continued work with the patterns of association of bivariate data reveals that students can use what they have learned about the slope and the y-intercept of a linear situation to solve problems (8.SP.3). The teacher in an eighth-grade math class decided she would try to make a point about why it was important to do their homework. She collected data on the number of missed homework assignments students had for a particular unit and correlated it to their quiz scores for the same unit. Students used the table of data to create a scatterplot and then draw a line of best fit through the data. Recognizing there was a negative correlation between the number of missed homework assignments and the quiz scores, students went on to determine an appropriate linear equation for their line of best fit. The data from one class resulted in a y-intercept of 94, meaning that when there were no missed homework assignments, students would score about a 94% on the test. The more homework assignments missed, the lower the score, by about 6 points for each missed assignment, as the rate of change was −6.

MP4
Model

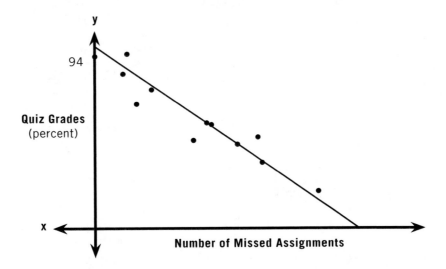

Correlation Between Missed Homework and Quiz Scores

Students learned to recognize that, given the fact the data are clearly related, they could use their linear model by substituting in values for the number of assignments to predict a quiz score. As well, they could find this ordered pair on their line of best fit, allowing them to see a pictorial representation for their result.

To this point, students in grade 8 have used scatterplots to analyze measurement or numerical bivariate data. The final standard in this domain requires students use two-way tables to relate categorical bivariate data. (8.SP.4) Although not required by the standard, students may find it helpful to first see the data in a Venn diagram. One group of students thought that it might be interesting to see if there was a relationship between interest in reading and writing. They asked the students in their classes whether they liked to read and then asked them if they liked to write. They tallied their results in the Venn diagram shown in Figure 9.8.

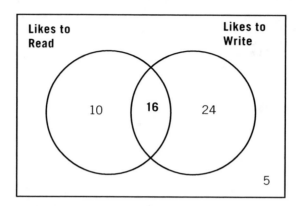

Figure 9.8 Venn Diagram of Categorical Data

Transferring this information to a two-way table required the students to show the categorical data classified in two different ways as in Figure 9.9.

Figure 9.9 A Two-Way Table

	Likes to Write	Doesn't Like to Write
Likes to read	16	10
Doesn't like to read	24	5

Building on the initial two-way table, students extended their knowledge of the data by first finding the totals for each category and then determining the relative frequency, or ratio of the number in the subtotal to the total, of students who fell in each category. An analysis of the data in this sample reveals that there is a weak positive correlation between those students who like to write and those who like to read as 62% of the students' surveyed liked to do both. Students may, alternatively, choose to state that there is about a 62% chance that students who like to read also like to write. Tasks in which students must interpret the data from a two-way table through relative frequencies and percentages gives students the opportunity to see practical and purposeful reasons for using these numerical calculations.

MP6
Precision

Figure 9.10 An Extended Two-Way Table

	Likes to Write	Doesn't Like to Write	Total
Likes to read	$\frac{16}{26} \approx 0.62$	$\frac{10}{26} \approx 0.38$	26
Doesn't like to read	$\frac{24}{29} \approx 0.83$	$\frac{5}{29} \approx 0.17$	29
Total	$\frac{40}{55} \approx 0.73$	$\frac{15}{55} \approx 0.27$	55

Probability

The formal study of probability begins in grade 7. Some state standards previously required students to begin study of probability concepts in the earlier grades, yet research has shown that younger students have had great difficulty in engaging in probabilistic thinking. Garfield and Ahlgren (1988) have stated that students need to, first, understand ratio and proportion before they can understand probability. In the Standards, students prior to grade 7 focus on displaying data rather than how the data is collected. The Standards connect how the data is collected with probability, hence the likely reason for introducing the two topics in one grade (Schwols and Dempsey 2013). The focus in this grade is on the probability of chance, through study of both simple and compound events. Students engage in an understanding of sample space while comparing experimental and theoretical probabilities. Early investigations with chance draw upon students' understanding of numbers between 0 and 1 as represented on a number line (7.SP.5).

One group of grade 7 students is given a list of situations, some of which always happen, some never happen and some happen ½ of the time. The students learn to record those events which never happen, such as "It will be September 2, 2005 tomorrow" at 0 on the number line, events which always happen, such as "The sun will rise tomorrow", are recorded at 1 and those which will usually happen half of the time, such as "When this penny is tossed, it will land on heads" are represented at $\frac{1}{2}$. As students become more adept at understanding how probability is represented as a rational number between 0 and 1, they learn to place other events on the number line, as more or less likely to happen.

MP3
Arguments

As students learn to collect data from a probability experiment, they learn that the more trials they conduct, the closer their results from the experiment will be to the theoretical probability that the event will occur (7.SP.6). Simulation software may be used to collect experimental data, which students then use to find the relative frequency for the sample. Relative frequency means finding the number of times that an event occurred out of a total number of trials. For example, most graphing calculators include probability experiments as applications, in which students can choose to toss a coin a prescribed number of times and the number of times it lands on heads or tails is displayed. If the coin was tossed 500 times and the coin "came up" heads 210 times, the relative frequency of the coin coming up heads is $\frac{210}{500}$. Students may complete tasks in which they compile their results of their experiments, determining that the more trials they conduct, the closer the relative frequency will be to $\frac{1}{2}$.

MP5
Tools

Although this critical area in grade 7 primarily focuses on the concept of chance, students in this grade learn standards requiring them to explore a variety of probability models as well. As probability allows for predicting what happens over time, students can use theoretical probability to predict the frequency of an outcome. Experimental data may be collected using random generation software or experiments by hand using chips, spinners, number cubes, or coins (7.SP.7; 7.SP.7a; 7.SP.7b).

Students learn to create probability models to answer such questions as:

- ✏ What is the probability that each time a student wants to use the school's elevator, it is on the wrong floor?

- ✏ Find the probability that a seventh-grade girl will be chosen to be principal for the day from amongst all the students in the school.

- ✏ Find the probability that someone in the class will have been born in March.

- ✏ Determine the likelihood that two cards, chosen at random from a deck, will be the same suit.

Known as the sample space, students first learn to determine all possible outcomes. If these outcomes are created based on the structure of the situation, such as listing all possibilities when a coin and a number cube are tossed, this probability is considered as *theoretical* and is written as {T1, T2, T3, T4, T5, T6, ...}. A probability model necessitating the collection of data, known as *empirical*, may come from creating a model to determine the probability of a cup landing up when it is tossed. While it may seem as though the probability of this occurring is $\frac{1}{2}$, this is not necessarily true and empirical data must be collected to determine this probability.

Grade 7 students complete their study of probability by finding the probability of compound events (7.SP.8; 7.SP.8a; 7.SP.8b; 7.SP.8c). In order to best visualize events in which more than one event is being compared, students first learn to record the probability of these events using organized lists, tables, or tree diagrams. While previous state standards required students to learn the counting principle, or rule, the Common Core Standards do not require the use of this rule beyond simple events. Rather, the standards encourage the use of tree diagrams and tables to determine the total number of possible outcomes, providing an organized model, allowing for visual representation of the total. For example, students may use a tree diagram to represent all of the possible choices that can be made for buying frozen yogurt in their school cafeteria, given two choices of cones, three choices of frozen yogurt, and two choices of toppings.

MP4
Model

Figure 9.11 Tree Diagram

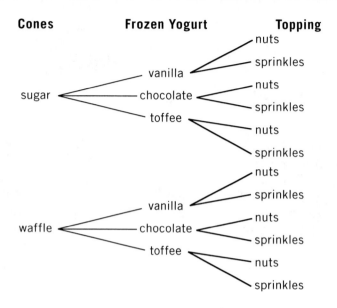

As students become more adept at creating visual models to represent compound events, they learn to ask more practical questions such as "If 20% of the students in the school are walkers, what is the probability that it will take at least 10 students to find one who is a walker?" Using simulation tools will assist students as they determine an appropriate model to use and then collect their data.

Conceptual Challenge

Students often expect that the results of their experiments will be equal to the theoretical probability. They often think that whatever occurred one time is what will occur all the time. As well, many students think that the theoretical probability will occur naturally in their experiment. For example, students often believe that, when a coin comes up heads one time, the next time it will come up tails, as though it has a memory that heads were tossed in the last toss. Students should be given the opportunity to conduct the same experiment numerous times so that they see that the experimental data is not the same each time.

Assessment Note

Assessment tasks in this domain must focus not only on the skills involved in finding statistical measures through calculation but also determining how well students can formulate good questions and then learn to answer them. As described in the work of the Mathematics Assessment Project (Mathematics Assessment Project 2011), students should engage in activities ranging from:

- ☞ **Novice Tasks**: These tasks focus primarily on gaining knowledge of the skills as related to the standards.

- ☞ **Apprentice Tasks**: These tasks are more substantial in nature, yet they are structured so that all students may gain access to the material. The steps in the task increase in the level of difficulty, whereby students and teachers can access how well the students have performed the task to a particular level. Because the tasks are structured, they do not rely heavily on the standards for mathematical practice in order to assure success.

> **Expert Tasks**: These tasks are not highly structured and success with them requires students to use significant problem solving as well as knowledge of the content involved. The tasks are primarily application-based and they rely heavily upon the standards for mathematical practice for success.

Authors of the materials written for the Mathematics Assessment Project believe that, in order for students to successfully accomplish college and career readiness they must engage in all three types of tasks. These tasks may be a part of formative or summative assessment activities and are described as performance tasks. Standardized test items are likely to include all three types of tasks, so the more practice students have with them as part of their daily classroom activity, the more likely they will be to fully engage in completing them on a standardized test. A sample standard test question may look like:

In a random sample, a researcher collected data from 1,000 drivers and 1,000 passengers about whether or not they use their seat belt while in a car. The researcher made a two-way table of the data:

Figure 9.12 Standard Test Question

	Driver	Passenger
Wore a Seat Belt	782	576
Didn't Wear a Seat Belt	218	424

Question 1: Write a valid statement about the conclusions that can be made from the results of the study.

Question 2: Write a statement to the Registry of Motor Vehicles recommending a study to further investigate the relationship between drivers and passengers and their seatbelt use.

These questions may be associated with "expert" tasks, requiring use of the skills learned as well as application of the statistical concepts, providing little to no structure for how to approach the task.

Voice from the Classroom

Quite honestly, when I first saw the grade 6 CCSSM standards for statistics I panicked. Some of the vocabulary was familiar, for example, I did know what histograms were and I was fairly knowledgeable about dots plots, or line plots, because we had taught those when we were teaching our previous standards. Median and mean were familiar to me as well, although I realized that there was a lot more to understanding and learning to use these measures of center than I had ever taught my students before. However, I truly had never heard of "interquartile ranges" or "measures of variability." I couldn't believe that it was going to be necessary to teach my grade 6 students how to calculate the mean absolute deviation (MAD) of a set of data when I hadn't a clue as to what it was myself.

As my training was originally in elementary level mathematics, I was not required to take a statistics course in college and so these concepts were all new to me. We didn't have any materials in our school to help us with these topics as not even the eighth grade teachers had to teach mean absolute deviation to their students.

I really didn't mind having to learn to teach something new to my students, as I did find that, after teaching sixth grade for about 15 years, I was tiring of primarily teaching about fractions, decimals and percent for practically the entire year. But, I knew that I had better see if I could get ahold of some materials to help me understand these new statistics concepts before I had to teach them to my students. We were not yet ready to make a purchase for a new textbook so I couldn't rely on prepared curriculum materials that taught concepts found in the new standards.

So, my sixth grade colleagues and I did an extensive internet search and found that there were a lot of great materials online. We "dug into" a number of the sample units that various states across the country were putting on their state websites. We also used some materials from some websites related to the Common Core initiative, such as illustrativemathematics.org and insidemathematics.org. It was by actually going through these units and doing a good number of the tasks that would be assigned to our students that we began to understand the material. One of my colleagues said that he actually liked the content found in this domain because it seemed so real-life oriented. Most of what we found in the resources was data that were quite relevant to kids, such as information about animals, geography, and space. They were also able to collect data they were interested in and make some predictions and inferences about their own school population that they didn't know before.

We decided that it was important to gain recognition for our efforts to learn new content, so we decided to form an official study group on the content of statistics and invited our colleagues in the other grades to join us.

This allowed us to not only receive in-service credits but also to work as an entire department of mathematics educators to "best fit" (pun intended!) the progression of the standards from grade level to grade level. While we have only been teaching these standards for about a year, we are finding that our students are truly engaged in the material as well. These statistical models are so realistic; we are hopeful that students will truly see the relevance of mathematics as a result of these new standards. The concept of mean absolute deviation is not easy for them, but we anticipate that it will get easier as we get better at finding the best ways to teach it. I think that we are going to learn from our students in this domain as much as they will learn from us.

—6th-Grade Teacher

Let's Think and Discuss

1. What topics do you think would most interest your students as you help them to choose surveys to conduct?

2. What do you think would be the best way to go about learning content you have not studied in this domain?

3. What are some ways you have found to assist your students when they find a concept to be difficult?

Chapter 10

Engaging Parents and Supporting Your Own Work

 **Snapshot**

Some teachers are meeting to discuss plans for the upcoming Back to School Curriculum Night for parents and guardians. This planning group would like to present a consistent message regarding their current work with the standards in the classroom. One of the teachers suggests that they do a short activity with the parents, perhaps highlighting the focus on conceptual understanding of math and how that differs from rote learning. Another teacher shares his thinking that a broader focus would be appropriate, providing an overarching list of the curriculum changes at their grade levels. One of the veteran teachers brings up the point that it might be difficult to make too detailed a presentation, given the fact that they only have a relatively short period of time that evening in which to make their points. One of the teachers found a presentation online, on their state's department of education website, which provides a good, short summary of the shifts in the standards. The group decides to use that presentation, tweaking it a little to make it more specific to their grade levels, and then to do a very short activity to provide a classroom example.

One of the teachers thinks that the "Guess My Number" game would be fun to play in order to give parents an idea of what the standards could look like in the classroom and would not take too long. While several of the teachers do know the game, two of the newer teachers have not played it before, so she asks the group to play the game together to see if they agree that it would be appropriate for the evening event. As leader of the game, she tells the group that she is thinking of a three-digit number that they must guess. She writes on chart paper, shown on the next page, and asks the teachers to make a guess as to what the number could be, in this case, without repeating any of the digits. One teacher guesses *three-four-five*. The game leader says, "Let's use the base ten number name *three hundred forty-five*, and then writes into the chart how many of those digits are correct and how many digits are in the right place. Another teacher guesses 352 and explains that she thinks the 3 and the 5 are correct, with the 3 in the right place and the 5 should remain but be moved to the tens place. The game leader writes the responses to this guess on the second line in the chart and asks for another guess. Someone pipes up and suggests 524, providing an explanation to the group as to why, and the game leader again writes the responses in the chart. She then asks everyone to stop and talk with a neighbor about what they know and how they know it. Several partnerships are considering all the different arrangements of these three digits and checking them against the previous guesses and responses. Another guess is made and the teacher tells the group that they have found the number. The group agrees that it is an enjoyable game that is engaging and would not take a long time to play. They also know that it can be played with fewer or more digits or even decimals. Moving on, they discuss how best to present why this game is appropriate for students and how it incorporates the standards. The group decides that the necessity to correctly name the numbers and refer to digits by their place value names is related to early grade standards on our base-ten number system and the logic and problem solving aspect of the game incorporates what the standards for mathematical practice are about, with a focus on making sense of problems and discussing viable arguments.

At the end of the meeting, the teachers feel satisfied they have found an appropriate presentation to offer the parents that will engage them in some initial thinking about how these standards are different than what and how their children have learned mathematics in the past. They decide to create directions to the game in English, Portuguese, and Spanish for parents who want them.

Guess	Digits	Place
345	2	1
352	2	1
524	3	1
542	3	3

This example of how teachers collaborate to present the Common Core State Standards to a group of parents and guardians raises many questions. Is there one way that is better than another to communicate about these standards to parents? Should it be done at a curriculum night or through a special presentation on another evening? While it may not be ideal to make the presentation on such a busy evening with lots of other things to talk about, it is also a good opportunity to take advantage of the captive audience. Teachers are faced with these kinds of dilemmas on a regular basis, as they consider how best to get an important message to parents regarding expectations for their children.

Many parents have heard of the Common Core, but they may not be well informed about how the standards will impact their children's education. These parents often want to know the information, but they need presentations that are clear, concise, and in laypersons' language. Finding ways to work with parents and guardians as a team is essential to your students' success, and so it is one of many things you must attend to in relationship to these standards. This chapter is intended to provide you with a variety of ways you can engage parents in these curricular changes as well as ideas for supporting your work overall during this time of change.

Engaging Parents

We all recognize the important role of parents in their child's education. A school, parent/guardian, and community partnership is a significant factor in student achievement (Epstein, et al., 2009). We should recognize parents and caregivers as experts on their children and view them as our partners in their children's learning (Aubach 2011). To form respectful relationships with parents, we must be culturally sensitive to expectations for roles and interactions (Delpit 2006; McKenna and Millen 2013). No doubt your school has specific routines, protocols, scheduled meetings, and other events to promote parent engagement. Here, the focus is on establishing school, family, and community partnerships to increase students' success with the Common Core State Standards.

What Do They Know and Hear?

What do parents know about the Core? In a summary of the 45th Annual Phi Delta Kappan Gallup Poll in 2013, Bushaw and Lopez state that, "Almost two of three Americans have never heard of the Common Core State Standards, arguably one of the most important education initiatives in decades, and most of those who say they know about the Common Core neither understand it nor embrace it" (9). We do not always make sure that parents understand and are able to engage in educational initiatives. Your school and state had learning standards before the Common Core was adopted. How much attention did you and your school administrators give to those standards as you communicated with parents? Yet, this situation is different. Because of its national impact and political polarization, some parents and members of the community may have particularly strong views and, at the same time, have access to incorrect information.

So informing parents about what the standards are or are not is an important place to begin. Parent/teacher organization websites are also helpful in providing information about the standards. It is most important to establish that it is still teachers who determine how to facilitate students' learning of these standards. Also, it is advantageous to avoid lengthy explanations, as they may initially make information about the standards difficult to understand.

Parents need to know that:

- Your state has always had standards;
- These standards are intended to cover fewer ideas at each grade level, more deeply;
- There are critical areas of focus for your grade level; and
- They are critically important in helping their children succeed, to be college and career-ready.

How Can Parents Help?

As President of National Council of Teachers of Mathematics, Linda Gojak (2013) encouraged teachers to view planning how best to engage parents in the learning process as important as planning instruction in the classroom. There are specific ways that parents can best support the likelihood that their children will meet Common Core State Standards. Parents and caregivers should:

1. **Set clear expectations for their children to work hard at their mathematics homework and to convey the message to their children that they believe that mathematics is important to learn.** In today's busy world of extracurricular activities for many students, it is often challenging for them to juggle all of their responsibilities. Urge parents to support their children by finding the space, time, and needed materials to complete their home assignments. Encourage parents to provide adequate time for their children to engage in the math they are learning in a meaningful way, rather than just trying to get their homework done quickly. Suggest to parents that they contact you if their children are struggling at home with the required work.

2. **Connect mathematical ideas to everyday tasks and interactions.** One of the key shifts in the mathematics standards is the emphasis on applying mathematical ideas to real-life problems and exposure to such thinking is important at home, as well. Suggest that parents engage their children in such tasks as reading a bus schedule and deciding which bus to take to get to an event or appointment on time; estimating the cost of items when grocery shopping; cooking and planning nutritious meals; and setting and planning budgets.

3. **Support fluency expectations and engage with their children in the playing of mathematical games.** Support expectations for students to model mathematics and engage with their children how to use such models. New models, such as tape diagrams or pictorial models for solving percent problems could be introduced at a Family Math Night and parents could take home examples of how to solve problems using these models to refer back to when working with their children at home. Tell parents that it is not possible to solely learn and practice mathematics in school, that practicing mathematics concepts at home is as important as practicing the piano or how to hit a baseball.

4. **Ask their children to explain their thinking about a math problem that comes up naturally in their household or in connection to a homework problem.** Tell parents that this will give them access to how their children are being taught to solve problems as well as provide students practice with justifying their thinking. Explain that such explanations will be included in new standardized tests.

5. **Model for their children how to engage in the learning process.** Help parents understand that if their child is uncertain as to how to do a particular problem or is struggling with a concept, parents should encourage their children to persevere and to seek out a variety of strategies for problem solutions. Remind parents that their children will be more successful if they learn to be self-reliant and take responsibility for their own learning.

Supporting Your Work

Perhaps there has been a time during your teaching career when you have switched grade levels, changed school systems, or been told to use a new textbook purchased by your school. You may have found such changes exciting, worrisome, stimulating, or exhausting. You may have experienced all of those reactions to the same change, at different points in the process. Regardless of which response was prominent, it is likely that the change required an additional time commitment, at least in the beginning.

As a teacher, your attention is pulled in many directions, and it's challenging to know how to prioritize your tasks. You know that you need to use your time wisely. More commonly now, professional development opportunities are spent analyzing test results of these standards, rather than on defining best teaching practices. And, although you may have teacher meetings intended to learn more about the standards, you will likely agree that these meetings don't give you nearly enough time to learn all there is to know. So what can you do to continue to support the important work of finding the best ways to help every one of your diverse students meet these standards? What could you do to keep your energy strong and support a positive attitude?

Get a Standards Buddy at Your Grade Level

Have you ever heard friends or colleagues talk about finding a new walking partner? Suddenly their exercise program has been reinvigorated. They are excited to get up in the morning to exercise. They claim that the time flies by. The same kind of benefit can be achieved from finding a *standards buddy*. Here are some ways you might want to work together:

- ✏ Read an article about the Mathematical Practices and meet to discuss it. You could even talk about what the practices mean to you while you go for a walk!

- ✏ Meet before you begin the next unit and review the related standards and critical areas. Decide what preparation you most need to make the unit successful and divvy up the work.

- ✏ If you have a "free" or a preparation period, use it once in a while to visit each other's classroom while your buddy is teaching a new lesson. Talk about what you learned and enjoyed. Once a level of comfort is established, talk about another visit where you focus on one aspect of your teaching you would like to improve.

- ✏ Watch a classroom video together and then talk about the evidence you saw of engagement and learning.

- ✏ If you are asked to teach a new mathematical topic you don't completely understand, work with your buddy to learn the new math content by doing some research together and practicing the idea prior to teaching it.

- ✏ Take advantage of local workshops by attending them together so that you can talk about what you both learned.

Connect Across Grade Levels

With the immediate demands of preparing and assessing your students, it can be challenging to think about the mathematics at other grade levels, but working across grade levels is a way to help you and your students. Consider forming a study group, including teachers who are interested in meeting together just once, to look at how one of the domains develops or how one of the Mathematical Practices might look different across grade levels. If it is helpful, you can always decide to meet again. Perhaps teachers from each grade level could bring a few samples of student work and, as a group, you could look at the samples to consider the following questions:

- What similarities and differences are there among the mathematical tasks we brought?

- What progression of learning do the work samples suggest?

- What do we notice about the ways in which students represent their mathematical thinking at different grade levels?

- What common errors or misconceptions do we notice and how can we help students avoid them?

- What evidence is there that students are developing the expectations of the Mathematical Practices?

Take Advantage of Online Resources

There are a variety of tools online to support implementation of these standards. For the first time, national websites and those from other states are helpful and relevant to the standards of your state. Due to the plethora of choices available, it helps to rely on sites that have connections to well-known, highly-respected organizations and individuals. Here are some ideas you might want to pursue for learning more about the standards. If you have not already done so:

- **Read the progressions documents for yourself.** They are available at http://ime.math.arizona.edu/progressions/. You can also participate in discussion forums hosted by Common Core State Standards writer Bill McCallum at http://commoncoretools.me/forums/forum/public/.

- ✏ **Join the National Council of Teachers of Mathematics (NCTM).** An E-Membership is more affordable and gives you access to a variety of online resources, current and back issues of *Teaching Children Mathematics*, and discounts for NCTM meetings and resources.

- ✏ **Receive a daily update from a professional organization**. You can sign up for the ASCD SmartBrief or the NCTM SmartBrief at http://www2.smartbrief.com/.

- ✏ **Listen to a TED talk**. As educators we can become so focused on educational resources that we miss ideas in other disciplines. TED is a non-profit organization that began in 1984 with the mission of spreading good ideas. The best talks are available online at http://www.ted.com/.

- ✏ **Watch videos of classrooms**. The Teaching Channel has dedicated a good number of its videos to demonstration lessons that support the work of the standards at all grade levels. Their videos can be found at http://www.teachingchannel.org.

- ✏ **Look at your state's website**. Most state departments of elementary and secondary education are posting quality resources for teachers on state websites as they become available. Do some research on available Common Core materials as provided by these leading state education agencies.

Resources are also needed to supplement or replace outdated materials. Most classrooms are filled with texts published before the Common Core. Though there will be useful sections of those books, it is unlikely that they will provide the deep focus needed, and a good number of books include topics that are now taught at different grade levels. Even those published shortly after the Common Core may not be as robust as necessary. The following sites have specific curricular suggestions:

- ✏ Illustrative Mathematics offers tasks, videos, plans, and curriculum modules at http://www.illustrativemathematics.org/. The work is funded by the Bill & Melinda Gates Foundation.

- ✏ *Illuminations*, a NCTM resource for teachers at http://illuminations.nctm.org/, was started before adoption of the Common Core, but its resources have been vetted by experienced mathematics educators.

✏ The website for the National Council of Supervisors of Mathematics (NCSM) has a link to Common Core resources on their main web page: http://www.mathedleadership.org, including a sample of "great tasks."

✏ Consider materials made available to you from www.achievethecore.org. Student Achievement Partners, founded by several of the lead authors of the Core Standards, has created a website resource which includes tasks and assessments, lessons, ready-to-use modules, and year-long planning materials. This website also has bilingual materials available for teacher and parent use.

✏ PARCC items and test prototypes can be found at http://www.parcconline.org/ and Smarter Balanced practice tests are available at http://www.smarterbalanced.org. Both consortiums are likely to continue to release items that can be used in your classroom.

✏ There are numerous formative and summative assessment tasks as well as freely available professional development modules on the Math Assessment Project website at http://www.map.mathshell.org.

Finally, with an emphasis on fluency, students need practice. Online games can often motivate some students in ways that nothing else seems to do as well. It's important to remember, however, that *drill and kill* can happen through technology as easily as paper and pencil. Such practice can support automaticity, only *after* a conceptual framework is established and *before* recall has been established. Consider online activities that encourage students to learn their facts in interesting ways rather than just becoming online flash cards. We must also remember to include games that support higher order thinking.

Look for Opportunities to Use Project-Based Learning

Our greatest challenges may be to find appropriate tasks as well as the time for students to pursue them. In light of the Common Core's expectation that students apply their mathematical knowledge to real-world problems, many educators have suggested that we give more attention to project-based learning (PBL). PBL offers students authentic questions and problems to pursue. As they are authentic, they are also complex and require a variety of concepts and skills. Usually explored with others, authentic projects give students opportunities to learn how to work collaboratively as they research and synthesize information. John Larnier, Director of Product Development at the Buck Institute for Education, (2011) suggests that PBL is appropriate for students of all ages, for ELL students, and for students with learning disabilities. Despite the fact that these kinds of projects do take more time to complete, they are most often very engaging for students, who tend to learn a good number of skills and concepts while doing them. The work of such projects could be started in class by collaborating with others and then continued at home or you could choose to fully dedicate in-class time for such work.

Mathematics and science are often connected. If your students were studying birds, projects could focus on their migration, their sizes, or counting and categorizing the number of birds that approach a bird feeder over time. Older students might investigate soil quality and other questions related to establishing a school vegetable garden. Another approach would be to ask how mathematical understanding informs a book being read in literacy learning, or a topic in the social studies curriculum. Projects such as *How could mathematical information help us better understand the Revolutionary War?* can engage students in interesting interdisciplinary learning endeavors.

School-wide projects can support school unity and provide opportunities for multi-age interactions. A project such as creating a school garden can connect to various components of the 6-8 mathematics curriculum as shown in Figure 10.1.

Figure 10.1 Sample Across Grade Explorations Related to a School Vegetable Garden

Grade 6	Grade 7	Grade 8
How much will the garden cost? (computation with decimals) How much space do we need for the garden? (area measurement) What was our yield in, for example, tomatoes, for each package of seeds that we planted? What portion of the garden should each type of plant get? (fractions, area measures)	How much water do the plants need? How can we measure the water they get from rainfall? (liquid volume measures) When can we harvest the plants? (line plots) How big are the vegetables? (length and mass measures, bar graphs) What percent of the garden contains each type of vegetable? (percents)	How much compost do we need? (volume measures) How will we use the vegetables? (fractions and measures in recipes) How many of .... (one type of vegetable) would we need in order to serve our whole school for one lunch period? (computation with greater whole numbers) Consider such questions as: Is the amount of zucchini yielded in the garden a function of the number of sunny days? (functions)

Write Your Own Professional Goals

Goal setting is common in education and with good reason. Intentionality gives us focus to our work. Many teachers are required to set goals every year, and some do so based on an evaluation calendar. When changes such as adoption of the Common Core State Standards occur, we all need to reflect on our practice and establish clear, meaningful goals that seem doable to us. Such goals might begin with one of the following sentence stems:

✐ By using strategies found within resources listed on the website of the National Council of Supervisors of Mathematics website, I will incorporate...

✐ By examining PARCC exemplars [or Smarter Balanced practice tests] I will create...

You may wish to begin with the practice standards. You could start by completing the following activity sheet (Figure 10.2).

Figure 10.2 Practice Activity Sheet

Name: _____ Date: _____

Mathematical Practice:

Two goals I have in relation to this practice are:

Evidence that I have met my goal would include:

A specific action I will take is to:

Resources I will use include:

In six months I will have:

Being a teacher can bring great sources of satisfaction as well as great challenges. When you are inspired and passionate about your teaching, chances are your students feel energized and excited about learning, too. So it is important that you find ways to support this work. Always remember, standards are only as valuable as the teacher implementing them.

Voice from the Classroom

My communication with parents seems to be "feast or famine." I either get lots of communication from them about their children or not enough. I've learned by now that this isn't unusual. This year's phone calls and emails seem to be focused on what the new standards mean and how their children will do on the new tests that they must take soon. Thankfully, most of them also want to know how they can be helpful at home. So, I've done a lot of thinking about what I could tell parents about suggestions for home activities. Some of the parents are open to my suggestions and some of them seem to resist my ideas about letting their children figure things out on their own at home and not jumping in to help too quickly. They seem to be almost afraid to let their children struggle at all, as though it is a strike against them if they don't understand something right away. I've tried to portray a message to parents that the more they let their children persevere on their own, the better off their children will be in the future. They need to know that it is imperative for their children to make connections between what they are learning in school and what they are practicing at home. Their children must learn ways to figure out what to do when it is not readily apparent. I am encouraging them to have conversations with their children about what they understand about a problem and to ask them to describe what makes them feel stuck. Such conversations are so much better than jumping in with an answer. I am asking parents to encourage their children to use their resources wisely to give them ideas on how to approach a problem, sometimes using handouts they got in school or notes they took, rather than just looking up the information for their children. A few days after a long conversation with one parent, she called to tell me that, in the midst of a long conversation about a problem with her child, they both had an "aha" moment about the problem and the child felt extremely satisfied about the solution in the end. She believes that her child felt very proud of himself that he figured it out on his own.

It turned out to be a great bonding experience for them and the parent felt as though she was able to help her child learn on his own more, rather than just telling him what to do. I hope that I can encourage more parents in such a way that they, too, have more of these "aha" moments with their children.

I must admit that I do get a little frustrated by not hearing from some parents at all, especially when I would like to talk to them about their children's progress. However, I think that I've found some other productive ways to let them know what is happening in the classroom. I've been writing some weekly bulletins that I send home with the students about what the math standards are about and how they will impact their children. I've also found some good games that the children can play with any of their family members. I've made some take-home math game "packages" that include everything necessary to play the game, along with a set of directions and a list of the standards that the students are practicing when they play the game. Students check them out like a library book and take them home for as long as they would like. I've included a blank card and an envelope in the package so that families can write me a note about anything they'd like regarding the game. It's been fun to think of some more creative ways to reach out to some reluctant families and I've been pleasantly surprised by the responses. One parent let me know that she appreciated being given the directions in Spanish as well as in English and one of my students' older brothers came to my open house night because he read about it in the newsletter that I sent home.

I feel as though these conversations and more varied communications with parents are helping me to grow as a teacher as well. I am gaining confidence about how I want to teach these new standards to my students, how to empower my students to be responsible for their own learning more than I ever have before, and how best to communicate with parents to make it a positive school-home partnership.

—7th-Grade Teacher

Let's Think and Discuss

1. How will parents in your district best engage with the goals of the Common Core Standards?

2. What sources of support have you found during past educational initiatives? How might they help you with this one?

3. What are two "I can..." statements that you can make about yourself in relationship to teaching and learning with the Common Core's mathematics content and practice standards? What are two you could make about your partnership with the community and parents?

The Standards for Mathematical Practice

Standards for Mathematical Practice, (National Governors Association Center for Best Practices [NGA] and the Council of Chief State School Officers [CCSSO] 2010)

MP1 Make sense of problems and persevere in solving them.

Mathematically proficient students start by explaining to themselves the meaning of a problem and looking for entry points to its solution. They analyze givens, constraints, relationships, and goals. They make conjectures about the form and meaning of the solution and plan a solution pathway rather than simply jumping into a solution attempt. They consider analogous problems, and try special cases and simpler forms of the original problem in order to gain insight into its solution. They monitor and evaluate their progress and change course if necessary. Older students might, depending on the context of the problem, transform algebraic expressions or change the viewing window on their graphing calculator to get the information they need. Mathematically proficient students can explain correspondences between equations, verbal descriptions, tables, and graphs or draw diagrams of important features and relationships, graph data, and search for regularity or trends. Younger students might rely on using concrete objects or pictures to help conceptualize and solve a problem. Mathematically proficient students check their answers to problems using a different method, and they continually ask themselves, "Does this make sense?" They can understand the approaches of others to solving complex problems and identify correspondences between different approaches.

MP2 Reason abstractly and quantitatively.

Mathematically proficient students make sense of quantities and their relationships in problem situations. They bring two complementary abilities to bear on problems involving quantitative relationships: the ability to *decontextualize*—to abstract a given situation and represent it symbolically and manipulate the representing symbols as if they have a life of their own, without necessarily attending to their referents—and the ability to *contextualize*, to pause as needed during the manipulation process in order to probe into the referents for the symbols involved. Quantitative reasoning entails habits of creating a coherent representation of the problem at hand; considering the units involved; attending to the meaning of quantities, not just how to compute them; and knowing and flexibly using different properties of operations and objects.

MP3 Construct viable arguments and critique the reasoning of others.

Mathematically proficient students understand and use stated assumptions, definitions, and previously established results in constructing arguments. They make conjectures and build a logical progression of statements to explore the truth of their conjectures. They are able to analyze situations by breaking them into cases, and can recognize and use counterexamples. They justify their conclusions, communicate them to others, and respond to the arguments of others. They reason inductively about data, making plausible arguments that take into account the context from which the data arose. Mathematically proficient students are also able to compare the effectiveness of two plausible arguments, distinguish correct logic or reasoning from that which is flawed, and—if there is a flaw in an argument—explain what it is. Elementary students can construct arguments using concrete referents such as objects, drawings, diagrams, and actions. Such arguments can make sense and be correct, even though they are not generalized or made formal until later grades. Later, students learn to determine domain to which an argument applies. Students at all grades can listen or read the arguments of others, decide whether they make sense, and ask useful questions to clarify or improve the arguments.

MP4 Model with mathematics.

Mathematically proficient students can apply the mathematics they know to solve problems arising in everyday life, society, and the workplace. In early grades, this might be as simple as writing an addition equation to describe a situation. In middle grades, a student might apply proportional reasoning to plan a school event or analyze a problem in the community. By high school, a student might use geometry to solve a design problem or use a function to describe how one quantity of interest depends on another. Mathematically proficient students who can apply what they know are comfortable making assumptions and approximations to simplify a complicated situation, realizing that these may need revision later. They are able to identify important quantities in a practical situation and map their relationships using such tools as diagrams, two-way tables, graphs, flowcharts, and formulas. They can analyze those relationships mathematically to draw conclusions. They routinely interpret their mathematical results in the context of the situation and reflect on whether the results make sense, possibly improving the model if it has not served its purpose.

MP5 Use appropriate tools strategically.

Mathematically proficient students consider the available tools when solving a mathematical problem. These tools might include pencil and paper, concrete models, a ruler, a protractor, a calculator, a spreadsheet, a computer algebra system, a statistical package, or dynamic geometry software. Proficient students are sufficiently familiar with tools appropriate for their grade or course to make sound decisions about when each of these tools might be helpful, recognizing both the insight to be gained and their limitations. For example, mathematically proficient high school students analyze graphs of functions and solutions generated using a graphing calculator. They detect possible errors by strategically using estimation and other mathematical knowledge. When making mathematical models, they know that technology can enable them to visualize the results of varying assumptions, explore consequences, and compare predictions with data. Mathematically proficient students at various grade levels are able to identify relevant external mathematical resources, such as digital content located on a website, and use them to pose or solve problems. They are able to use technological tools to explore and deepen their understanding of concepts.

MP6 Attend to precision.

Mathematically proficient students try to communicate precisely to others. They try to use clear definitions in discussion with others and in their own reasoning. They state the meaning of the symbols they choose, including using the equal sign consistently and appropriately. They are careful about specifying units of measure, and labeling axes to clarify the correspondence with quantities in a problem. They calculate accurately and efficiently, express numerical answers with a degree of precision appropriate for the problem context. In the elementary grades, students give carefully formulated explanations to each other. By the time they reach high school, they have learned to examine claims and make explicit use of definitions.

MP7 Look for and make use of structure.

Mathematically proficient students look closely to discern a pattern or structure. Young students, for example, might notice that three and seven more is the same amount as seven and three more, or they may sort a collection of shapes according to how many sides the shapes have. Later, students will see 7×8 equals the well remembered $7 \times 5 + 7 \times 3$, in preparation for learning about the distributive property. In the expression $x^2 + 9x + 14$, older students can see the 14 as 2×7 and the 9 as $2 + 7$. They recognize the significance of an existing line in a geometric figure and can use the strategy of drawing an auxiliary line for solving problems. They also can step back for an overview and shift perspective. They can see complicated things, such as some algebraic expressions, as single objects or as being composed of several objects. For example, they can see $5 - 3(x - y)^2$ as 5 minus a positive number times a square and use that to realize that its value cannot be more than 5 for any real numbers x and y.

MP8 Look for and express regularity in repeated reasoning.

Mathematically proficient students notice if calculations are repeated, and look both for general methods and for shortcuts. Upper elementary students might notice when dividing 25 by 11 that they are repeating the same calculations over and over again, and conclude they have a repeating decimal. By paying attention to the calculation of slope as they repeatedly check whether points are on the line through (1, 2) with slope 3, middle school students might abstract the equation $(y - 2)/(x - 1) = 3$. Noticing the regularity in the way terms cancel when expanding $(x - 1)(x + 1)$, $(x - 1)$ $(x^2 + x + 1)$, and $(x - 1)(x^3 + x^2 + x + 1)$ might lead them to the general formula for the sum of a geometric series. As they work to solve a problem, mathematically proficient students maintain oversight of the process, while attending to the details. They continually evaluate the reasonableness of their immediate results.

Unpacking a Particular Standard

Standard:	Organize by Nouns and Verbs:
Relate to Other Standards:	**Vocabulary/Symbols:**
How Does This Idea Develop?	**Learning Target Examples:**
Curriculum/Instruction:	**Student-Friendly Language:**

Frayer Model Diagram

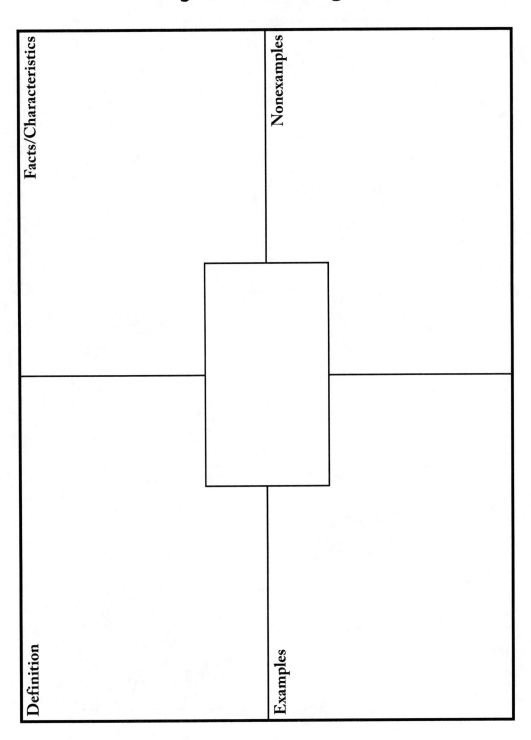

Facts/Characteristics

Nonexamples

Definition

Examples

Is It Proportional?

The situation: _____

_____

_____

_____

My representation using color cubes:

My representation using my picture model:

My representation using the applet:

Here's what I think about whether or not it is a proportion:

Rules for Operating on Same Base Numbers with Integer Exponents

Operation	Example	Rule
Multiplication		
Division		
Raising a power to a power		
Zero as an exponent		
Negative exponents		
Distributing an exponent		

Practice Goal Activity Sheet

Name: _____ Date: _____

Mathematical Practice:

Two goals I have in relation to this practice are:

Evidence that I have met my goal would include:

A specific action I will take is to:

Resources I will use include:

In six months I will have:

References Cited

Afflerbach, Peter, and Summer Clark. 2011. "Diversity and English Language Arts Assessment." In *Handbook of Research on Teaching English Language Arts*, 3rd edition, edited by Dianne Lapp and Douglas Fisher. Newark, DE: International Reading Association.

Aspinwall, Leslie, and Julie Aspinwall. 2003. "Investigating Mathematical Thinking Using Open Writing Prompts." *Mathematics Teaching in the Middle School.* 8: 350–353.

Association of American Colleges and Universities. 2010. *Quantitative Literacy Value Rubric.* Washington, DC.

Atkin, J. Myron, Paul Black, and Janet Coffey. 2001. *Classroom Assessment and the National Science Standards.* Washington, DC: National Academies Press.

Aubach, Susan. 2011. "Bridging Cultures and Building Relationships: Engaging Latino/a Immigrant Parents in Urban Schools." *Educational Leadership.* 68: 16–21.

Balliett, Blue, and Brett Helquist. 2006. *The Wright 3.* New York: Scholastic Press.

Barlow, Angela T., and Michael R. McCrory. 2011. "Three Strategies for Promoting Math Disagreements." *Teaching Children Mathematics.* 17: 530–539.

Beckmann, Sybilla, and Karen Fuson. 2012. "Standard Algorithms in the Common Core State Standards." NCSM 22: 14–30.

Bill, Victoria, and Pam Goldman. 2012. "The CSS and the Importance of Assessing the Mathematical Practices." http://ifl.lrdc.pitt.edu/ifl/index.php/blog/index/the_ccss_and_the_importance_of_assessing_students_mathematical_practices.

Bresser, Rusty, Kathy Melanese, and Christine Sphar. 2008. *Supporting English Language Learners in Math Class, Grades 3–5*. Sausalito, CA: Math Solutions Publications.

Bushaw, William J., and Shane J. Lopez. 2013. "The 45th Annual PDK/ Gallup Poll of the Public's Attitude Toward the Public Schools: Which Way Do We Go?" *Kappan Magazine* 96: 9–17.

Carpenter, Thomas P., Megan Loef Franke, and Linda Levi. 2003. *Thinking Mathematically: Integrating Arithmetic and Algebra in Elementary School.* Portsmouth, NH: Heinemann.

Cawley, John F., Rene Parmar, Lynn Lucas-Fusco, Joy Killian, and Teresa Foley. 2007. "Place Value and Mathematics for Students with Mild Disabilities: Data and Suggested Practices." *Learning Disabilities: A Contemporary Journal.* 5: 21–39.

Chapin, Suzanne, Catherine O'Connor, and Nancy Anderson. 2009. *Classroom Discussions: Using Math Talk to Help Students Learn.* Sausalito, CA: Math Solutions.

Collins, Anne. 2012. *Using Assessment to Improve Student Learning: Math Problems Aligned with NCTM and Common Core State Standards.* Reston: VA: NCTM.

Colton, Connie. 2010. "Justifying Answers and Providing Explanations for Mathematical Thinking: The Impact on Student Learning in a Middle-School Classroom." http://scimath.unl.edu/MIM/files/research/Colton_AR_FinalLA.pdf.

Common Core Standards Writing Team. 2011. "Progressions for the Common Core State Standards in Mathematics: 6–7, Ratios and Proportional Relationships." http://commoncoretools.files.wordpress.com/2012/02/ccss_progression_rp_67_2011_11_12_corrected.pdf.

Common Core Standards Writing Team. 2011. "Progressions for the Common Core State Standards in Mathematics: 6–8 Expressions and Equations." http://commoncoretools.files.wordpress.com/2011/04/ccss_progression_ee_2011_04_25.pdf.

Common Core Standards Writing Team. 2011. "Progressions for the Common Core State Standards in Mathematics: 6–8 Statistics and Probability." http://commoncoretools.files.wordpress.com/2011/12/ccss_progression_sp_68_2011_12_26_bis.pdf.

Common Core Standards Writing Team. 2012. "Progressions for the Common Core State Standards in Mathematics: K–6, Geometry." http://commoncoretools.files.wordpress.com/2012/06/ccss_progression_g_k6_2012_06_27.pdf.

Common Core Standards Writing Team. 2013. "Progressions for the Common Core State Standards in Mathematics: The Number System, 6–8." http://commoncoretools.me/wp-content/uploads/2013/07/ccssm_progression_NS+Number_2013-07-09.pdf.

Crowe, Marce and Pokey Stanford. 2010. "Question for Quality." Delta Kappa Gamma Bulletin Summer: 36-41.

Darling-Hammond, Linda. 2012. *Creating a Comprehensive System for Evaluating and Supporting Effective Teaching*. Stanford, CA: Stanford Center for Opportunity Policy in Education.

Delpit, Lisa. 2006. *Other People's Children: Cultural Conflict in the Classroom*. New York, NY: New Press.

Demi. 1997. *One Grain of Rice: A Mathematical Folktale*. New York, NY: Scholastic Press.

Denman, Greg. 2013. *Think It, Show It Mathematics: Strategies for Exploring Thinking*. Huntington Beach, CA: Shell Education.

Driscoll, Mark. 1999. *Fostering Mathematical Thinking*. Portsmouth, NH: Heinemann.

Dweck, Carol. 2012. *Mindset: The New Psychology of Success*. New York, NY: Robinson Publishing.

Epstein, Joyce, Mavis G. Sanders, Steven Sheldon, and Beth S. Simon. 2009. *School, Family, and Community Partnerships: Your Handbook for Action*, 3rd Edition. Thousand Oaks, CA: Corwin Press.

Flanagan, Dawn, Jennifer Mascolo, and Steven Hardy-Braz. 2009. "Standardized Testing." www.education.com/reference/article/standardized-testing.

Flores, Alfinio. 2002. "Profound Understanding of Division of Fractions." In *Making Sense of Fractions, Ratios, and Proportions: 2002 Yearbook*, edited by Bonnie Litwiller and George Bright, 237–246. Reston, VA: National Council of Teachers of Mathematics.

Frayer, Dorothy, Wayne C. Frederick, and Herbert J. Klausmeier. 1969. *A Schema for Testing the Level of Concept Mastery. Technical Report No. 16.* Madison: University of Wisconsin Research and Development Center for Cognitive Learning.

Friel, Susan N., Frances R. Curcio, George W. Bright. 2001. "Making Sense of Graphs: Critical Factors Influencing Comprehension and Instructional Implications." *Journal for Research in Math Education* 32: 124–158.

Garfield, Joan and Andrew Ahlgren. 1988. "Difficulties in Learning Basic Concepts in Probability and Statistics: Implications for Research." *Journal for Research in Mathematics Education* 19: 44-63.

Gojak, Linda. 2013. "National Council of Teachers of Mathematics. Partnering with Parents." http:// http://www.nctm.org/about/content.aspx?id=39367.

Goodwin, K. Shane, Lee Ostrom, and Karen Wilson Scott. 2009. "Gender Differences in Mathematics Self-Efficacy and Back Substitution Multiple-Choice Assessment." *Journal Of Adult Education* 38: 22–41.

Hancock, Chris, James K. Kaput, and Lynn T. Goldsmith. 1992. "Authentic Inquiry with Data: Critical Barriers to Classroom Implementation." *Educational Psychologist* 27: 337–364.

Hancock, Melisa J. 2012. *Sixth Grade Common Core State Standards Flip Book*. Kansas: Kansas Association of Teachers of Mathematics.

————. 2012. *Seventh Grade Common Core State Standards Flip Book*. Kansas: Kansas Association of Teachers of Mathematics.

————. 2012. *Eighth Grade Common Core State Standards Flip Book*. Kansas: Kansas Association of Teachers of Mathematics.

Heritage, Margaret. 2008. *Learning Progressions: Supporting Instruction and Formative Assessment*. Washington, DC: Chief Council of State School Officers.

Huang, Ron. 2005. "Verification or Proof: Justification of Pythagoras' Theorem in Chinese Mathematics Classrooms." Paper presented at the Conference of the International Group for the Psychology of Mathematics Education. *PME 3* 29: 161–168.

Hufferd-Ackles, Kimberly, Karen Fuson, and Miriam Gamoran Sherin. 2004. "Describing Levels and Components of a Math-Talk Learning Community." *Journal for Research in Mathematics Education* 35: 81–116.

Hughes-Hallett, Deborah. 2010. *Applied Calculus*. New York: John Wiley and Sons.

Hull, Ted H., Ruth Harbin Mills, and Dan S. Balka. 2012. *The Common Core Mathematics Standards*. Thousand Oaks, CA: Corwin Press.

Kansas Association of Teachers of Mathematics. http://katm.org/wp/wp-content/uploads/flipbooks/6FlipBookedited22.pdf

Kazak, Sibel, and Jere Confrey. 2006. "Elementary School Students' Informal and Intuitive Conceptions of Probability Distributions." In *Proceedings of the Seventh International Conference on Teaching Statistics*, edited by Allan Rossman and Beth Chance. Salvador, Brazil: International Statistical Institute and International Association for Statistical Education.

Khan. 2013. www.khanacademy.org

Lamon, Susan. 2012. *Teaching Fractions and Ratios for Understanding: Essential Knowledge and Content Strategies for Teachers*. New York, NY: Routledge.

Larnier, John. 2011. "Debunking Five Myths about Project-Based Learning." http://www.edutopia.org/blog/debunking-five-pbl-myths-john-larmer.

Lutsky, Neil. 2008. "Arguing with Numbers: Teaching Quantitative Reasoning through Argument and Writing." In *Calculation vs. Context: Quantitative Literacy and Its Implications for Teacher Education*, edited by Bernard L. Madison and Lynn Arthur Steen, 59–74. Washington, DC: Mathematical Association of America.

Ma, Liping. 1999. *Knowing and Teaching Elementary Mathematics Teachers' Understanding of Fundamental Mathematics in China and the United States.* Mahwah, NJ: Lawrence Erlbaum Associates.

Martin, Michael, Ina Mullis, and Pierre Foy. 2008. *TIMSS 2007 International Mathematics Report: Findings from IEA's Trends in International Mathematics and Science Study at the Fourth and Eighth Grades.* Chestnut Hill, MA: TIMMS & PIRLS International Study Center, Boston College.

Mathematics Assessment Project. 2011. www.math.mapshell.org.

McCallum, Fuson, and Beckman. 2012. http://commoncoretools.me/forums /topic/division-and-multiplication-algorithms-in-the-progressions.

McKenna, Maria K., and Jessica Millen. 2013. "Look! Listen! Parent Narratives and Grounded Theory Models of Parent Voice, Presence, and Engagement in K–12 Education." *School Community Journal* 23: 9–48.

McManus, Sarah. 2008. "Attributes of Effective Formative Assessment." http://www.dpi.state.nc.us/docs/accountability/educators/ fastattributes04081.pdf.

Mullis, Ina V. S., Michael O. Martin, and Pierre Foy. 2008. *TIMSS 2007 International Mathematics Report: Findings from IEA's Trends in International Mathematics and Science Study at the Fourth and Eighth Grades.* Chestnut Hill, MA: TIMSS & PIRLS International Study Center, Boston College.

Murray, Miki. 2004. *Teaching Mathematics Vocabulary in Context: Windows, Doors, and Secret Passageways.* Portsmouth, ME.

National Council of Teachers of Mathematics. 2013. "Position Paper on Formative Assessment." http://www.nctm.org/uploadedFiles/About_NCTM/Position_Statements/Formative%20Assessment1.pdf.

———. 2000. *Principles and Standards for School Mathematics.* Reston, VA: NCTM.

———. 1995. *Assessment Standards for School Mathematics.* Reston, VVA: NCTM.

National Governors Association Center for Best Practices, and Council of Chief State School Officers. 2010. "Common Core State Standards." Washington, DC: National Governors Association Center for Best Practices, Council of Chief State School Officers. Accessed January 14, 2014, http://corestandards.org/math.

National Governors Association (NGA) and Council of Chief State School Officers (CCSSO). 2010. *Reaching Higher: The Common Core State Standards Validation Committee—A Report from the National Governors Association Center for Best Practices and the Council of Chief State School Officers.* Washington, DC: NGA Center and CCSSO.

National Mathematics Advisory Panel. 2008. *Foundations for Success: The Final Report of the National Mathematics Advisory Panel.* U.S. Department of Education: Washington, DC.

National Research Council. 2009. *Mathematics Learning In Early Childhood, Paths Toward Excellence and Equity.* Washington, DC: National Academy Press.

———. 2001. *Adding It Up: Helping Children Learn Mathematics.* Washington, DC: National Academy Press.

Page, Michael, Cynthia Guevera, and Edward Walton. 2012. "Concept Based Instruction for Stoichiometry: The Balanced Molecular Equation and Proportional Reasoning." *National Study of Education in Undergraduate Science*: 1-6.

Parker, Frieda, and Jodie Novack. 2012. "Implementing the Common Core Mathematical Practices." http://www.ascd.org/ascd-express/vol8/805-parker.aspx.

Posamentier, A. S., B. S. Smith, and J. Stepelman. 2006. *Teaching Secondary Mathematics: Techniques and Enrichment Units.* Upper Saddle River, NJ: Pearson Merrill Prentice Hall.

Ramdass, Darshanand, and Barry Zimmerman. 2008. "Effects of Self-Correction Strategy Training on Middle School Students' Self-Efficacy, Self-Evaluation, and Mathematics Division Learning." *Journal of Advanced Academics* Fall: 18–41.

Ray, Max. 2011. "Problem Solving Strategies and the Common Core Practice Standards." http://mathforum.org/blogs/max/problem-solving-strategies-and-the-common-core-practice-standards/.

Rowe, Mary Budd. 1986. "Wait Time: Slowing Down May Be a Way of Speeding Up." *Journal of Teacher Education* 37: 43–50.

Russell, Susan Jo. 2000. "Developing Computational Fluency with Whole Numbers." *Teaching Children Mathematics* 7: 154–58.

Saunders, Alicia F., Keri S. Bethune, Fred Spooner, and Dianne Browder. 2013. "Solving the Common Core Equation: Teaching Mathematics CCSS to Students with Moderate and Severe Disabilities." *Teaching Exceptional Children* 45: 24–33.

Schwols, A., & Dempsey, K. 2013. *Common Core Standards for High School Mathematics: A Quick-Start Guide.* Alexandria: Association for Supervision and Curriculum Development.

Selmer, Sarah J., Johnna J. Bolyard, and James A. Rye. 2011. "Statistical Reasoning Over Lunch." *Mathematics Teaching in the Middle School* 17: 275–281.

Shaughnessy, Meghan M. 2011. "Identify Fractions and Decimals on a Number Line." *Teaching Children Mathematics*, 17: 428–434.

Siegel, Lee. 2012. "Rise of the Tiger Nation." *The Wall Street Journal*.

Silver, Edward. 2010. "Examining What Teachers Do When They Display Their Best Practice: Teaching Mathematics for Understanding." *Journal of Mathematics Education at Teachers College*. 1: 1–6.

Smarterbalanced.org. 2013. http://www.smarterbalanced.org.

Smith, M., E. Hughes, R. Engle, and M. K. Stein. 2009. "Orchestrating Classroom Discussions." *Mathematics Teaching in the Middle School* 14: 548–556.

Swanson, Kristen. 2013. "5 Tips for Explaining Common Core to Parents." http://thejournal.com/articles/2013/10/01/how-to-explain-common-core-to-parents.aspx.

Thomas, John W. 2000. "A Review of Project Based Learning." http://www.bie.org/research/study/review_of_project_based_learning_2000.

Thompson, Tony D., and Ronald V. Preston. "Measurement in the Middle Grades: Insights from NAEP and TIMMS. *Mathematics Teaching in the Middle School*. 9 (2004): 514–519.

USD. Wichita Unified School District 259, Learning Services. 2011. http://mathprojectsjournal.files.wordpress.com/2013/02/questionstodevelopmathpractices.pdf.

Van de Walle, John A., Karen Karp, and Jennifer M. Bay-Williams. 2013. *Elementary and Middle School Mathematics: Teaching Developmentally*, 8th edition. New York, NY: Pearson Education.

Vanhille, Lee S., and Arthur J. Baroody. "Fraction Instruction that Fosters Multiplicative Reasoning." *Making Sense of Fractions, Ratios, and Proportions: 2002 Yearbook*, edited by Bonnie Litwiller and George Bright, 224–236. Reston, VA: National Council of Teachers of Mathematics, 2002.

Wedekind, Kassia Omohundro. 2011. *Math Exchanges: Guiding Mathematicians in Small Group Meetings*. Portland, ME: Stenhouse Publishers.

Weiss, Iris and Joan Pasley. 2004. "What is High Quality Instruction?" *Educational Leadership* 61: 24-28.

Wormeli, Rick. 2005. *Summarization in Any Subject: 50 Techniques to Improve Student Learning.* Alexandria, VA: ASCD.

Wu, Hung-Hsi. "Teaching Geometry According to the Common Core Standards." 2012. http://math.berkeley.edu/research/areas/geometry-topology.

Zorin, Barbara, Patricia D. Hunsader, and Denise R. Thompson. 2013. "Assessments: Numbers, Context, Graphics, and Assumptions." *Teaching Children Mathematics* 19: 480–488.

Zucker, Joshua. 2012. http://mathprojectsjournal.files.wordpress.com/2013/02/questionstodevelopmathpractices.pdf. Circle Network (Autumn 2012): 4-7. http://www.mathteacherscircle.org.